Salt 2

salt 2

boatbuilding, sailmaking,
island people, river driving,
bean hole beans, wooden paddles,
and more Yankee doings

edited with an introduction
by Pamela Wood

ANCHOR PRESS/DOUBLEDAY
GARDEN CITY, NEW YORK
1980

Pamela Wood, who started *Salt* magazine with a group of her students in 1973, runs a boatyard in Kennebunkport, Maine, where she and her colleagues teach students how to make magazines, video productions, and fine photographs, as well as boats, cabinetry, and energy-efficient constructions using principles of appropriate technology. A working journalist-teacher, she is the editor of *The Salt Book* and the author of *You and Aunt Arie: A Guide to Cultural Journalism.*

The Anchor Press edition is the first publication of *Salt 2* in book form. It is published simultaneously in hard and paper covers. Portions of this collection first appeared in *Salt* magazine, Copyright © Salt, Inc. 1974, 1975, 1976, 1977, 1978, 1979.

Library of Congress Cataloging in Publication Data
Main entry under title:

SALT 2: boatbuilding, sailmaking, island people, river
  driving, bean hold beans, wooden paddles, and more
  Yankee doings.

  1. Maine—Social life and customs.   2. Country life—
Maine.   3. Handicraft—Maine.   I. Wood, Pamela.
F26. S25   974.1
Library of Congress Catalog Card Number 80–553
ISBN: 0-385-14346-x

Contents

To Reid Chapman,
  who loved to grow things,
and Herb Baum,
  who loved to make things.

Acknowledgments

As the years pile one upon the other and I continue to spend—with my students—the better part of my creative time collecting the sort of material in this book, it has become increasingly clear to me how I gained the palate for what I am doing. My taste was whetted long ago in childhood by two people.

The first to introduce me to the heady pleasures of listening to the people of my town talk was my father, Elgar Dowess Holley, a country attorney in the best traditions of "country." (He practiced preventive litigation, handing out advice more willingly than the succession of Baptist ministers who drifted into Maud, Oklahoma. Payment came in the form of milk, chickens, and free passes to the Arcadia Theater.) From the time I was three years old, my father let me trail after him as he traveled in southeast Oklahoma, talking to oil riggers and farmers, bootleggers and Indians. We took our time and listened well.

The second person to encourage me to become an active listener was my grandmother, Ella McClinton, to whom I was loaned as a gift for a year when I was ten, after the death of my grandfather. Grandma Mack ran the Eureka Hotel in Stigler, Oklahoma, and she let me sit in the lobby listening hour after hour to the stories of the "regulars" who lived in the hotel. If I maintained unbreathing silence and a small presence, I could usually make it through all the best stories before being sent to bed.

In addition to these debts of experience, I want to acknowledge some practical debts. Four students spent patient, tedious hours in the final stages of putting this book together. Julie Watson and Jane Whitten replaced aging photographic prints collected over the years, while Sheryl Lane and Dorothy O'Keefe helped with the important job of piecing together the manuscript and identifying photographs. Without the four of them, I would still be struggling to complete *Salt 2*.

Pamela Wood

Introduction

Sprawling on the mud flats near the mouth of the Kennebunk River on the coast of Maine lies a hulking tramp steamer of a building that has come to represent the tides and fortunes of Salt.

She is windscarred, rusty, pugnosed, laden to the gunnels and listing southward, a rugged and willing workhorse of the sea. She is a fitting vessel for us at Salt as we evolve from a small home-grown magazine into a teeming, exuberant center for generating human growth and achievement.

This vessel of ours—this old boatyard building—flies no flag. Those of us who are aboard her need no passports. Our masthead is a four-letter word without political significance. The "salt" in the title of *Salt 2,* as well as in that of its predecessor, *The Salt Book,* the *Salt* journals we publish, and the salt of all Salt endeavors is generic, elemental salt. It is the salt of sweat, of tears, of life, of the sea, crossing boundaries of place and time, belonging to all worlds. It is the salt of our cultural base on coastal Maine.

For most of her lifetime, the cavernous building that now launches all of Salt's productions and educational efforts has been the hub of an active boatyard in the fishing community of Kennebunkport, sending several hundred vessels down the saltwater river to the Atlantic. She is a plain and unpretentious symbol of a long succession of boat-builders, craftsmen, and fishermen who have worked and achieved along the banks of the Kennebunk River.

What could have been more natural than for Salt to add its youthful energy to that succession in 1977, when the boatyard fell silent, as Herb Baum retired after thirty years of crafting fine wooden boats.

With Herb's blessing, and the bravery born of a recently published book (*The Salt Book,* 1976), the young student trustees of Salt, Inc.

and their advisors voted to raise the funds for a down payment on the boatyard and acquire the awesome burden of a five-year mortgage. It was a daring thing to do and we looked to two sources for fortitude: our conviction that Salt needed a home to survive and to grow; and our confidence that young people were learning and achieving within Salt's structure by leaps and bounds just short of the miraculous.

Here on the banks of the Kennebunk River, Salt has burst the bounds of the printed page. Young Salt apprentices are now practicing the skills and crafts that other Salt apprentices write about, as we grow from a promising publication to a bustling center dedicated to extending the limits of human endeavor. The evolution is almost predictable, given the energy of the idea that lies at the heart of Salt.

The concept is neither new nor complicated. It has been in existence for as long as one generation has passed on to the next linking generation its practical skills, experiences, and day to day knowledge of life.

It is an idea as old as mankind, an idea having to do with the ways in which young people learn, grow, and become productive. We believe that young people cannot become skilled craftsmen simply through talk or textbooks. In order to learn to write, they must write. In order to learn to build boats, they must build boats. In order to learn to navigate, they must steer.

And they must do so in the company of good writers, good boatbuilders, and good seamen who have mastered their skills and are willing to pass on what they have learned.

So the idea that pervades the boatyard, as well as the magazine, *Salt,* is that learning is an active, doing process—not a passive, receiving process over which the learner has no control. Energy is generated by the very nature of such an idea.

Most people who walk through the doors of the old boatyard are struck by the energy that electrifies it.

It is the energy of many young apprentices learning a craft—learning drafting, lofting, boatbuilding, photography, writing, graphic design, television production, cabinetry, construction, and a proliferating number of other skills.

It is also the energy of the fine craftsmen and practicing professionals who train these young people—energy unleashed as craftsmen work to make what they like to make.

And finally—floating with the sawdust in the air, compressing with the boatyard's present energy—is the energy of the past. It is the energy of one of the best boatbuilders in the trade, Herb Baum, and the craftsmen who worked with him over the years. It is the energy left behind by thirty good years of boatbuilding.

How do we harness the rampant energy that courses through the boatyard, how does one turn the wheel, make a magazine, build a boat, construct a television production, restructure a decaying boatyard building?

My colleagues and I at the Salt Boatyard let the natural lure of making a good product be the principal conduit for directed energy. Making the product becomes the incentive, reward, mechanism, and symbol for learning and growth.

It is an incentive and symbol no less compelling for us as artisans and professionals than for the students we teach by example. I am as challenged and activated by the making and shaping of a new story idea, new magaine, or new book as any of my students. Indeed, if I am not, I fail as their teacher, for they will not learn from me the solid pleasure I take from doing my work.

I have no patience with people who face me with "either-or" questions about my work and my students. Questions that ask: which is more important to you, the progress of your students or the quality of the product you and your students make together? What nonsense! My students are the first persons who are going to smell me out if I don't care as much about the quality of the product as they do. To be a legitimate artisan, I must have a legitimate absorbing care for what I do. That is an important part of the teaching process here at the Salt boatyard.

And my students? What about their achievements, their progress? Don't I care about that, too? Of course I do, so much so that I want my students to experience the same sense of achievement I have when I make a product. It is a circular process, this making and learning. To make a product, the student must learn and the product is his learning, his achievement; in the end, product and learning become one. It is an exhilarating union.

Beyond this basic product approach, what are some other fundamental approaches to learning we use in the Salt Boatyard? Peer teaching is an important one. Young people who have just mastered a skill or gained an idea are often the most convincing teachers for those who are a step behind them. For the young peer teacher, sharing a skill or a concept is an important affirmation of his learning.

Or, as the signed graffiti of one seasoned Salt apprentice put it not so long ago on the newly whitewashed boatyard bathroom wall: "SALT is *S*eeing
        *A*cknowledging
        *L*earning
        *T*eaching"

Corollary to our use of peer teaching is our refusal to use "tracking," or grouping students according to similar skills levels and experience levels. My colleagues and I go to considerable effort to mix and mingle young people. We find that variety in levels of experience brings the greatest growth rate for the individuals involved. This puts learners in a position to spur each other onward and to aid each other as they make a common product or explore a common concept.

Self direction is another important given at the boatyard. Youths who are on the threshold of making big decisions about their lives are hungry to recognize and define their own needs, hopes, and goals. As we work together in the boatyard, we recognize this hunger and seek to satisfy it.

Unless we look to the stirrers and tenders of this churning, ever-changing educational mix, we will not understand how it works. The nature of the staff at the Salt Boatyard is quite unlike those stern, condemning figures who populated my childhood imagination at the time I swore I would never be a teacher.

I would venture to say that most of us are more nearly like that fellow down the street you remember so well when you were a kid because you liked hanging around him, talking to him.

Most of the staff here at Salt can tell good stories. Most of us laugh quite a lot. Most of us have a fair understanding of what we are as people and most of us can pretty easily imagine ourselves in another person's shoes.

All of us are tough and demanding when it comes to the quality of the work we expect from ourselves and from those around us. None of us have ever been entirely satisfied with our final product as we continue to struggle to find a way to make it better next time. All of us are learners.

The last crucial ingredient that goes into the potent educational broth we serve here at the Salt Boatyard is our reliance on the community for learning experiences. This book is nothing if it is not a demonstration of the richness of the natural teaching faculty that exists in every community in New England if we but take the time to search and listen. The content of the learning is demonstrated on every page.

Not only content, but some fine instances of effective teaching "methodology." Let me simply hope that those of us who are teachers within the boatyard can match the natural teaching techniques of Ken Campbell as he tells about caulking a boat. More important, let's hope we as teachers and students are always as lucid as he is about that time when telling should end and doing should begin.

"There's a lot to it," Ken concludes about the craft of caulking. "But as you do it, you learn a lot by yourself. You get into a few messes, but you learn a lot every time you do.

"There's a few things you can show anybody, and from then on you've got to practice and experience it. Experience and practice will teach you more than I can."

Boatbuilding

Boats That Come Naturally

By Dorothy O'Keefe
Photography by Julien LeSieur

Ralph Stanley charted his course early in life. "Ever since I was a little boy I was fiddling around with boats. It just came natural to want to build them."

He is reminiscent of the hand-hewn masts of yesterday—sturdy, tall, and windcarved—he has a sense of purpose in this life. Ralph is a master boatbuilder. A builder of wooden boats. After years of exposure in a changing world, he remains constant. His boats are built to standards of perfection. They have to be. He will settle for nothing less.

Ralph was born in 1929, the eldest of eight children and only son of Chester and Bertha Stanley. His father was a fisherman, as were many people of the community in which he lived his life, Southwest Harbor, Maine. "I always thought that I would like to go fishing, but it's pretty hard work and I wasn't ever very strong. The only fishing I did was in the spring. A little hand-lining. And that was for the fun of it, not to make any big money. You see, I had a summer job with the summer boats."

Sitting on a spool of rope, completely relaxed and comfortable in his surroundings, he spoke of his younger days. His form was bent over as he spliced ropes—a silhouette against the morning sky. His hands played out a natural rhythm as future rigging took shape. His stories

1. (*Photo by Lynn Kippax, Jr.*)

were interrupted by the sound of an occasional fishing boat leaving the wharf. The gulls wailed in frustration as they accompanied a boat into the harbor or soared around the nearby sardine factory in search of their next meal. He talked of sailing, an activity that has dominated a good deal of his time.

"When we were little kids we had a sailboat. Fooled around a bit.

"I can remember being a young boy and just watching the boats. I was always around watching and wondering how they were put together and that sort of thing. I drew out my first lines plan when I was —gosh—fourteen years old, I guess.

"I was seventeen before I got on a big boat to sail. It was on an old schooner. The *Niliraga*. The original owner had her then. He was an old man and couldn't go out by himself. He had a captain. I went as a cook and deckhand. I sailed all that summer on her. And I sailed with him all the next summer on a yawl. They did a lot of racing and stuff like that.

"After I got out of high school I went to junior college for two years. Up in Houlton. I'd have probably gone a lot further if I'd had any more money, so I thought I'd come home and build a boat.

"So I came home and made enough money that summer to buy up some lumber and materials to start a boat. Then I started it. Got her planked up that winter, then I worked and made enough money to finish her off and make a down payment on an engine. I got the boat off.

"By the time I finished that first boat I was so glad to get it done that I thought that I would never get the courage to build another one. I thought, 'I'm glad that's over.'

"Generally when you're building a boat you can't wait to get it finished so you can start another one. You get awful sick of working on the same boat.

"So another couple of months, a fella come along and said that he wanted me to build him a boat. I had taken him for a ride in it that day and he said, 'Go ahead and build me one.' I just couldn't wait to get started. I been doing it ever since."

Ralph built his first boat in 1951, and for years he continued to build out of the old barn located beside his father's home. Since the barn was not situated on the water, the conventional means of launching a new boat took a slightly different turn.

"We used to drag 'em down the road. Get a big truck and drag 'em right along in the cradle. Some of them we had to drag to Manset to get to the beach. On a dry day they would smoke quite a bit," he said, laughing. "On a wet day they would drag right along real easy. Nothin' to it!"

2. Ralph Stanley. (*Photo by Sheryl Lane*)

With his first two boats completed by the time he reached the age of twenty-four, Ralph was pretty much established in his new business. However, his course was altered sharply when he became seriously ill.

"I didn't do anything for a year. I was twenty-four years old and I had TB.

"I had had a tooth pulled out. I suppose I had the tuberculosis bug in me. A lot of people have it and it doesn't bother them. I had a lung abscess from the tooth extraction. I suppose that's what happened. When I had the lung abscess, the TB took right ahold.

" 'Twas in the right lower lobe. That's an unusual place for tuberculosis to strike. It's generally in the upper part of the upper lobes.

"I knew I was sick, but the doctors didn't know. They couldn't find out what was wrong with me. I went down to the Massachusetts General Hospital. They turned me inside out and found out what the trouble was. I don't know as I'd have found out if I hadn't done that.

"I was laid up a whole year. I didn't build another boat until after I was married. Then I had to do something!

"In the wintertime I would build a boat or two. Summers I was on the old schooner. I went back on the old schooner to work when I was, I guess, twenty-six or twenty-seven years old. Mrs. Florence Montgomery had inherited it from the original owner.

"Once I went over the side of that old schooner. I got hit by the boom. We were coming into Northeast Harbor, not too much wind, and we had let the sails down. We jibed over and I shifted the jib sheet from one side to the other. I was about ready to let the jib sheet go and go up forward and pull the jib down.

"We were sailing quite close, almost by the lee. We were in danger of a jibe at almost any minute. I looked up to see where the boom was. It was all right. I was a little longer than I intended to be or something, so I thought everything was still all right and I stood up without looking.

"The next thing I knew that boom was right alongside my head! And it didn't hurt a bit. I felt as if I were floating in the air. I thought, 'My goodness, I'm not floating, I'm falling!' By that time I'd come to my senses. I suppose it stunned me, knocked me out a bit.

"But it felt wonderful just floating along in the air—nothing holding you up. It felt great!

"I reached out for something and I grabbed ahold of a rail. I didn't have any strength. I couldn't hold on. It seemed as if I couldn't hold on. I just couldn't get a grip on it. My feet hit the water and I went down to about my waist.

"That cold water! I could feel my strength coming back. I hung on the rail and pulled myself back up. I thought I was okay. I got the people back in and the boat tied up at the mooring. When I came home I began to feel kinda funny. Dizzy. I laid down for a little while and felt better. I probably had a little concussion. But what a funny feeling just floating in the air. It felt great!"

In 1956 Ralph married Marion Linscott in the Congregational Church. Marion remembers it was, "just the immediate family. We had no reception afterwards. We got married, changed our clothes, and went right onto the boat and went sailing off. As it was, they had time enough to put rice in our suitcase and streamers all through the rigging.

"Somebody put a dried fish under one of the bunks." She laughed. "A dried fish! We never found it until we hauled her up for the winter and cleaned the boat. I wish I had known. I love dried fish!

"We had a wonderful honeymoon. We went sailing all along the coast. That was the first time I ever went sailing. I had been on boats before, but they'd always been motorboats. I fell in love with it the first day.

"I'd lot rather sail than go on a motorboat," she continued. "When you sail, there's no sound of a motor. A quiet sail is so nice.

3. Ralph and Marion Stanley.

"Boats have always been a part of my life, but not the building of them until I married him. I knew that this was his life and love, and it got so that it was something to me. It's fascinating. Each boat is different, and it's great to watch the boat begin from paper to the real thing. Each step. I never get tired of it.

"But then they got to mean even more—the insides of them and everything. I came to love them, really, as much as he does.

"I knew what I was getting into. It's had its ups and downs, just like anything else. I kind of encouraged him. I knew he loved doing it.

"His father never, never got into boatbuilding. Ralph did all the boatbuilding. That was his. I think it comes from generations way back. From his great-grandfather. It's way back in the family.

"It was either boatbuilding or going on boats to other places. He's always been interested in building boats. When he was a youngster, he used to just sit on the rocks and look at the boats and wonder how they were drawn out. Finally it came to him how. And he used to go to the other boat shops in the area and watch. And then ask questions and see what they done.

"His father would let him build in his barn only. Ralph had asked his father if he could build a place to build his boats, and his father said, 'No. Not while I'm alive.'

4. Ralph's storage workshop.

"Well, he died in 1970. I said to Ralph, 'Your father's gone now. You can build here.' That was the year he rebuilt the *Dictator* and the *Amos Swan* over to Jarvis Newman's shop. Well, he got the *Amos Swan* partly rebuilt, and he built these buildings here at the house.

"He started in on his first boat here in one of the buildings before the other one was finished. He just dived right in! He's been here since 1973 when he finished the last one. Been happy as can be right here, too. I still don't know to this day why his father wouldn't let him have those buildings. But it's the only thing I would have changed.

"I wouldn't want to live any other place but here. And I know that about Ralph. The water is where he wants to be. If he could go somewhere by car or by boat, he'll take the boat every time. He won't go anywhere by car on account that it makes him 'all lamed up.'

"There's some places I'd like to go. Scotland, Holland. The Scandinavian countries and places like that. But I doubt very much that I'll get there unless we go by boat."

Building Friendship Sloops

Ralph harbors a particular passion for Friendship Sloops, wind-powered lobstering vessels of the past. To date he has built or completely restored nine of them. "I don't know what it is—it's got to be a special kind of person that wants a Friendship," he revealed. "I suppose it's the shape of it, the feel of it. Maybe it's the way they sail. It's the looks for some. Others seem to be obsessed with the thought of having one. I always said you had to be kinda crazy to want one.

"Seems if I've always known what a Friendship Sloop was. I remember the last working Friendships around here. They were a good boat that people were using at that time. They seemed like the right thing. Had a good feel to them.

"But they were on the way out then, the old ones that were working. Most of them were on the beach falling apart. I thought that we'd never see them again—that some other boat would take their place. And I still figured that I'd like to have one someday.

"Then along come Albie Neilson and told me that he wanted me to build him one someday. To keep it in mind, he'd let me know. And I thought to myself, 'Now, that would be interesting.' Finally he did. And that was the year of the first Friendship Sloop race. In 1961.

"That summer I read in the paper where they were going to have the regatta. I told Mrs. Montgomery about it and she said, 'Let's go!' So we took the schooner down to the race. There were seventeen boats that year. And that was quite something to get that many of the old sloops together.

"Bernie MacKenzie kind of started the race. He had an old sloop named the *Voyager*. And he put her in a race amongst a whole lot of fancy racing yachts. Fast racing yachts. Anyways, he put this old Friendship in the race. Come along a gale of wind and here come the yachts, losing their masts and limping home. Well, that old Friendship kept right on agoing. He won the race!

"He got the idea of having a race up in Friendship every year for all the old Friendship Sloop owners he could round up to make the trek to Friendship each year. And he did.

"I like to build Friendships."

He set out the middle of February 1979 to do just that. He wanted construction of the wooden sloop *Endeavor* to be as traditional as the old working vessels he had known.

"She has a big open cockpit. It's not watertight. If I get some water in it, it's going to run through the floor and into the bottom of the boat.

5. Ralph sending
a plank through
his planer.

That's the way the old fishermen wanted it. If they got water on board, they didn't want it on top of the boat 'cause of the weight. They wanted it to run to the bottom of the boat as quick as it could. Then they would heave to and pump her out and continue on.

"The cabin's small just like they used to be. It's just like the older ones. They had a low profile. And a round coaming." (A coaming is a piece of wood that is placed around the top of the inside edge of the cockpit. It can be used comfortably as a backrest while sailing.)

Endeavor has inside ballast. Rocks were used. "Small ones," Ralph explains. "Small round ones. They fit nicely. A lot of the newer sloops have outside ballast. A lead keel. But the older fellas wanted the inside ballast because it weren't so quick a motion. It [inside ballast] had an easier motion. They might roll deeper, but they'd roll easier. They didn't want that quick motion to wear them out before the day's over.

6. Ralph Stanley on the cabin of his *Endeavor*.

"And a tiller. You have a better feel for the boat with one. Some people get so they can't even use a wheel.

"I did change the construction of the keel structure from the old ones. The old ones were built with a stern post and no engine. The plank ran out from the rabbet to the stern post. I built mine with a shaft log and built up the deadwood for a more rugged construction.

"The old fellas weren't fancy. They had no use for fancy frills. Didn't want to have to paint an extra stripe on their boats. They left out all they could get away with. Like having a boot top [a stripe between the water line and the hull] isn't traditional. The old fellas built theirs practical. They built the quickest way. Priced to sell, you know.

"They figured a boat was gonna last them about ten or twelve years. I build mine a lot ruggeder. Nowadays people want their boats to last a little longer.

"I didn't use a metal fitting in the boom or anything. The mast and boom are spruce. It's simpler and serves the purpose. One old lady owned a woodlot that I used to go and cut trees for masts. She was my schoolteacher in school. She's dead now.

"She was about ninety years old the last mast I got. Gladys Whitmore. Well, I used to go get these trees and then tell her what I got and pay for them. She never liked the idea of cutting all the trees, but one or two every year could be cut. She always said, 'You want more, you be sure and come back.'

"Every time I went down there she liked having me come in and talk with her. She'd get me to sit in her easy chair and see how nice it felt. And then she'd keep me there for two hours! If somebody would call her on the telephone, she'd answer it, 'Can't talk now . . . I got company!' "

"I knew that when he was going down there I wouldn't see him for two hours," Marion said, smiling.

Two elderly gentlemen that Ralph had the pleasure of visiting in the area were Eben and Guy Romer. "They were old bachelors," Marion chuckled. "They never walked together." Ralph added, "One always used to walk about ten to twelve feet behind the other.

"Once they was mixing up a cake. I think they had something like six eggs in it. So they mixed the batter all up. They they decided that they got to put baking powder in it so they grabbed the can and got it up over the cake, just shaking some in, you know.

"Well, the cover came off and dropped the whole can of baking powder into the batter! 'We'll scoop it right out and stir in the rest,' they said. So they did. They stirred it right into the cake and put the cake in the oven.

"The oven door hinge was broken so they had to prop it shut with a brick. They had it propped up, the cake was baking and everything was going along just fine.

"Well, they sat there awhile and decided that they better look to see if it were done. They very carefully moved the brick to one side and opened the door and peeked in there.

"That cake had risen so that it rolled right out and over the edge of the pan! It was up like a loaf of bread. And it was all wiggling, you know. But it still wasn't quite done. It wasn't brown.

" 'Oh, don't that look good,' they said. They very carefully put the cake back in the oven and propped the door back up.

"Well, the minute he turned his back, that brick came crashing down, the oven door fell off, and that cake sunk right back in the middle of the pan!

"So one of 'em says, 'Oh well, I don't like those light fluffy cakes anyway. At least when I eat this, I'll know I'm eating something.'"

Marion remembers those days in Southwest Harbor. Days when people like the Romers and Gladys Whitmore were around. "It used to be that you knew everybody in town. Now we hardly even know our next-door neighbors!"

But then neither can Ralph's home be the same as it was just nine years ago. He leaned against the partially built cabin on *Endeavor*. His hands adjusted the hat that most people have come to associate him with. The same hands that have known hard work for years and have painstakingly carried out the precise measurements that make Ralph Stanley's boats so special.

Here in the high-ceilinged and sawdust-strewn buildings flourishes a mutual respect between employer and employee that is evident in the absence of harsh orders, time clocks, and constant supervision.

7. (*Photo by Julien LeSieur*)

"The fellas that work here, they all seem to be one big happy family," said Marion. She also handles the bookkeeping for the business. "It's a small place. Ralph is careful who he gets. We try to stay small. They all get along good. Everybody can kid around and we all like that. We'll keep it that way."

Ralph recalled a good example to illustrate the advantages of having a small crew that works well together. He laughed about the film team that visited his boat shop to document the building of a Friendship Sloop.

"When we timbered out, they expected to hear a lot of noise—orders and talking and all that. So they wired us up with the microphones around our necks and radios in our pockets. They had a remote tape recorder to pick up the sounds from the radios.

"And all they got was a lot of grunts and groans. Everybody knew what to do, see. They'd just pass the hot timbers and bend 'em, clamp 'em, and nail 'em in. Nobody said a word. Everybody just worked. They knew what to do. If we switched around, it may have fouled things all up," he admitted. "But everybody had their job. We timbered up and planked her in a week's time."

Reggie Durgin, Renato Saavedra, and Peter Basley are three of his employees that attended the boatbuilding school in Eastport, Maine. His son-in-law, Tim Goodwin, also works there. Here they have the opportunity to utilize their skills, as well as the freedom and space to expand their knowledge.

"A lot of people want to be a boatbuilder," says Ralph. "I always tell them that the best thing to do is to get a job doing something and get money enough to start a boat on their own. Find a place to set it up and build it. Because if they have enough gumption to do that, they're probably going to carry it through.

"That's the way I did it, more or less. Come to getting stuck on something, I'd figure it out or go look to see what someone else had done.

"I learned not to ask. Some builders, especially thirty years ago, were awful jealous about their trade. They wouldn't tell ya. Or else they'd tell ya wrong. I learned it was best to go and look. Or I'd just think of it. I'd go off for a while and figure it out.

"But had I gone to boatbuilding school, I'd have learned the basics. Anybody would get a lot out of it by going to school, though. They'd stand a better chance of being able to build a boat on their own. They'd see what I do and know why I do it. I don't have the time to sit down and teach them.

"In a case like that, anybody come here to learn boatbuilding probably wouldn't learn how to build a boat. If I get a boat to build, I can't

8. (*Photo by Lynn Kippax, Jr.*)

take the time out to show them how to get out a plank or build the transom. If I get a boat that calls for sixty timbers and I get seventy to have ten spares, then I can't afford to break any.

"So an apprentice in a shop like this gets all the routine jobs that there's no danger of fouling up. Like driving plugs or reading lines. It's good to be able to go to school. And if you want to build a boat, just go and build it."

Mastering the Trade

Ralph is a master in his trade. And like all other masters, he has developed ways to perfect even the most difficult skills in boatbuilding.

"Fitting the tuck planks is a tough job. That's where the plank comes up on the stern post. You got to fit 'em in the rabbet on the horn timber. Have to steam the planks to fit the rabbet. It's quite a job.

"Making the transom by eye. It's work. A lot of people couldn't do it. They'd have to loft it out," Ralph continued. "As you're planking up, you finally get it so they're running out by the stern.

"Before you do the transom, you have a plank already picked out for the bottom. That gives you the shape to work with. You steam it and bend it around the form. Let it stand for a week. It cools off and stays in that shape. Now that determines the curve of the transom. You can't put any more curve in and you can't take any out. That's it. You work from there.

"When you bend the timber in, twist it when you bend it. You can find ways of stretching it a bit. See, you bend it a little more in places. Then when you get it to just about where you want it, bend it a little harder than you have to and let it spring back. It seems to lay in a lot better that way. Then as it cools off, it doesn't pull away. You'll find a lot of little discoveries as you work.

"I'm quite fussy about the model. I want the boat to turn out the shape I want it to be. If I'm setting the boat up and something goes wrong, I go to great lengths to make it right. And if a boat is *all* set up, you can shimmy it up, touch it up, and make it do. But it might change the shape of the boat, and I don't like that. I want the boat to be the shape of the model that I've already made.

"In the case that I don't make a half-model and just lay the lines down on paper, I want the boat to be like the plan. A lot of them don't. If something comes out wrong, they just make do. Maybe that's where the most skill is.

"Some of them wasn't very true. I'll bet some now aren't very true. That's a skill of a boatbuilder. Getting a boat true. But a boat doesn't necessarily have to be true to still be a good boat. That *Dictator* is an inch and a half wider on one side than she is on the other. But you'd never know.

"One thing on the replicas or on the ones that are being rebuilt. You're bound to change the shape of the boat from what it originally was. Most of these boats are built from a model. The bilge on the model will be a little bit harder than the boat built from that model. It's just a natural thing—when you build with wood it straightens out some when you use it. It changes some. And if you rebuild a boat it's going to change again. It's going to slack that bilge a little more.

"In the case of the *Dictator,* it may have made her faster. The *Dictator* was in this harbor back in the 1920s, and she wasn't considered to be a very fast boat. Yet Jarvis can take her up to Friendship and win the race. So she's probably a lot different shape than she originally was. And sharper, too."

His boat shop has given rebirth to such sloops as *Amos Swan,* the *Venture,* and the *Morning Star*. "If there was enough of the shape left,

9. Ralph
finishing a part
of the *Endeavor*'s
cabin.

it might be worthwhile to rebuild the older ones. If you restore them, they're still called Class-A boats, even though it's all new.

"I think it's kind of nice for an old existing one not to lose it. Some of them are so bad that you have to throw them away. There's no shape left. But if the shape is left and you can save the model, then it's worth the time.

"I think that the *Dictator* was the oldest [1904]. The *Venture* was 1911, the *Amos Swan* was 1912, and the *Morning Star* was right around there.

"The *Amos Swan* was so bad. There was nothing, no shape left to her at all. All the bilge was gone. Somebody just sawed off the stern and boarded it up with boards. It was a mess. So we took a chainsaw to her, sawed her up, threw the pieces in a truck, took her to the dump, and built a new one. I don't know anyone else that would tackle rebuilding one like that.

"Now *Morning Star* still had her shape. One side was better than the other, but she had a good shape transom and she hadn't gone out of shape too bad. She still had some left.

"We also rebuilt that R-Class racing sloop *Jack Tar*. Now that was quite a different construction.

"It seems like a lot of people that want a Friendship Sloop think that they can't afford one. Bill Pendleton, once the owner of the *Black Jack* and past president of the Friendship Sloop Society told me, 'By all means have one. Go without something else, but have a Friendship.'

"What I'd like to have is one on this model here." He points to the *Freedom,* a sloop he built in 1976. "I'd like to have it finished off with the open cockpit and the smaller cabin, though. It's a little faster. Maybe a bit sharper. It's a nice sailing boat.

"It seems like a lot of people are out to get off on the competition. I don't go for that. Maybe I appear to be, but I don't go out just for the competition. It seems that I've only raced on other people's boats, or I'd be in the crew."

"It's kinda hard," agreed Marion. "There's an art to it. I like to when I can, but he knows what he's doing and I don't, so he gets kind of frustrated at me once in a while. He gives an order and expects it to be carried out right that second."

"Naturally, when I speak you're supposed to jump!" Ralph joked.

Marion proceeded to compare Ralph to a Simon Legree on the water. She teased, "He's one of them. In a race he's terrible."

Ralph continued to talk about racing. "I've raced on the *Freedom,* the *Morning Star,* the *Peregrine,* and the *Amos Swan.* I've been in races for the Northeast Harbor Yacht Club. A regular monthly series, but I was a hired hand.

"I like the Friendship races. I suppose that the Friendship race is the best race I've ever been in. The best part is to sail around, show off the old sloops, and stuff like that. And that's more so than the actual racing. So many of them get there and try and be real competitive. That kind of takes the fun out of it.

"But I'd rather build them than sail them. I'll always build, as long as I can pick up a hammer, probably. If I were incapacitated and couldn't build boats, I'd build fiddles. I'd have to use my hands."

A colorful poster on the door in his office makes reference to "Fiddling Ralph Stanley." Along with the pictures of the many boats that have known the touch of Ralph's hand, can be seen a fiddle in the last stages of completion.

"I just built one. I had a lot of old ones that I put back together, so I knew pretty much how they were made.

"There's one up there that I made. I had to scrape it down. And I got parts of others that I'm making. I've made just the one, but I don't know how many I've put back together.

"There's quite a few people that make 'em. They're getting real valuable. Mine are a little rough, but they have a good tone."

Ralph puts himself into everything he builds, be it a fiddle to entertain or a boat to sail. He builds with simple lines that work. They must. They are the same ideas and methods that have been used for years.

Marion is proud of her husband's talents. "His boats will be around long after he's gone. There's not too many that can build a boat and do it right. He can. And it's quite a talent. But he's very definite on fiber glass. He won't do it. He's allergic to it. But he still wouldn't even if he weren't allergic. Wood means more to him than fiber glass ever will. With wood he can do what he wants. With fiber glass he can't."

Ralph thought a minute before speaking. "I don't like the stuff. Not even for a cabin top. I just don't trust it. I wouldn't feel secure in a fiber-glass boat. If I had to be out in a storm in a fiber-glass boat, I'd kind of worry.

"I've worked on some fiber-glass hulls, and no matter how good it's laid out, it's still all full of little bubbles. I'd rather have a wooden boat that I built and I know that every joint fits and every fastening is where it ought to be. I want to know that all is where it should be.

"I know how much a wooden boat will take. I don't know how much a fiber-glass boat will take. Some of them have cracked apart. Somebody told me the other day that he always had the feeling that one day it would go POOF! and disintegrate. I don't know about that, there are some that are twenty years old or so, but they're getting awful hard and brittle. I just don't know what will happen to them.

"I think that there'll always be people that want a wooden boat. I don't know how many, but I think they'll have to have a lot of money to have one. There'll still be people that will want a wooden boat. It's like buying diamonds. You can have a man-made diamond that you can't tell the difference, but there'll always be somebody that'll want a real one. It's the same with boats."

10. (*Photo by Lynn Kippax, Jr.*)

11. (*Photo by Nicholas Hollander*)

Felling the Wood Keel and Stem

By Suzanne Emery and Greg Violette

"Why don't we cut that one? That's a good big one."

"It's a straight one, too."

"How tall would you say that tree is?"

"Eighty to a hundred feet. You'll get one, two, three logs at least before you get to that first limb up there. That'd be forty or fifty feet, and then there's another fifty feet alone. A hundred feet, I'd say."

George and Roy Cole of East Kingston, New Hampshire, were felling a giant locust tree for us one sunny day in May. The two of them, father and son, have been logging together since George was a boy, and they continue to operate as Roy Cole has always logged, hauling the trees out of the woods by horse and scoot. Afterward, George mills the logs in his own small farmyard sawmill, rough cutting them according to the specifications of his customers.

Most of the people who come to them for lumber are boatbuilders or fishermen. We had gone to their farm and sawmill to get the wood for the backbone assembly of a forty-five-foot Herreshoff Ketch to be built by Tim Dowling at the Salt Boatyard on the Kennebunk River, Maine.

Tim explained what is so special about the wood for his boat that we had to go so far for it. "It's locust wood. It's hard. It's rot resistant. It's pretty clear [of knotholes]. Cheaper than white oak. It's the Cadillac of boatbuilding wood."

George contrasted locust to mahogany. "Oh, much better. You can use it almost anywhere in a boat, as opposed to mahogany, which can't be used in the frame. It's more rot resistant. It has a natural chemical makeup of something like creosote already in the wood.

"Some people call it creosote. I don't know what you call it. Mother Nature will mix together something, but you don't try and question Mother Nature. Some days you're better off.

"Hickory, theoretically, is harder than this stuff, but hickory does not take water. This stuff will take water. You plant one of these [logs] in the ground, it'll last longer than you or I.

"Locust is a native wood of New England. You have to look for it, but it is around. There isn't much of a market for it, anyway. It's a specialized market, and the bigger lumber companies won't touch it because of costs. You take a brand new mill [which] today is about two hundred and fifty thousand dollars and set it up to saw fifty thousand feet a day. Now they can't go in there and saw five hundred or a thousand feet a day. That doesn't even pay their interest.

"So only the small guys play with it. The little guys can well afford to do it," George said.

A large, straight locust tree rising from the side of a hill was chosen by the builder and the loggers to become a part of Tim's boat. "Isn't there a way of measuring the girth of it that you can figure out how much you're gonna get out of it?" Tim asked George.

"I've got a [scaling] stick," George replied. "I didn't bring it, though. It's a shame. It will give approximately how many feet you're getting within five feet. You take the stick, hold it a certain way, you walk back away from the tree on level ground and it'll tell you within five feet how tall it is." This method of measuring trees is called scaling. (See Plate 12.)

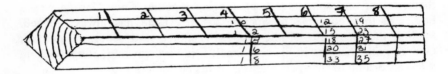

12. Close-up of one end of a scaling stick. This tool is used to approximate the number of board feet in a log or tree. (*Diagram by Greg Violette*)

George and his friend, Lennie Dube, chose the direction they wanted the tree to fall.

Then the near silence of the forest was split by the steady, high pitch of George's power saw starting to "notch," which is the beginning step in felling a tree. George sawed from the tree an almost wedgelike piece of wood, thus creating the "notch." (See Plate 13.)

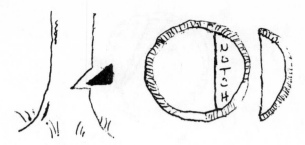

13. Making the notch. (*Diagram by Greg Violette*)

He told us this gives a logger control over where the tree is going to fall and helps it to break clean. Without notching, the tree will fall anywhere the wind blows it or split in half from the cut up.

George now placed the saw next to the notch. He sawed into the tree in a circular motion, going back to the notch on the opposite side, and leaving a little ridge of uncut wood to hold the tree. (See Plate 14.)

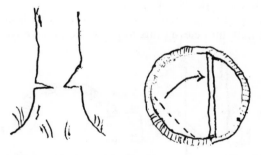

14. Normal procedure for directing the tree. (*Diagram by Greg Violette*)

"Hold it," Roy Cole yelled to his son.

"Is one of you actually going to hold that tree?" we asked incredulously.

"No, no, no, no. What we mean by holding is when you get back to your notches [with the saw], you don't cut one of 'em. You leave something here and nothing there and when it starts falling, this side will break first because there's nothing here to hold it, right? So she'll have a tendency to twist in this direction." (See Plate 15.)

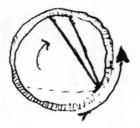

15. Changing the direction of the fall. (*Diagram by Greg Violette*)

"She's leaning that way! She's leaning!" people yelled.

"Yeah. Perfect," Lennie said to George.

"But Mother Nature isn't cooperatin'," replied George.

"The wind. The wind is holding it. Things go wrong. When it rains, it pours. What does the man say? Murphy's law. When nothing goes right, nothing goes right.

"She ain't come back yet. To be safe and not sorry, we'll put a wedge in it," George said. His father had already cut two wedges from deadwood while George was talking.

Lennie pounded in the first of the two wedges with an ax head. (See Plate 16.) It took him eleven hits to place the first wedge.

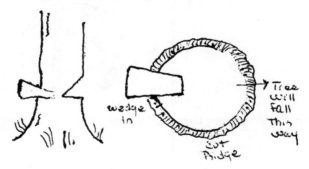

16. Using wedges. (*Diagram by Greg Violette*)

"This tree is ready to go. You get back. It's gonna be a reaction. Something that springs back from the other trees. They're not supposed to, but they will occasionally spring back."

George started the saw again to finish the cutting of the tree, while

17. (*Photo by Sheryl Lane*)

Lennie drove the wedge in more and more. Thirty-six pounds of the ax, fifty pounds, seventy pounds at a steady pace, while the saw sheared the last strands of the tree fibers.

The pounding continued at one hundred fifteen smacks of the ax. People started to yell, "There she goes! There it goes! She's lifting right up, right now! Watch your horse!" One hundred twenty-nine pounds. "She's goin'!"

A loud CRACK pierced the forest air as the last splinters separated. Then the tree angled and fell, not crashing to the earth downhill, but clattering into the arms of its fellow trees. Slightly off track from where the men had wanted it to go.

Branches and bark fell while the tree toppled and chips continued to fall, even after the tree stopped. In a minute all motion in the trees ended. Up in the air at about a forty-five-degree angle the locust tree rested.

George walked up the slanted trunk to measure out the length and thickness Tim needed for the cut: seventeen feet, figuring on twelve inches diameter of wood beneath the thick bark.

Lennie and George then got the tree down from the others by cutting the intertwining branches and other obstructive wood. The locust fell

18. Roy Cole hooking the chains of the woofle bar to the logs. (*Photo by Sheryl Lane*)

to the ground, not with the full crash of a falling giant, but with a hollow drumming thud.

With the power saw, George cut off the limbs and branches. Then he cut the tree into logs. Clyde, a huge old 1,360-pound Clydesdale horse, was harnessed to a "woofle" bar, which is used to drag logs.

Roy hooked the chains of the bar to the logs and then Clyde was guided out of the woods to the side of a road, where the logs were rolled onto a flat-bed trailer. George referred to this as "yarding" the logs.

More trees were dragged out, and then we gathered around the loggers to ask some questions.

"Trees are just like anything else," George told us. "Like a garden, they need to be thinned out and trimmed. If this has been done for a while, you can see the differences in the annual growth. They like to be taken care of, too."

We asked if logging has changed much since George and Roy began logging. "Tremendously in the past twenty years. Like everything else, it has become more mechanized. Twenty or thirty years ago, it was strictly a horse operation. The cost of labor has driven it up so that it's become mechanical.

19. George Cole leading Clyde out of the woods to the flat-bed trailer. (*Photo by Sheryl Lane*)

"In the old days when I was a kid, we used to cut logs with a two-man saw, and I remember when we got our first power saw. That was quite an adventure, and now you don't see nobody using crosscut saws. The first [power saw] we had, it was a two-man saw, basically. It was so heavy two guys had to lug it. I mean today what they weigh, fifteen or twenty pounds. Like everything else, modern times have caught up with the logging business.

"We don't see a lot of the more modern equipment. We see some, but if you go into the backwoods, where logging is done professionally, there's probably very few power saws used. It's so mechanized.

"A tractor, what I call a tractor, goes in and a pair of shears grabs the tree and they have what they call a 'monkey.' It's a hydraulic thing that goes up the tree, clips all the limbs off just to a certain size at the top. It stops there, cuts the top off, comes back down, and jumps off.

Push a button [the shears are] just like a pair of scissors. It cuts the tree and lays it down and goes on and takes another tree.

"It's essentially a two-man operation [in modern logging]. One man running that [monkey] and another man has a tractor or skid or whatever you wanna call it. He hauls 'em all aside the road to the place where they're picked up. That's the only place the power saw is used.

"We use the power saw. We use a horse, because that's what my father wants to use, and we use what he wants. He enjoys it. It's not for me to say he can't. I'm not going to change him.

"We've always logged. That was always a supplement to our income. We always farmed basically. And the reason I got the sawmill was I went to build a house and I didn't have enough lumber and couldn't get no mill, no lumber at that time. So I found a mill.

"I enjoy working outdoors. I don't miss much of anything going on, airplanes going by, helicopters or anything else. I can tell you pretty near every bird that flies by of any size or quality. I don't miss too much."

Some of us rode on the horse-drawn cart with Roy Cole, and the rest of the group hopped on the flat-bed trailer drawn by George Cole's tractor. The horse and tractor moved slowly along the well-worn muddy trail, through the woods and fields of East Kingston, New Hampshire, and back to George's house and sawmill.

As we rode along we asked, "Isn't there less damage to the forest when you go in with a horse to pull out your logs?" George pondered a moment and his answer reflected the balance he has struck between old and new ways of logging.

"It depends on what school of thought you use. Oh, surfacewise it appears that little or no damage is done with horses, but this also creates another problem."

George said that pulling logs by horse fails to stir up the forest floor and does not help in the reseeding of trees. "Reseeding is like planting a garden in the forest. If we go in and chew up the bottom of the forest, you know, the surface of the ground, the leaves and needles and what not . . . there the seeds have a better chance of getting into the ground and actually growing, replanting themselves.

"But if you take and make a path and you take and drag logs out the same path a hundred fifty, two hundred times, pretty soon you have a rut there and that rut means erosion and it will erode. You can't help it.

"If they go in and they don't use the same path continuously, they do a good job. They are successful.

"So I mean there's things that can be said for both sides. It's like anything else. Common sense in some cases is not used, and that's what gives the bad names to people who go in and don't do a good job.

"Common sense tells you this, but a lot of work isn't done on common sense. It's done on money. Basically money. They're more worried over the dollar, and so it makes a bad name.

"Yet there are people go in loggin' who do an excellent job, and they're not gettin' credit. It's like listening to the news. You're always hearing the bad things, not necessarily the good things about what goes on."

20. George Cole's sawmill. (*Photo by Mark Emerson*)

21. George moves the log to his mill. (*Photo by Mark Emerson*)

Country Sawmill— Cutting the Stem and Wood Keel

By Greg Violette

It was an early spring day at the farm of George Cole in East Kingston, New Hampshire, when we arrived to watch him cut the wood for the stem and wood keel of the forty-five-foot Herreshoff Ketch that Tim Dowling is building.

As we walked down past the barn, we caught the distinctive smells of the farmyard and realized that soon we would be enjoying the highly pleasing aroma of freshly cut wood.

"Let's take a look at what you want to be sawed here," George said. "One thing about locust. You can tell. It's yellow. It has a very thick bark." The reason for using locust in a boat is that it is hard, rot resistant, and fairly free of knotholes, according to George.

Tim and George measured and compared a number of logs in the stack of locust. They checked out length and diameter (which is measured from the inside of the bark to the opposite inner side), and they also looked for quality. They referred to Tim's blueprints many times.

While they did that, some of us looked at the sawmill. We could not help but notice its makeshift, slightly dilapidated appearance.

"The mill is a little unsettled. The frost pushed up the other side. It's a little cock-eyed, but what we're gonna do today, it won't bother us," George explained cheerfully.

The building was made of weather-grayed timbers and boards. The left side of the structure was a largely open place that was cluttered with piles of scrap and lumber in stacks. A truck was parked halfway inside the building. It was used to deliver lumber.

A door stood in the center of the building with a sawdust-encrusted window nearby. The door opened into the immediate area where the gasoline motor to run the mill was placed.

To the right of the structure, flanked by enormous clumps of bushes, was an open doorway, and beside this was a large three-sided stall holding a mountain of sawdust.

When the logs were chosen for milling, George climbed onto his bulldozer-tractor, which had two long, metal, tusklike extensions bolted to the bucket, designed for lifting logs like a forklift.

It came to life with a loud roar. George shifted the gears and it sprang forward. The large metal tracks it rode on picked up and sprinkled dirt about. He lowered the bucket and the extensions dug slightly into the ground as they slid under the logs. He raised the bucket, put the 'dozer in reverse, and turned his head around. He backed past the open doorway, shifted, and took a right turn through it.

Inside the doorway were two large parallel wooden beams. George lowered the bucket between them, placing the logs on top. He backed, shifted again, parked the bulldozer near the truck, and hopped down to join us.

We stepped through the doorway of the sawmill where the logs had been deposited. Hanging overhead was a ragged, sun-bleached, sawdust-coated, oriental-style carpet with a beautiful design that could still be faintly seen.

As we ducked under this and around the line of logs waiting to be cut, our eyes took in a great variety of objects.

There were fourteen tin plates fastened to a ceiling beam, variously colored—black, green, purple, red. Many were mottled with rust and some were totally illegible. The younger plates plainly denoted that they were *"State of New Hampshire Wood Processing Mill Registration. Class One."*

Extra saw blades rested against the far wall, and four or five fire extinguishers stood here and there in the sawmill.

To be expected—but still surprising because of the degree of its presence—was the layered coating of sawdust, wood chips, and bits of bark on and over everything, everyplace, throughout the building.

Dominating the interior of the sawmill were the large saw and the log carriage. The carriage has six tiny wheels which ride on a forty-foot stretch of track. It has a locking device which clamps the log down, holding it in place as it moves through the saw.

George told us the history of his mill. "This mill originally came from Kingston. It was built around 1880, burnt down at the end of World War I, and I rebuilt the mill. This is the original kind of mill that came out at that time.

22. "I can set the log the way I want it." (*Photo by Nat Bailey*)

"This is one of the first rope mills. The real old mills were what they call 'ring and pinion.' Instead of the carriage running on a track, it ran on a set of rollers.

"Now they reversed it. They put six [wheels] on the carriage and they put it on a track, like a train track, and it runs back and forth. The only reason they call it 'rope' is there's a cable to pull it back and forth.

"Now, I can't tell you why they changed the name from a 'ring and pinion' to a 'rope' mill, where they always had a cable to pull the carriage, 'cept in the old days they pushed 'em down by hand and pulled 'em back by hand. They don't do that no more!

"Even the modern mills today are basically the same way, except they're all steel. They don't use no wood in them and the guy normally sits around the corner so he can't see the saw. That would be what they call a live log pen!

23. Changing tooth on blade. (*Photo by Nat Bailey*)

"In other words, when the logs come in, there's a chain that keeps turning and he has a series of buttons to push, and once it rolls on the carriage, he has no control over the log, and everything's automatically clamped on there.

"I can fool around. I can set the log the way I want it. In the new mills they don't do that. When they hit the carriage that way, the things keep turning all the time. The guy lets one log slide on. It jumps on and everything . . . WHOOSH!" George gestured, showing how fast the logs go through the new mills.

"Believe it or not, when they get done with a day's work, they have a man or a lady come in. They use a vacuum cleaner and they vacuum the whole works because they have hydraulic equipment."

George walked over to his saw blade to check its teeth. "I just bought two boxes of teeth. They've jumped in price up to around forty-five cents a piece. This is a three-piece saw. A tooth, a ring, and a blade."

He picked up a tool that somewhat resembled a can opener. He placed it on a tooth and with a bit of tugging he snapped it off the blade. Then with a bit more straining he replaced it.

"There," he said. "Snug little fit. If I was sawing a large amount of lumber every day, I would probably sharpen the teeth maybe twice a day. If I sharpen it once a week, I do well."

George and Tim gave the logs another check to see which way they should be cut. Then he and his friend Lennie Dube each took a "peavey," or cant dog, and hooked them into the bark of the first log in line.

They rolled it off the wooden beams onto the carriage and continued to roll it around until they got it on the side that George wanted to cut first. Having done this, he clamped the holding device onto the log and locked it. This device, besides holding the log secure, could also make the log inch out as far as George wanted it to when he pulled on a handle.

George got his oil squirt can and spurted oil on various bolts and hinges. Then he lubricated points in the motor that provided the power for the saw blade, the carriage, and the "sawdust remover."

He started the motor, which made a very loud noise while running. Slowly it began to turn the drive belts which came in direct contact with the machinery. Then the saw blade started to circle, and as it gained momentum, the teeth seemed to disappear, to become a solid, flat plane like the rest of the blade. A whirling whine was its voice.

The "sawdust remover," a suction vent located under the saw blade, began to absorb the wood particles, which went up across the ceiling and were deposited onto the heap in the stall outside.

George got at his station, put his hand on the lever and eased it forward. The cable pulled taut, the carriage edged forward, and the log neared the saw. Then the teeth of the saw ripped into the fibers of the log, making an awful staccato sound.

Quickly it was through and the carriage rolled back, as Lennie threw onto a scrap pile the first piece, which is called a "slab," because it consists mainly of bark with a thin slice of wood.

George and Tim examined the wood that the first cut had revealed. They looked for possible signs of decay, insects, or soft-centered knots, none of which are good to use on the construction of a boat.

The log was good. George sent it through the saw again and again while Lennie stacked the boards. Occasionally, George would lean his hip against the log to get just a little bit less wood on the board.

When the log got to a certain size, or a certain number of boards were cut, he would stop the carriage, unlock the clamps, and turn the log over with a peavey to the exact opposite side, make a "slab," check

24. George sends the log through the saw again and again. (*Photo by Nat Bailey*)

the underlying wood, and send it through again until the log was finished.

This was not the only procedure he used for dividing the logs. Occasionally, when there was an exceptionally fine log, George would simply square off the log, leaving it looking like a rectangular cylinder. This thick block of wood is called a "timber." Tim used these in the backbone assembly (keel) of his boat.

Later George told why he runs the sawmill. "I did it for a living. I was married and had three children, so I had to do something as a steady income. Now I do this as a hobby.

"I enjoy the work. Basically it's a physical job and I work where I am. I have to physically work, but I'm not pressed."

Master Boatbuilder

By Herbert Baum III and Kathi Preble Peck
Photography and interviewing by Anne Gorham, Herbert Baum III,
Kathi Preble Peck, Anne Pierter, Sandy Frederick, and Gerald Dickson

During his thirty years of building boats on the Kennebunk River in southern Maine, Herbert Baum, Sr. has launched over a hundred boats. When asked the exact number, he replied, "I tried to figure it out one time how many boats I have built, and I thought I got them all. Then I would think of another one."

Herb is a master boatbuilder who has been building boats the better part of his life. He comes close to being a legend in his own time, one of the keenest eyes in the business, according to some of his admirers.

He grew up on the sea, but lost his taste for the seafaring life as he became older. "I went fishing when I was a kid," he began to explain. "See, I lived on Matinicus [an island off the coast of Maine], and I always was out on a boat. I went herring fishing for five summers. Then I went dragging for five trips, and then I went back to herring. I did like water when I was a kid, but not much when I was older.

"You have to be a different person to work on the water. You might get one dollar one day and one hundred dollars the next day and nothing the day after that."

So Herb took jobs on the land instead of becoming a fisherman. He worked for several years in a lime plant outside Rockland, and he worked in a woolen mill in Camden.

While working at the woolen mill, "I just fooled around in my garage on Saturdays." One of the things he "fooled around" doing was building small boats. "The first boat that I built was a peapod.

"Then I worked in South Portland for a shipyard. After working in the shipyards building steamers, another man and I decided in 1945 to buy a boatyard of our own. [The wartime shipbuilding had stopped.] We hunted for a place, and I found one in South Portland, but they

wanted a hundred dollars a month for rent. So I gave up looking and
went back to fishing.

"Then one day my wife was looking through the Sunday paper and
she ran across an ad that said there was a boatyard for sale in the Kennebunk area. So we came down here to look at it, and we decided to
buy it. That was in 1945 and we moved up here and started to build
boats that same year."

As Herb remembered that first year, he started to count off on his
fingers the number of boats he built. "When we came here in 1945, we
built one . . . two . . . three . . . four . . . five . . . six . . . seven
. . . eight, and we were on our ninth boat in two years. We were really
building.

"We built like the devil at the first of it. We were building lobster
boats and small pleasure boats then, but later on people began to get

26. First sailboat, the *Lark,* built by Herbert Baum, Sr.

more money and they were spending more money and they wanted bigger boats. Some of those big boats took almost a year to build."

We asked Herb if he thought today's boats are as good as the ones that were built years ago. "It's according to how good they take care of them. The old boats used to last longer than the new boats because they were narrower. The wider they are, the more they lug and carry. Same as a big man or a big woman. Your body can't stand that extra weight."

We knew that Herb had been in the Coast Guard for a time, and we knew that he had lived as a boy on Matinicus Island, but there were some gaps in his life before buying the boatyard that we were curious about. "Well, I lived everywhere like a wandering Jew," he grinned. "I went to high school in Rockland [Maine], and then after high school I went into the Coast Guard.

"We graduated on a Wednesday or a Thursday, and the next day we were in the Coast Guard," Herb told us. "I came home from school one day and my aunt says to me, 'What are you doing after you get out of high school?' I says, 'I don't know.' She says, 'Em'—that's her husband—'I got the boy going to the Coast Guard.' I didn't do nothing about it.

"Then in school one day I was talking to Fred Knight, he was graduating, too, and he says, 'What are you doing?' and I said, 'Let's go down to the Coast Guard.' Fred says, 'No, Christ, no.' Well, we had an assembly, and during the assembly three of us went over to the Coast Guard. Fred, Ludwig, and myself. We took three bicycles from the grammar school and they said we stole them. I didn't think we done nothing. We just borrowed 'em and brought 'em back.

"Well, we had another assembly and the principal had this letter, and she brought it up and it was about the bicycles. And she says, 'I know who two of the boys are, but I don't know the third one.' And this other guy got right up and he turned around and said to me, 'Tell 'em, Baum, it is you.' He says, 'She thinks it is me.'

"So when the thing [assembly] was over, she says, 'I want to see Mr. Baum, Mr. Knight, and Mr. Ludwig.' So she says, 'You get me a written note from the owners saying that everything is all right or I won't sign your diplomas.'

"So away we went and I found the kid whose bicycle I had, and he said everything was all right. Then we went to the one that Fred had and, Jesus, the guy wouldn't sign it. It belonged to his son and his son was going to the University of Maine and we would have to wait until he got home. It was funny. They gave us our dinner, but he wouldn't sign it.

"Fred says, 'You can't. I got to get my diploma.' Well, the guy kept stalling off. We must'uv been there two or three hours, and finally he signed it. So he wrote it right on the back of the paper that I had. So Fred and I brought the paper back to the principal and he gave her the paper and she read it and she says to me, 'Where's yours?' I says, 'Right on the back of that one.'

"Wasn't she wild then! She thought we had ganged up. Naturally you would think so. Ludwig, oh, he had to buy the kid new wheels and a new tire because he got a flat. Oh, it was funny!"

Herb finally did get his diploma, along with the other two boys, and they all joined the Coast Guard together. He told us that he didn't like the Coast Guard. "Eighteen years old and tied down and can't do anything. We was only down to White Head for two months and then we went down to Salisbury Beach. A year was enough."

We were curious about what Herb did at Salisbury Beach, and he told us that he chased rum runners. "We never caught any," he said. "They was like a bunch of spiders in a nest. They would all run away when they saw us coming.

27. Herb and crew steaming in the frames. "You can't drive every nail or saw every board."

"I had nothing when I went into the Coast Guard, and I had a hundred dollars when I come out. One hundred dollars. I wouldn't 'uv had that if I hadn't sold . . . another guy and I, we bought a car together. We bought a Cadillac at first. Then we bought an old Ford, and I sold my half for two hundred and fifty dollars. I come home with a hundred dollars."

Next came the years with the lime company and the woolen mill. He was married in 1927 and moved to South Portland during the wartime shipbuilding years of the 1940s.

Throughout his years as a boatbuilder, Herb said, he has had a crew of fine men working for him. Asked if there is any one man that stands out in his mind as a skilled worker, he replied, "All of them. I don't think you could beat them anywhere. They were really good men.

"Your product is no better than your men are. I get all the credit as long as things are good. But if things are the other way around, it's the men that does the work.

"You can't drive every nail or saw every board. It's up to you to try to get them to do it the way you want it done.

"I had some very good men. They were good. I don't know how it would be to start out with young people. Some would be better than others. I have had several young people, and they weren't interested. Of course, today all they think about is money. That's the whole story.

"Everyone has to have money. We were interested in money— enough to live, yu' know. But they [his men] had pride in their work. A lot of men would go home and try something. Others would go to the library and find something out. Some would go to different boat-yards and see what they were doing wrong.

"I used to sneak up and down other yards to see how other people do it. When I first started out, I did that. When I got older, you don't get around as much."

We asked Herb if he learned anything from sneaking around in different boatyards and he replied, "Yeah, then you was looking for something you were doing wrong. You might think that you are doing it right, and you go to some place they are doing it different. You might think that you are doing it right. That is only natural.

"Getting your money is the biggest problem with boatbuilding . . . no, the biggest problem is getting labor. I was lucky I had men stay so long. Francis Clough came in 1951 and Doane [Lawrence] came here that same year. Francis got through the same time I did, 1974, and Doane got through a few years before that. Dwight Robinson, he was the first man that I hired, and he worked a few years and then he would go away, then come back. Amirault and Bill Towne worked for me, and Byron Swett was here for a long time. Herb [his son, Herb, Jr.] worked quite a bit, and Milt Maling [his son-in-law] worked for me. I was lucky they all stayed."

Other than the men who did the physical work of building the boats, Herb was helped by his wife, Kay, who kept the books and files for thirty years. His dog, Baumbie, also helped in the business. Every Friday Baumbie delivered the payroll, running from the house to the boat shop with a bag tied around her neck.

28. "Baumbie" delivering paychecks weekly to the workers of Baum's Boatyard.

29. Herb feeding his geese.

Herb also has ten pet geese who have served him over the years. "I bought four of them just for pets. That was way back, and they are all gone now. These that I have here now I just keep them because they make good watchmen. They make a noise when anybody is around."

We had come to Herb to learn about the craft of boatbuilding, and during a half dozen interviews in his cavernous frame boatyard, he answered questions, explained patiently, and demonstrated, all the while darting quickly from one section of the big building to another.

First we wanted to know what kind of tools he would use to build a boat.

"You would need everything. I mean we had everything. Some people don't have everything. We had two of everything because there was four or five of us working, and one saw wasn't enough. We had two saws and two planers, three bandsaws, and two jointers. I don't know how many sanders we had, but we had two of everything—sometimes more."

As Herb talked, our eyes followed the walls of his boat shop lined with rows of tools and materials. We saw scores of clamps ranging from one half inch to two feet. Dozens of graduated bits stood on narrow shelves.

"A lot of people, all they need to build a boat is an ax and a hammer. I don't know, some people don't have very much and they still do a good job. Some people don't have but a dozen to twenty clamps, but I have over two hundred clamps.

"In some places men had their own tools. My men just had their hand tools, saws, planes. A lot of places, the men even have their own SkilSaw."

30. Behind a small pram, *Kathy 2,* Herb's tools hang on the walls.

31. The *Lady Elayne,* a fifty-three-foot luxury cruiser.

32. The *Maine Maid,* a fifty-foot luxury cruiser.

Steps in Building a Wooden Boat

Herb took us step by step through the process of building a wooden boat. We will explain the major steps, but it is important to remember that each major step involves dozens of smaller steps. Much of the photography for the step-by-step demonstration follows the construction of a forty-five-foot wooden sailboat, the *Edleweiss*.

First the buyer of the boat tells Herb what kind of boat he wants. From the owner's ideas, Herb makes a model of the hull, which is the backbone or frame of the boat.

"Well, you just take a piece of wood," Herb explained as he told us how to make a model. "Someone tells you what they want, and I take and rough it out on a piece of wood, or I just sketch the shape of the hull on the wood.

"If this is what the man wants, well then I take the wood and put it on the bandsaw and cut it out and have the model." Some people will take this model and finish it and stain it and display it in their homes.

"The whole story is that you have a picture, and then you have to develop this picture. Some people have the picture, but can't develop it."

Herb designs many of the boats he builds, drawing up the blueprint himself. If the model for the boat is one of Herb's designs, he draws the plans from the model. If the boat design is patented by another marine architect, he contracts with that architect for the plans.

"Every draftsman draws differently. Sometimes you have to learn all over again [to read the plans]. Some guys draw up the plans one way and you can read them or understand them, and then you get somebody else and he'll do a little different. I have had a lot of men draw for me. There was Eldredge McInnis, George Stedell, John Alden, Stoner and Crocker, Winthrop Warner, Dwight Simpson, Philip Rose, F. C. William, and Miles Fitch." These men are all well known in the field of marine design.

After the plans have been drawn up, Herb paints a cross section of the hull on the floor of a pattern room or "lofting" room, as it is more commonly called. The pattern room is a long room on the second floor of Herb's boat shop. For each new cross section of a hull, he uses a different color of paint. To the untrained eye, these lines mean nothing, but to Herb each line is a reminder of the many boats he has built.

From this cross section, or pattern, he makes the molds that support and mold the shape of the hull while it is being built. The molds are made from plywood.

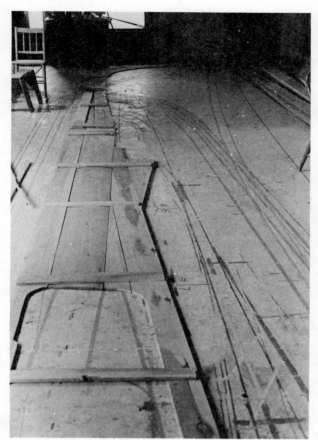

33. The pattern room, better known as the "lofting room."

One of the most important decisions in building the boat is the decision about what kind of wood to use. Many kinds of wood can be used. Herb has used mahogany, redwood, Alaskan cedar, pine, and Maine cedar. "I think cedar is the easiest and softest wood to work with," he told us.

Mahogany is the only wood he uses that does not have knots in it. "Look at the knots in this one," Herb said, while pointing to a piece of Maine cedar. "Too knotty. You can use wood with knots in it, but some wood is too knotty."

We asked him why he couldn't use wood that is too knotty. He explained that if he came to that knot when cutting a board, the knot would crack and fall out and he would have a hole where the knot was.

34. Molds before
being set in
place.

35. Molds set in
place.

Herb told us some of the special characteristics of wood that a boat-builder needs to know. We had not realized that a boatbuilder prefers to work with rough-cut planks that still have the bark on them rather than finished planks. Herb explained that a rough-cut board does not have straight edges. When he uses a rough-cut board, the edges are already partly curved, making his work easier since most of the boards in the boat need to be curved. Trimming his own planks, Herb says he has less waste than when the boards are pretrimmed.

After the patterns have been drawn on the floor and the molds have been made, Herb makes a keel plug out of wood and sends it to a foundry to be cast in lead. "The plug doesn't weigh much," he told us. "All the plug is, is just a form. You make it out of plywood and you send it to the foundry and they put it in the sand [to make a mold] and they pour lead into the sand [mold]." Although the keel plug doesn't weigh much, Herb said that the keel itself can weigh up to five thousand pounds or more.

The lead keel balances the boat. It is the center section of the bottom of the boat and is connected on each end to a piece of wood called the wood keel. This wood is then connected to the stem (front) by a forefoot and to the stern post (back).

36. Timbers and battens in place.

37. The stern post.

The stem, which is the backbone of the bow, and the stern post, which is the backbone of the stern, have to be connected to the keel by pieces of wood. Several pieces are joined to connect them, because one piece of wood won't run the entire length of the boat. The forefoot serves as sort of a joint between the stem and the keel. Herb likened it to a knee, which connects the thigh to the calf.

After the keel is made, Herb lays wooden blocks on the floor of the building room. These blocks serve as supports for the keel while the boat is being built.

Once the keel is laid and the stem and stern posts are put in place, the molds are put up. The molds control the shape of the boat as it is built. These molds have a notch in the bottom that fits over the keel.

The battens are put on next, and these help to hold the molds in place. The battens are horizontal beams that run from the bow to the stern, and they are the first beams put on in building the boat.

After the battens are in place, the timbers go on. The timbers are the vertical boards that go to the inside of the battens, extending from the keel up. The timbers are steamed before they go on so that they will bend. Timbers and battens are nailed where they cross.

Now that the timbers are in place, Herb starts planking, or boarding up the side of the boat. The first board that he nails on is called the

38. Dwight Robinson drilling holes for stopwaters, which are dowels of softwood driven into the seam between the keel and adjoining parts.

39. Byron Swett continues planking.

40. Floor timbers in place.

garboard plank. He then continues planking until the side of the boat is completely sealed.

Herb says that everyone does planking differently. "Some people start at the top and come down, and also start at the bottom and work up. Then they come together in the middle.

"I always start at the bottom of the boat and then go right up to the top so that my top board is the last board that I put on. Some people say it takes a little more figuring to start at the bottom and that it is harder.

"Probably that is why I do it that way. I like to do things the hard way," he said, grinning.

When Herb has finished planking, he removes the molds. Next he puts braces up along the sides of the boat. When the braces are in place, he builds the engine bed. This holds the engine in place while it is set into the boat by a block and tackle.

The next step is to build the deck. First Herb lays the floor timbers and bolts them down. The floor timbers are the beams that support the weight of the deck. The beams run from the starboard (right) side to the port (left) side. The decking is laid down from the stern to the bow.

41. Finishing the deck.

42. The ways.

As the deck is finished, the visible features of the boat take shape. Herb builds the cabin next and then he starts the finishing touches. The deck is coated with fiber-glass resin to keep the water from seeping in. The interior design is done.

When the boat is finished, preparations must be made for the launching. First packing is placed under the sides of the boat. Packing consists of planks used to support the boat while it is being prepared for launching. The packing is two to six inches thick and ten to twelve inches wide in random lengths.

"If she was going to be launched on Saturday," Herb told us, "then on Monday we would start to build her up [put the packing under the boat]. We would take them [the packing planks] out and grease everything down, and then that same day we would put them back in for keeps, until the boat is in the water."

The ways are runners on which the boat slides into the water. Each of the runners is about twelve inches wide with raised edges that extend from under the boat down into the water. On the back side of the boat shop are tall barn doors that swing open when it is time to launch a boat.

Now Herb drives wedges under the packing the entire length of the packing. This lifts the boat about one half inch off the blocks, which are then removed from under the keel. Temporary cradles with shoes on each side are slipped beneath the boat for it to rest on as it slides down the ways.

The shoes of the cradle sit on the top of the ways and the packing is on top of the shoes. Since the ways are greased, the boat will slide down on the shoes into the water.

"Fasten the shoes to the ways with a piece of rope. This will hold the boat and packing to the ways and keep the boat from running away," Herb explained.

Christening is the traditional ceremony of breaking a bottle of champagne over the bow of the newly built boat. "The owner will get a bottle of champagne. Usually this is a gift from someone, and if not, then it is usually the cheapest he can get. We fix up the bottle, decorate it with red, white, and blue and then put netting around the bottle so no one gets cut. Then we make a place for the person christening to stand on.

"Friends of the owner and our own friends come to the launching," Herb continued. "When people would hear we were having a launching, they would come from everywhere. Some people come from a long way away. After we had the launching, they usually had a party at the boat shop. We try to have the party afterward and not have any drinking before the launching, but sometimes you can't help it. People sneak drinks if they can."

43. "It is something that you just can't work on for only eight hours a day."

44. "I christen thee . . ."

45. A boat sliding into the water.

After the bottle has been broken over the bow and the ropes cut, the boat slides into the water. "Francis Clough was our official rope cutter all the time that he was here.

"I have always done it that way," Herb said as he talked about the launching. "Sometimes the person christening the boat might miss and then they are up on a staging. If the boat is already sliding down the ways, they might fall off the damn thing and get hurt, trying to hit the bow of the boat and getting themselves together. So we wait until the bottle has been broken, and then we cut her adrift."

Herb began telling about some launchings he remembered. "There was this boat, oh, the owners were oddballs. They brought a bucket of water and they said it was from Lake Winnipesaukee. And they came with that bucket. They probably took it out of the faucet. Then the girl threw the water on the boat, and that is how they christened it. Oddballs. Jesus, were they oddballs!

"We had a priest who bought a boat once and he first put on his robes and blessed the boat. Then he changed back into his clothes and christened the boat. He went into the back room and changed and then came out and said, 'I christen thee'—that is what you always say when you hit the boat—and then he said the name of the boat. I don't remember it now.

"I remember one launching and George Cooper was down to it and we launched the boat. He came up to me after and he said, 'You know that in twenty minutes after you launched that boat, you had another keel laid in there.' He couldn't understand it. But I figured I had help there, so I got the keel laid for the next boat."

Herb has built all kinds of boats, from draggers to houseboats, lobster boats to sailboats—just about everything. There is one exception. He has never built a Friendship Sloop.

"I always wanted to build a Friendship Sloop, and the nearest I came to building one was when a man in New Jersey wanted a small sailboat. He had already had a big yacht built, the *Maine Maid*.

"I told him that the cheapest one to build was this Friendship Sloop and he said no, and he had to go and have me make another one. And someone killed him in Boston before she was ever finished."

Another boat that interested us was a sixty-five-foot dragger that he built for Harold Day in 1951. The dragger, *Rita and Olive,* was started in July of that year and finished by January of the next year.

46. The *Rita and Olive*

47. Herb's crew in 1960.

There was a crew of ten that worked on that boat at all times. The boat was so big that Herb had to build it outside. The shop just wasn't big enough.

"The first sailboat that we built, we took her out into the water, and want [weren't] it some rough. That is me hanging on there [pointing to picture of the boat]. There was no air, but want it some rough, and one of the guys . . . the rigging was loose, and he went up to the rigging to tighten it and he loosened it. So we went up there and we had an awful time with her.

"We were taking her over to York Harbor, and the boat, she had two owners. One of them was up forward with a lead line [a line used to measure the depth of the water], and he threw the lead line over and we had twelve feet. And he threw it back and hauled it, and we had ten feet, and he did it again and we had eight feet. He says to the captain, 'You want me to let go of the anchor?'

"The captain, he says, 'I'll tell you when to let go of the anchor. LET GO OF THE ANCHOR!' It was funny. He says, 'I'll tell you when to let go of the anchor. LET GO OF THE ANCHOR!'

"We built a boat for a guy in New Hampshire and he called up and he says the bank wanted a number of the boat. So I said to him, 'What do they want a number for?' and he says, 'I don't know, but they want a number of the boat, so give me the number, will ya?'

"I says, 'One hundred eleven.' That's the easiest number I could think of. You couldn't say one, we've built more boats than one, so I chose one hundred eleven. I tried to figure it out one time how many boats I have built, and I thought I got them all. Then I would think of another one."

We asked Herb if he would encourage young people to become boat-builders. He told us that there were just as many around now as ever, but many people were building with fiber glass now. We asked him what he thought about fiber glass and he replied, "Nothing. It is all right if you want it." We had expected a sharp answer, but he fooled us.

His son, Herb, Jr., was willing to talk a little more about fiber glass. "They haven't proven bad yet, so it is hard to say. Maintenance is why they are buying them. If you want a fiber-glass boat, you can haul it out and scrape it and paint it in the next day. Also paint seems to hold better on fiber glass. With a wooden boat you have to scrape it, paint it, and let it dry out. It isn't that a fiber-glass boat won't get a hole poked in it, though. But who's to say? I always will believe in wooden boats."

Herb, Sr. then went on to tell us more about the future of the business of boatbuilding. "If a person wants to work, it is all right.

"It is something that you just can't work on for eight hours a day. You have to work twelve hours a day, and there are so many days that you can't do anything.

"Once in a while I took a Sunday off, but not very often."

Epilogue

Shortly after this article about Herbert Baum, Sr. was first published, the master boatbuilder retired and the big old boatyard stood silent for many months. Then on December 23, 1977, the boatyard was bought

by Salt, using revenues from *The Salt Book* as a down payment. The
Baum Boatyard has become the Salt Boatyard and once again it rings
with the sound of hammers, now joined with the clack of typewriters,
as young people build boats on the ground floor and other young people make magazines on the second floor.

At the time of Herb's retirement, his grandson, Herbert Baum III,
wrote the following commemorative to his grandfather's work which
was published in *Salt:*

After thirty years of building boats on the Kennebunk River, my
grandfather has retired. To those of us who watched him build boats
for most of our lives, this was a sad time. To the local fishermen who
have brought their boats to the boat shop for repairs every year, this
was a time when they remembered all the hard work Gramp and his
crew did for them on every boat that was hauled up at the boatyard.

The people of Kennebunkport will miss hearing the sounds of hammers and the smell of fresh wood every time a new boat is being built.
The local people will remember the excitement and the shouts of joy
every time a new Baum-built boat slid out of the boat shop and
plunged into the water for the first time.

His family will remember how proud Gramp looked when one of his
boats was completed and the rope was cut, sending the boat out from
his careful sheltering into the rough seas that would follow. We will

also remember the look of relief that came across his face when the drawbridge across the Kennebunk River was opened and the boat was on its way to our great Atlantic.

I will remember the times that I have seen one of my grandfather's boats ride smoothly across the water and the times I have seen the same boat return to the river in which it was built for a visit with the builder, like a salmon returning to its spawning grounds.

Although there will be no more new Baum-built boats sliding out of the shop, they will still be with us, somewhere in the vast miles of ocean, with the look of quality that, in our eyes, no other man can match.

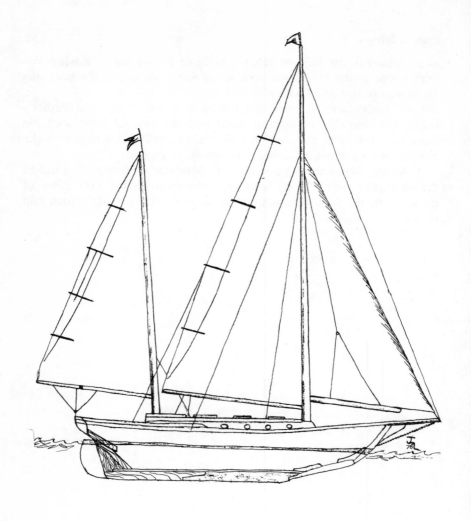

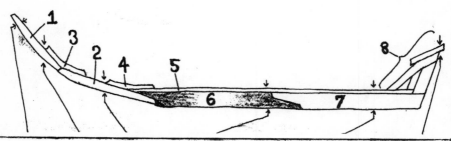

50. 1. Stem   3. Knee   5. Keelson   7. Wood keel   2. Forefoot   4. Knee   6. Lead keel   8. Deadwood

Laying the Keel

Story, photography, and sketches by Julien LeSieur

This is a sketch of a forty-five-foot Herreshoff Ketch which is being built at the Salt Boatyard by boatbuilder Tim Dowling, with the help of several apprentices. Tim has dreamed all his life of living on a boat and sailing around the world, and that's a good enough reason to build a boat.

In boatbuilding, the first part to build is the keel, the backbone of the boat. Before it was built, the boatbuilders drew a full-size plan of the ketch, transferring the lines of the boat from a set of scale plans.

In boatbuilders' terms this is called lofting, and this procedure is done on a whitewashed floor of a room known as the mold loft or lofting room. The name of this room derives from the time when boatbuilders used barns for boatbuilding. In the barns were haylofts that were quite useless for boatbuilding, so they used this area for planning their vessels.

The plans for Tim's ketch show the dimensions of each individual part full size, and from these plans the dimensions are transferred onto timbers to be cut according to their shapes and sizes.

The keel of the boat has three major sections, two of which are wooden and the other of which is lead. Roughly speaking, the lead section is in the center of the boat and serves as ballast to steady the vessel in the water. The two wooden sections fit around the lead sections extending foreward and aft from the center. (See Plate 50.)

In general terms, the whole forward wooden section of the keel is referred to as the stem, although technically the stem is only the tip of that section. This whole wave pounding area is made up of four separate pieces of wood: the stem (1) attached to the forefoot (2) by a wooden knee (3), all of which are attached to the lead keel by another wooden knee (4). (See Plate 50.)

The whole rear wooden section of the keel is generally referred to as the wood keel, although technically (as with the stem) the wood keel is only one of two parts in this section. The other part is the deadwood.

Together these two form an immovable rudder that helps guide the boat through the water. The real movable rudder is attached to the deadwood and is used to direct the boat.

Running along the top of the lead and wood keel (but not the stem) is a long plank, called the keelson, that secures the lead keel permanently to the wood keel. (See Plate 50.) The keelson is chiseled to form a long groove, called the rabbet, which receives the planking from the hull.

The cutting process for the wooden sections of the keel begins on a machine called the surface planer. This machine is used to trim the timber's thickness evenly by means of an adjustable blade.

The blade is adjusted to a desired level and the timber is repeatedly passed through the planer. About every three passes the blade is lowered again. This procedure continues until the desired thickness is achieved.

51. Tim Dowling guides a timber across the bandsaw.

The bandsaw does the major cutting of the timbers. The large, fierce blade of this machine gives it a murderous appearance. When in use, the blade screams through the wood timber, and any mishap could lead to instant amputation for the operator.

After going through the bandsaw, the unfinished part is passed over a machine called a jointer which smooths the edges that the bandsaw has cut.

A wood preservative to prevent drying and cracking is applied to the piece after it has passed through these machines, which constantly shake the boatyard while in use.

When the preservative has dried, the piece is brought upstairs into the mold loft. As the pieces accumulate, they are fitted together like the pieces of a puzzle and hand-planed to make a flush fit. Piece by piece, the parts of the wood keel are fitted, and the structure takes a definite shape as it awaits the time when it can be attached to the lead keel.

Lead Keel

The first step in forming the lead keel is to build a mold that will hold the ten thousand pounds of molten lead which will be poured into it. This lead will form a keel seventeen feet by one foot by fifteen inches.

The mold, like the other parts of the boat, was lofted and built from plans. It consisted of a wood framework lined with asbestos sheeting to prevent the hot lead from cindering it.

After the mold was built, it was lowered into the ground. The hole in which the mold was placed had a bottom lined with concrete bricks. The bottom had to be level, because the mold was gravity fed and the slightest tilt would cause an improper fill. It took two weeks to dig that

52. Ten thousand pounds of lead for the keel.

hole and line it with two rows of bricks, keeping the bottom level at all times.

To help pour the lead keel, Tim had on hand for the day two professional lead pourers, Gordon Swift and Nickerson Rogers of Exeter, New Hampshire, who are also boatbuilders.

"Swifty," as Gordon Swift is called, had brought his own caldron for the event, an old-time cast-iron bathtub mounted on lion's feet that was four feet long and twice the depth of a modern tub.

The tub was placed on four steel rails (railroad rails), each approximately four feet in length, which were set on firebricks.

To heat the lead, three propane burners were set underneath the tub. About two thousand pounds of lead was loaded into the tub and then the burners were ignited. The sound of the fire-blasting burners somewhat resembled jet engines of an airplane warming up just before takeoff.

The roaring burners and the heat seemed to distract—but not drive away—the many people who had gathered to watch this great pouring event. (Among them, watching with great interest, was Herbert Baum, Sr., himself a highly respected boatbuilder and former owner of the Salt Boatyard.)

53. Tim removes impurities called slag which float to the surface of the boiling lead.

54. Tim puts a lead ingot into the caldron.

55. Using a steel rod, Gordon Swift pushes the ingots down.

As the lead reached a boiling point of 621 degrees Fahrenheit, the steel rails supporting the tub were red and white hot, and soon the pouring started.

It had to be done in one complete pour. If the lead hardened before the boatbuilders finished, the job would be ruined. That would mean starting back to another mold.

"You can't stop in the middle of it," Swifty said. "Should be one pour."

The pour was slow, and as it continued, Tim, Swifty, and the apprentices gradually added more lead ingots to the tub, one at a time to keep it full at all times.

The lead spattered as it fell into the mold and formed mirrorlike metallic streams that flowed along the inside and slowly solidified.

The temperature that day was about 90 degrees and the area around

56. Placing ingots in the mold.

the pouring was at least 20 degrees hotter. The shirtless bodies of the workers were perspiring heavily, and to prevent dehydration, each of them consumed two salt tablets.

As Swifty strode to and fro around the caldron, warning Tim not to put the lead bricks in too rapidly (which would reduce the temperature of the molten lead), he said, "It's a nerve-wracking operation. It looks so easy, but you never know what's going to go wrong.

"Old Bud and I were pouring one—about eight thousand pounds and it blew. Jesus, we had to start it all over again!"

To hasten the process, Swifty was trying a trick that Herb Baum had used successfully in the past. Solid-lead ingots had been set on the bottom of the mold and the liquid lead was poured around the ingots, like fillings around the stub of a tooth.

"I just stole a page out of your book," Swifty said as he paced by

57. The mold
full to the brim.

Herb. "Nobody's going to dig the inside of that lead out," Herb grinned back, as he watched the lead swirl around the solid ingots.

By noon, after three hours of steady pouring, the mold was full and the cooling process began. The lead keel was still too hot to work with the following day, but the second day after the pouring, work could begin again.

The lead keel was then raised from the ground, freed of its mold, and set onto timbers. Electric power tools were used to smooth its surfaces.

As these tools were used, sharp lead fragments flew about, stinging like buckshot. For safety precautions, the workers wore face shields to protect their eyes from the flying fragments.

First the top of the keel was smoothed; the keel was next leaned on one side and then the other to do the sides and bottom. The finished lead keel was now ready for the wood keel and stem.

Before the wood keel and stem were attached permanently, they were fitted and checked for any misfitting areas. The wooden parts were sculpted to a flush fit, requiring the skill of a boatbuilder to do the job right.

58. Smoothing the rough surface of the lead keel.

60. Sanding the lead keel (below).

61. With floor timbers attached, the keelson is fitted onto the keel.

62. Fitting the wood keel and deadwood onto the lead keel.

When the stem and wood keel had a tight, snug fit, they were permanently attached. First a marine adhesive sealer was applied to the surfaces of parts where they would join to stop any leakage there. Then all parts were bolted together.

Finally, the rabbet was chiseled. This is the last major step in laying the keel. The rabbet is a long groove running along the two sides of the keel close to the top edge.

This groove is where the planking for the hull will fit into the keel. Because the planking will come down along the keel at different angles, the rabbet had to be cut out by hand using a hammer and chisel. Over a hundred feet of chiseling was done by the boatbuilders.

Now the whole keel was painted with a lead-base primer to prevent it from cracking and to seal it from leaks. The rest of the ketch can now be built upon its backbone.

Building this boat is a long, hard task. However, as each part is completed, Tim's dream comes closer to reality.

63. "Can't you hear it ring? It's lively. A mallet without a ring is dead. It's no good. A dead mallet will tire you out in no time at all."

64. Left, small yacht mallet. Right, regulation mallet.

Caulking Boats

Story and photographs by Carl Young
Interviewing by Carl Young, Chuck Riley, and Paul Jackson

We heard that Ken Campbell was down caulking a boat at Baum's Boatyard, so we went down to see how it was done. Ken was at work on a lobster boat, and we all crawled under the bow to watch.

Ken has been caulking boats for nearly fifty years. We asked him how he learned.

"Well, my brother was a caulker before me. I got to working with him and I got to liking it. Well, it's just like anything else you get into. You just keep goin' and goin'.

"I've caulked some boats down south, working in the shipyard. And while I was in the Navy, I caulked a lot of boats, too. I've also done a lot for Herbie Baum [Baum's Boatyard in Lower Village, Kennebunk].

"I've done all of Herbie's boats, I guess. There might have been one or two small ones, I don't know. Seems though I have. I done the *Maine Maid*. I've done the *Lady Elayne*—she was a luxury cruiser.

"That was cotton and oakum together. Put two strands of cotton in, then a strand of oakum on top of it. But you can't do that with this boat here. You've got to have at least three- to four-inch planking to use oakum. This boat here has thin planking."

He explained to us about the tools he uses. They consist mainly of a mallet and irons of various shapes and sizes.

"A mallet just can't be made out of any kind of wood. A caulking mallet has to be made out of two kinds of wood. That's black mesquite or live oak.

"Either one of them is good, but I like black mesquite. They are both very tough. I've pounded them for years, and you can see they're not even battered up."

Mesquite is a shrub or small tree. The roots and trunk are used for the caulking mallet.

"Now you may be thinking why I have such a long mallet for. Well, the reason for that is this mallet has to have these slots in the head. These slots give what they call life to the mallet.

"It's lively. Can't you hear it ring? Well, a mallet without a ring is dead. It's no good. A dead mallet will tire you out in no time at all.

"You know what this handle is made of? You can tell just by looking at it. It's a cue from a pool table. The best handle for a caulking mallet is cherry wood. Cherry wood never makes your hand sore. I don't know what it is. It just doesn't make your hand sore.

"I know years ago everybody that got a piece of cherry wood to make a handle out of thought they had something—which they did. This handle here, after a while will get my palm sore, especially if it gets a little dirty. But cherry wood wouldn't do that. It's the best wood for a handle.

"The regulation caulking mallet is sixteen inches long. I got one at home and it's big and heavy. They use a sixteen-inch mallet for a boat with four-inch planking. This mallet here is a small yacht mallet. I don't think it's over fourteen inches long.

"You wouldn't use a regulation mallet on this 'cause it's too heavy. You'd probably break a plank or something.

"This little fellow here is ideal for this job here.

"Now, there are various kinds of irons, different shapes, thicknesses, and widths. It all depends on what you're doing.

"You'll notice that some of these seams are very close and some are quite open. Well, for these close ones you've got to have a thin iron. If you didn't, you couldn't get the cotton in the seam.

"If the seam is well open, you could use a thicker iron, but it don't make no difference. You could still do it with a thin iron. I got a whole box of irons at home, a mess of them, but I don't have many here.

65. Irons.

"The reason you hold your iron like that is you do it just with your wrist, like that, see. You more or less roll it in with your iron. You rock that iron as you caulk it.

"Course, when they plank a boat, the planking is supposed to fit tight on the inside and then supposed to leave me a caulking seam on the outside to put the cotton in. It's supposed to be tight on the inside so I can't drive the cotton and iron right through. If I drive the cotton right through, it's no good.

"Now, sometimes you'll have a seam that's so tight you can't get any cotton in it. You just got to get cotton in there somehow. Well, when you do, we have an iron that's thick here on the shaft and sharp on the edge. This is what we call a reamer iron. [See Plate 65.]

"With this iron I can ream that seam out. So you just drive that iron in there. That'll ream it right out so I can put cotton in there. What I'm doing, in other words, is making a seam. There are various thicknesses of these reamers. It depends on how much seam you need, how big a seam you want, and how much cotton you want to get in it.

"Now, here is what we call a garboard iron. When you are caulking you have to go with the bevel of these planks. The bevel of these planks change. They're not all the same angle.

"The bevels change as they go up. So some of the irons are shaped at different angles so I don't bang my knuckles against the hull.

"Now, here's an iron that's a little thicker. See the difference between the garboard iron and this one? Now, it don't look like much to you, does it? But it is. It's really quite a lot. When I come to a big seam I'll use this thicker iron, and I don't drive it through as quick as the thinner iron.

"Now, you might be saying to yourself, 'How much cotton do I know to put in there?' Well now, that's something I really can't tell you. That's something you've got to experience and learn.

"When you come to a seam that you can see right through, well, there I put more cotton in it. Now, when I come to those places I can tell by the feeling of this iron when I tap it whether that's tight or whether it's loose.

"I can tell by the feeling, but I can't tell you. If it's loose, I tap it a little closer, but if it's tight, I'll just straighten the cotton out so I won't get so much cotton in there. Now, it's not as good done that way, but sometimes that'll do it.

"The more you can just tuck it in the seam, the better it is, for the simple reason that when you tuck it in, the cotton wedges itself right in there tight. But if you straighten it out, it just goes in there and it could come out.

"The more I drive the cotton in, the tighter it gets. Course, I can

66. How to hold cotton and iron.

only drive it in so far till it comes up against the back of the seam, and I hope I can't drive it through.

"What you can do is hold your iron that way and use your finger as a gauge. I don't drive that iron beyond that. When my finger fetches up, that's the depth, and I can't drive that cotton anymore.

"Now, this is the way you hold your cotton. You take your cotton like that [see Plate 66] and put it over your finger, put your hand like that. That way you can just feed it right in the seam.

"Now, if you tried to do it the other way, the cotton would catch on that wood and you'd have fuzz all over the place. This way you hold the cotton away from the wood. Actually, you don't even touch the wood. See, I just roll that cotton right in there. This here and learning to caulk is about the only thing you can do.

"There's a few things you can show anybody, and from then on you've got to practice and experience it. Experience and practice will teach you more than I can.

"If you didn't put any cotton in this boat at all here, you could put her in the water. She'd sink, maybe fill up, but in two or three days that boat will be so tight she'd never leak afterward as long as you kept her in the water.

"If you took her out of the water, she'd leak like a sieve when you put her back in again. Caulking does away with all that."

We asked Ken how much cotton he went through on a boat.

"Well, let's see. I've used around five pounds on the other side and I just finished that side. I'll probably use nine or ten pounds of cotton on this boat by the time I get done.

"That's quite a lot of cotton. You get quite a lot of cotton in a pound. You stretch it right out. Course, the better they plank a boat the easier it is to caulk.

"If a boat is planked well, the seams are reasonably small, and they don't take so much cotton and are easier to caulk. But if the seams were wide open, they would be much, much harder to caulk and take a lot more cotton."

67. "That's quite a lot of cotton to pound," says Ken Campbell.

68. Beetle in left
center with irons
and a mallet on
each side.

"Another thing. It makes a difference on the width of the plank. The wider the planks are, the less seams you get. The narrower your planks are, the more seams you get.

"Now, if I was going to do this boat for contract, I'd count them seams and figure up how many seams and how long they are. This is what would determine how much I'd get for the job.

"This boat here is what they call a dead-wood boat, and there are less seams on this boat than on a down-plank boat."

A dead-wood boat has a solid oak keel and is built up from the keel. A down-planked boat is timbered down from a hollow keel and is built down from the keel.

"This boat [dead-wood boat] is easier to caulk than a down-plank boat. I figured I'd be done caulking this boat in six days. This will be my third day and I've just started on this side, but I got the stern to do. Course, another thing about caulking a boat makes it difficult is how thick your planking is. The thicker your planking, the easier for caulking 'cause you don't have to worry about driving it through.

"The boat here has only about an inch planking. If this was an inch and three eighths, like a lot of them, I'd have three eighths of an inch more and I wouldn't be hasslin' with it. With little planking boats you have to be a little more careful.

"If you break a plank on the inside, they've got to take the plank off, and that hurts. If I did that, Herb would have to take that plank out and put in a new one. But you take a heavy, thicker plank like an inch and three eighths, you aren't going to break that. You can tap it pretty hard and still not do it any harm.

"On the big ships after they had gotten all the cotton and oakum in, they'd take an iron and hawse it all in. They went right along the hull and set that in just as hard as they could, just set the whole business right in, oakum, cotton, and all.

"It would take two men, one to hold the iron and one to swing the beetle. I've done that, and that's a back-breaker of a job."

We asked Ken if there were many caulkers left around here.

"There aren't many left," he told us. "I don't know why there's not. Course, they're going into fiber-glass boats. There probably won't be any left after a while. Not many want to do it.

"As I say, there's a lot to it. But as you do it, you learn a lot by yourself. You get into a few messes, but you learn a lot every time you do."

69. The greased ways. (*Photo by Herb Baum III*)

I Christen Thee, Endeavor

By Dorothy O'Keefe

Ralph Stanley's boat shop was a hub of activity the morning his Friendship Sloop, the *Endeavor,* was launched. Coffee time came and went without one crew member taking even a moment to relax. There was too much work to be done yet. The ways needed to be prepared. The gold-leafer was expected any minute. Rocks were being collected for ballast, and the bowsprit was not secured. Crewmembers Tim Goodwin, Peter Basley, Reggie Durgin, and Renato Saavedra had much to accomplish.

Tim and Peter assumed full responsibility for the preparation of the ways, the wooden rails that extend from the boat shop thirty-five feet, well into the harbor. All old grease and dirt was scraped clean.

"You have to scrape all the old dirt off," said Ralph. "Then you put some grease on it." The ways were greased in order to help the boat glide in one smooth motion into the water. "They have to be done," Marion Stanley explained. "It's a must."

Ralph's eyes scanned his shop. Reggie and Renato were busy with all the last-minute touches that precede any major event. "Now we wait for the tide."

Amid greetings and shouts, with an "AKC registered 100 per cent golden retriever" at her heels, Alice Smith arrived. Her laughter reverberated through the shop in spite of the cigarette anchored between her lips. Her paint-stained shirt indicated she'd been in this line of work awhile.

Marion led her to *Endeavor*'s bow. Laughing, she removed a toy doll suspended from the cutwater. "That's one of the guys' doings."

Alice is an artist. "I was a commercial artist for twenty years, but I was primarily into lettering. I decided to make a business out of it or kill myself trying. So I started making signs.

"I spent one winter working down at Henry Hinckley's boatyard.

And while I worked there, I met an old gentleman by the name of Harvard Graham who is a master boat letterer. Because I was already doing signs, I was fascinated by watching him letter. And by watching him lay on gold leaf I picked up the idea of how to do it. I've been doing it ever since. About seven years.

"I started to do signs. I started to do boat lettering. I started to letter Ralph's boats. And now I letter boats other than Ralph's all over the place."

Alice wielded her brush and with deft hands she applied the varnish to the carved scrollwork on the cutwater. "Ralph cut it. He's a great whittler." The varnish went on in short, sure strokes. "This has a little yellow paint in it so I can tell where I've been and where I'm going.

"It doesn't want to get all the way dry. It wants to get tacky. When I lay my knuckle on it and take it away, it makes a sound, TCHUK!

"Now I lay on the sheets [3″ by 3″]. It's real gold leaf. Expensive. But it lasts a long while. This boat is very special. He's been wanting to build his own boat for years. Been working on everybody else's for years."

Alice took a sheet of the gold leaf from the packet. She handled this very delicately to take care that none was wasted. The sheet was laid onto the varnish, gold side down. The varnish was tacky enough that as she pressed the sheet, the gold would "lay off" onto the varnish. Often Alice had to repeat the process several times.

"These grooves are incised so deeply that in the first rub it doesn't all come off. I never can quite tell because I have the impression on here [sheet]. Yet sometimes the leaf does not adhere. So I go back and press very tightly into the grooves to make sure that it's well covered. I use each sheet until it's all taken off. It comes off just where the size [varnish] is.

"Now I'll go back and letter the stern. That's just with black paint. By the time I finish lettering the stern, this ought to be set up enough so I can burnish it with the cotton. It will really tighten the gold leaf onto the size and remove the excess. Put a real shine to it."

Alice lettered the stern and burnished the gold leaf. Her part of the pre-launching activities done, she left, "because I have another boat to letter yet today."

As Tim and Peter finished greasing the ways, Reggie secured *Endeavor* onto the cradle and began the strenuous job of moving her out of the shop and into the yard, onto the ways. Renato fetched the come-along, a device used to aid in the moving of large objects, such as boats. (The come-along was appropriately nicknamed the "click-clack" by a young spectator due to the noise it made while in use.)

People began to arrive at Ralph's. They spoke in subdued tones as

70. Alice Smith
lettering the
Endeavor.
(*Photo by E. J.
Blake*)

they watched *Endeavor* being guided out of the shop. Renato and Peter
controlled the movement while Reggie replaced the rollers under the
salt-stained cradle, which supported her hull.

"Is that quite tight, Peter?"

"A little bit wide, I think." Reggie moved *Endeavor* and continued
to guide her until she was no longer in danger of scraping her side
against the wall. Safely outside the shop, she rested while her bowsprit
was secured.

Her bowsprit secured, Renato and Reggie placed large rocks on the
outside bottom edges of her cradle. When launched, the weight of
these rocks will hold the cradle down in the water allowing *Endeavor*
to float freely from the wooden support she has always known.

Ralph's two sons, Richard and Edward, along with Tim and Peter,
began to collect the rocks for her ballast. After a short while, a sizable
pile had been accumulated.

71. Marion
Stanley
christening the
Endeavor.
(*Photo by Lynn
Kippax, Jr.*)

Endeavor patiently endured the constant placing of ballast rocks
deep within her hull. The sound of rock against wood soon converted
to rock against rock as the pile diminished.

She was surrounded by an air of splendor, seemingly delighted at
being the center of attention. She sat there, the perfect lady, all too
ready to accept the compliments that came her way. This was her day.

Marion chatted with a small group of people, Tim one of them. The
nervous edge in her voice was barely detectable. "I've got my champagne. I just hope it breaks. That's what I'm worried about. It's a wedding present. We said we were going to save it for something special.
This is special."

With the four words, "I Christen Thee, *Endeavor,*" the bottle gave
way amidst shards of broken glass and cheers from the spectators.

Endeavor patiently endured the constant placing of ballast rocks nervous about the water. Reassured by Ralph's presence on deck, she eased down along the ways. And with a triumphant splash, a dream that began thirty-one years ago was realized. Ralph Stanley's *Endeavor* was launched.

72. (*Photo by Lynn Kippax, Jr.*)

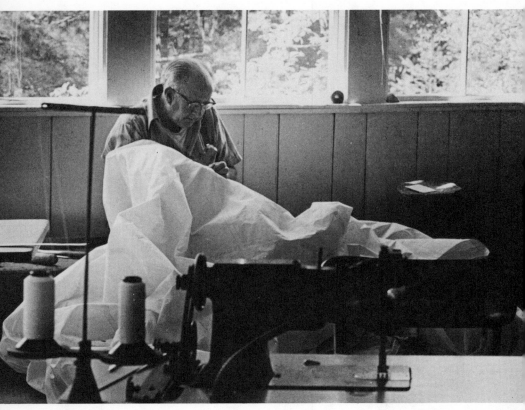

73. Don Hale's father, Clarence, mending a sail in his sailmaking shop.

Sailmaking

Story and photography by Anne Gorham and Anne Pierter

Don Hale of Sargentville, Maine, is a sailmaker. The day we went to see him he completed a sail, from chalking out its pattern on the worn, wooden floor of his shop, a converted one-room schoolhouse, to fashioning a sail bag for the finished sail.

His father, Clarence, is also a sailmaker by trade. Retired now, he still wanders in and out of the shop to repair a sail or chat with some of the local people and tourists who stop by.

Don has been making sails "for ten years or so. My father's been in it since 1933." Clarence Hale was the first sailmaker in the family. We asked what made him decide to go into that trade. "Well, the Depression came and I couldn't get a job. I had a wife and child, and I was starving to death. I was nothing for a job."

So he became an apprentice for the master sailmaker in the area, Frank Harding. "Yes, I got three dollars a day to start with, and them were big wages. I did that [apprenticed] for two years and Frank died. I really hadn't learned too much. Well, I could do things, but it's hard to learn yourself. I had to teach myself more or less. It used to bother me, but it straightened out. My son, he worked with me."

Don then told his side of the story. "Well, I started to work for him when I was probably fourteen or fifteen, off and on, helping him. I'd rather be out playing. But I'd have to come in to work. I started to work for him steady when I was, oh, twenty—somewheres around there. After I got married, I had to do something, of course."

Don has two boys of his own, and we wondered if they had been introduced to sailmaking. "Well, they haven't yet, and I don't force them into it. I didn't like to do it when I was young. But they come up once in a while. Course, the oldest one's fourteen. Probably when he gets fifteen or sixteen, I'll make him come up."

The sail that Don made the day we visited was for an El Toro class

74. Spools of rope, canvas, and other supplies cover the tables of the shop.

sailboat. The original sail was too old for any further repairs, so the owner was having Don sew a new one for the 12-foot boat.

To make a sail of this type you need the following: sail material, thread, a sewing machine, a headboard, battens, grommets, boat tape, a thimble, brass rings, and shackles. Each will be described in detail as they are needed.

The sail material is made of Dacron, and Don orders it in rolls from Bainbridge of Boston along with the rest of his sailmaking supplies. We asked him if he made canvas sails. "Once in a great while. Not very often. It's a hard job to get good canvas. The sails of the big schooners are usually canvas." The weight of the Dacron sail material varies according to the size of the sail. This sail was a small one, and the weight of the Dacron was 3.8 ounces. The smaller the sail is in size, the less the material should weigh.

Don measured the old sail that the owner had sent him as a guide for the new one. "The hoist [luff] was 10'1", the foot, 6'8", and the leech, 11'11"." Don marked out the dimensions of the sail on the floor in chalk. "Well, so far as I know all sails are cut out the same way. Any sailmaker I've seen, that's how they do it. Where they make them in mass production, some of 'em do this all day long [cut out the sail pieces], and someone will sew, and someone will cut patches all day long. This gets kind of hard on the knees after a while."

On the hoist side (the side nearest the mast), he chalked out the belly of the sail. The belly gives the sail a pocket in which to catch the wind more easily. He cuts the sail bigger than its finished size. Don explained he cuts a sail three inches wider than necessary on the leech side. He does this because after the pieces are all sewn together, he cuts a strip off the leech side, and sews it back on over this side for added reinforcement.

From the outline Don began to cut the sail. He did so by first marking a square on the chalked outline from the corner where the hoist and foot meet, straight across to the leech side. He placed his thirty-six-inch wide roll of Dacron on the squared off corner of the outline and cut the first piece of the sail. His scissors are like those found in upholstery shops. There were five pieces to this sail, each one cut to overlap the other piece by half an inch. This is the seam allowance when he sews the sail pieces together. Five pieces to a sail is relatively few. We asked Don how many pieces the main sail would be if he were making a sail for a Friendship Sloop. "Oh, usually about twenty-two, twenty-four." We wondered if he could cut it out on his shop floor. "No. I have to take it over to Brooksville. Over to the gymnasium. I can't cut too big a one in here." So Don goes from one school to another to cut his sails.

The sail pieces were sewn together on a 1959 sewing machine, one of four in his shop. Two spools of thread are placed atop a metal holder behind the machine, one spool feeding the machine, the other winding an unused bobbin beside the machine. Don said you could sew a sail on a home machine but, "You couldn't sew a very big one."

The thread he used for the sail was size ⚹24 cotton thread. Like the material, the weight of the thread depends on the size of the sail. "Well, a little small sail like this will use .69-ounce thread. And when you get to heavier stuff, you use heavier thread."

Don sews the five pieces of the sail together using the zigzag stitch. "They have machines that you can sew down just once, double needle." His needles are single, so he has to sew each seam twice.

Now Don is going to show you how the rest of the sail is made.

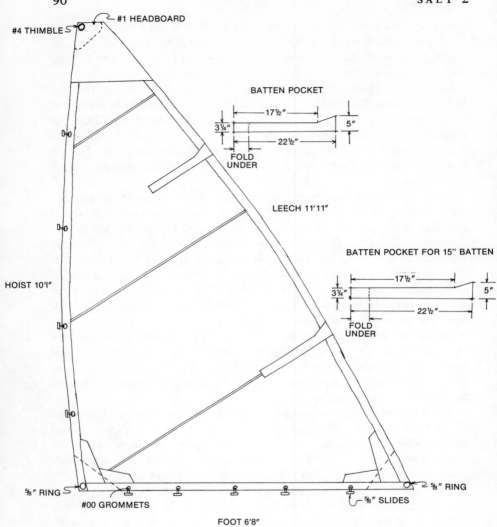

#4 THIMBLE — #1 HEADBOARD

BATTEN POCKET
17½″
3¼″
22½″
5″
FOLD
UNDER

LEECH 11′11″

BATTEN POCKET FOR 15″ BATTEN
17½″
3¼″
22½″
5″
FOLD
UNDER

HOIST 10′1″

⅝″ RING   ⅝″ RING
#00 GROMMETS   ⅝″ SLIDES

FOOT 6′8″

75. (*Diagram by Anne Gorham*)

76. Don makes the outline of the sail on the floor with chalk. The dotted marks show the belly of the sail.

77. Don squares up the pattern. The line he makes is where he places his material to be cut. We asked him if you have to be good in geometry to chalk out the pattern. "Well that's one thing I ain't good in," he answered.

78. Using awls to hold the material, he cuts the first piece of the sail. When cutting the four other pieces, he overlaps them half an inch for seam allowance.

79. The zigzag stitch is used to sew all the seams. Don sews down one side, flips the sail over, and sews up the other side.

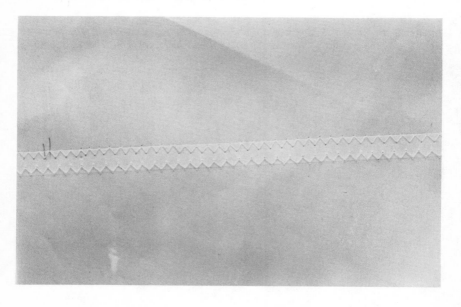

80. After sewing the pieces together, he cuts a strip 3″ wide off the leech side. He then creases the leech side ½″. This is done only on the leech side.

81. Now Don creases both sides of the strip he just cut off to make it 2″ wide. This strip will be sewn back on later.

82. Don cuts two patches and two reinforcements for the 2′ corners. "I try to make them so they're not too big or too small, so they look good." The reinforcements go under the patches.

83. "Next you sew your two reinforcements together" for the first corner. Sew them onto the sail with one edge on the foot, and the other on the crease of the leech. Then the two patches are sewn onto the sail over the reinforcements. Now sew the other set of patches and reinforcements on the foot and hoist corner.

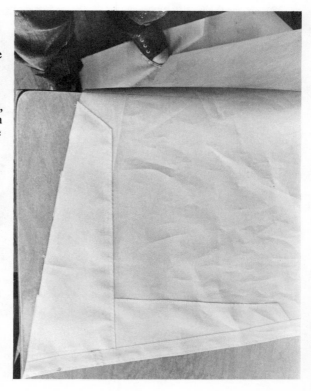

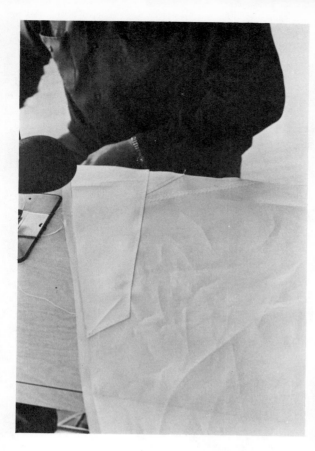

84. Now sew the strip back on the leech side, keeping all the edges folded under.

85. The next step is to sew on the pockets for the battens. The battens are made from white ash and are tapered at one end so they can bend in the wind. Photo shows batten pocket on the old sail Don is replacing.

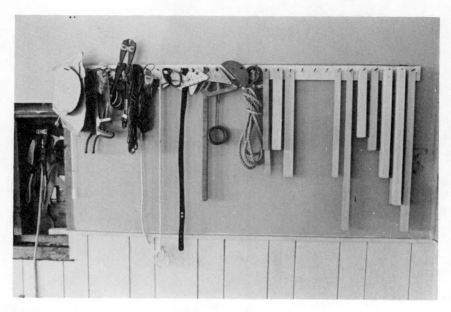

86. Left to right: tools, headboards, and battens.

87. The batten pockets are cut from the leftover material.

88. When you slide the batten in, the tapered end goes in first.

89. Don sews boat tape onto the hoist and foot sides. The Dacron boat tape comes in rolls 4″ wide. The weight is 6.5 ounces, and the tape is folded around the two edges of the sail. Some sailmakers use rope instead of boat tape. Don explained his reasons for using the tape. "It's just as strong. The days of roping has gone by."

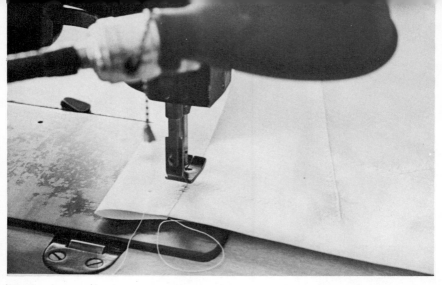

90. Sewing on the tape.

91. The headboard is sandwiched between the two reinforcements and two patches, also cut from leftover material. This leaves a large pocket in which the headboard is loose.

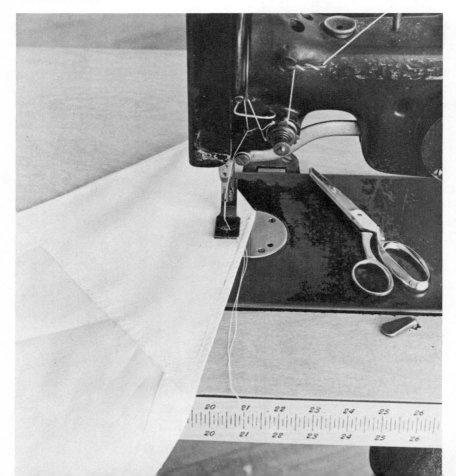

92. Don then moved to a different machine and sewed up the pocket using a straight stitch.

93. The headboard is now hand-sewn in place. Don used a different type of thread than that on the machine. "It's a Dacron braid. This is ⅟₁₆th of an inch wide. Clarence told us what the old sailmakers used. "This is Egyptian thread. It's got six strands to it. Then you had to wax it with beeswax."

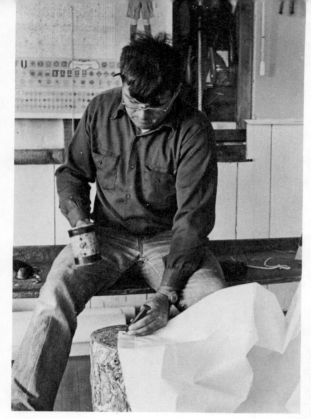

94. Using a punch, Don puts a ⅝″ hole in each corner of the foot.

95. Don now sews a brass ring around the hole so it looks like a shade pull.

96. With a die, Don puts a thimble inside the ring.

97. Using a carrot-shaped piece of wood called a fid, Don reams out the brass ring.

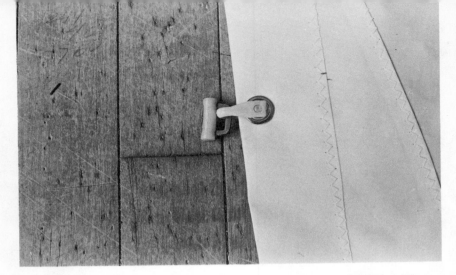

98. Five grommets are put on the foot side, and four on the hoist. These will hold the shackles and slides in place. The grommets on the foot are 12″ apart, and the ones on the hoist are 24″ apart. The slides fit a groove in the mast and boom. Sailmakers used to sew the slides directly to the sail, but now they use shackles. "The shackles take the place of sewing." We wondered if they ever came off. "They ain't supposed to. They'll probably come off after a time. Same as if you sewed 'em on."

99. After putting the slides on, Don uses a soldering iron to burn out the large hole in the headboard. He also uses the soldering iron to round and seal the corners.

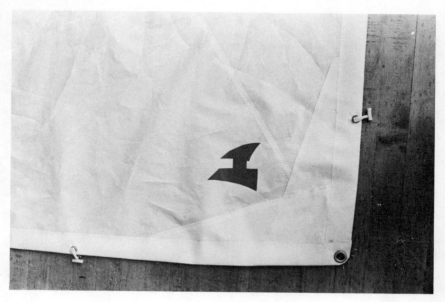

100. Don puts the Hale sail mark on the finished product. Then, he sews the sail bag. "That's it. That's your sail."

Stepping the Mast and Rigging

By Sheryl Lane

STEPPING THE MAST

Building and repairing the boats of others is what Ralph Stanley has always done for a living. His concepts of a finer boat and the best methods of building had to rest in the back of his mind while other specifications were followed. Finally, he found the time to unleash his own ideas, designs, and methods in his building of the Friendship Sloop, the *Endeavor*.

He believes in wooden boats and traditional ways of building. Ralph never considered putting a motor in his Friendship Sloop. Spending unnecessary money on premade parts seemed senseless to him. By handcrafting parts of his boat that are usually prepackaged, Ralph was able to derive a lot of pleasure and save a good amount of money without risking the quality of the sloop.

"I try to make it as simple and as uncomplicated as I can. Don't spend too much without sacrificing the look and performance."

Ralph realized the importance of every move he made. He planned and worked in quiet, thoughtful deliberation. The spruce trees chosen for the mast, boom, and gaff of the *Endeavor* had been aging in his yard for a year before he began to shape them. A wooded lot in West Tremont, not far from Ralph's home, was the source of his material.

"I have places in the woods where the trees grow straight—that I spotted. Well, I peel the bark off and I get four straight sides. After I get four sides, I'll get eight sides. Then I'll shape and taper the spar down some, I'll get the shape that I want, and then I'll round it. I use an electric plane mostly. Then the last step will be the sanding.

"I had a bandsaw and I had a little table saw. If we're making the mast or something like that, we did an awful lot of work by hand."

102. Ralph Stanley and his two sons carry the mast down to the wharf. (*Photo by Sheryl Lane*)

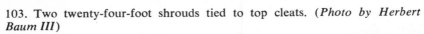

103. Two twenty-four-foot shrouds tied to top cleats. (*Photo by Herbert Baum III*)

Once the mast, boom, and gaff were shaped and varnished, they were placed in Ralph's storage workshop (behind his house). They remained there until the body of the sloop was launched. After the *Endeavor* was launched and docked at the Stanleys' wharf, the mast was carried down from the storage workshop and laid on the wharf with the mast top rested on a saw horse.

As the mast lay on the wharf waiting to be lifted into the mast hole in the bow of the boat, the four shrouds which would be its support were tied with marline (cord made from plant fiber which looks like leather and is usually used for lashing and seizing) to the four mast cleats. The two mast cleats on the starboard side of the mast and two on the port side were built in order to hold the rigging of the sloop intact.

Positioned about a foot from the top of the mast were the top cleats. Secured a foot and a half below the top cleats was the second set of cleats.

Two twenty-four-foot shrouds made of stainless-steel wire were tied to the top cleats, one on each side. The shorter twenty-two-foot shrouds were attached to the two lower mast cleats in the same fashion.

Also tied on before placement of the mast were two stays (same material as shrouds but serve a different purpose). They support the bowsprit and the sail for the two front jib sails. The longer twenty-six-foot stay (flying jibstay) was tied to the top mast cleat, and the shorter twenty-three-foot stay was attached with marline to the lower cleat.

All shrouds and stays were tied to the bottom of the mast with a single rope strand. This was done to prevent them from swinging dangerously in the air as the mast lifted.

Before the varnished spruce mast could be lifted and placed into the mast hole, a block pulley (has a grooved metal piece in the middle to allow rope to pass through it) had to be rigged around mid mast and a tall, thick wharf piling rooted into the ocean bottom two feet away.

The gut strength to support the weight of the mast was burdened on the piling as Renato Saavedra, Ralph's assistant, hauled the pulley rope. Just before Ralph and two other assistants, Reggie Durgin and Ralph's son, Richard, took their positions for maneuvering the mast into place, Ralph tenderly took the sleeve of a blue-cotton shirt and wrapped it between the mid mast block and the varnished surface of the mast. There was no way the mast could possibly be scratched.

Gracefully, in silent concentration, the three men stepped closer to the *Endeavor* slowly guiding the mast into the mast hole as Renato hoisted the mast with the rope pulley.

The only sound to be heard was the creaking of the rope as the massive weight of the mast struggled against the wharf piling and the rope strained through the blocks.

104. Shrouds and stays tied around bottom of mast. (*Photo by Herbert Baum III*)

As the three men guided the tapered foot of the mast through the mast hole, Renato eased the mast down the pulley rope. The foot of the mast was secured in a hole in the mast step under the cabin just the size of the tapered end.

Around the circumference of the mast hole on the underside of the deck was an extra five-inch layer of mahogany wood, the mast partner. It could be seen on the roof of the cabin, and it served to add strength around the mast hole as the boat moved and the mast shifted.

The spar of the mast is about six and three quarter inches in diameter while the mast is about thirteen and three quarter inches in diameter. This means that the circumference of the mast would be thirty-seven and three-quarter inches. To allow for the adjusting of the mast and mast-hole wedges, the mast hole was slightly larger than the mast.

Ralph sent Richard back to the workshop to get four temporary

105. Ralph wraps cotton sleeve between block and mast. (*Photo by Herbert Baum III*)

inch-and-a-half-thick wedges to be placed between the mast and the mast hole. The mast was cushioned with a wedge on all four sides. With the fitting complete, only the securing had to be done.

Ralph watched as Reggie attached the turnbuckles (used to adjust the tension in the shrouds) to the bronze chain plates. There was a chain plate for each shroud. One was placed one foot to the left of the mast and the other one foot to the right. The center between the two plates was also the center of the mast. Altogether, there were four chain plates. Reggie connected the portside shrouds first.

As Reggie was doing this, Richard and Tim Goodwin, Ralph's son-in-law, were traveling back and forth from the workshop to the wharf with a wheelbarrow full of rocks. The wheelbarrow was parked at the end of the wharf next to the *Endeavor*. Rocks were thrown into the hold of the boat for ballast. Each rock thrown in clapped as it landed

106. Guiding
mast toward
Endeavor.

upon the pile already loaded before launching. This happened sporadi-
cally throughout the stepping of the mast and the rigging. The clap was
occasionally interrupted with a splash. Richard was throwing some of
the rocks into the ocean. "They're greasy—might get the boat dirty,"
seventeen-year-old Richard said.

Reggie finished attaching the starboard shrouds. The mast had been
stepped and secured.

The ton of rocks continued to be placed in the hold for ballast.
Ralph had decided to have rock ballast in the hold instead of an outside keel. Early wooden boats had rock ballast. The rock ballast would
allow the *Endeavor* to draw about four and a half feet of water.

A rowboat was used to move the sloop to the town dock, two
houses down, so that the rigging could be started.

108. Ralph checks shrouds after the mast has been stepped.

109. Ralph adjusts flying jibstay to first eyebolt.

RIGGING

The fog lifted late the morning after stepping the mast. A 10:30 or 11:00 fog lift is a common occurrence in Southwest Harbor. Ralph Stanley waited for the morning to clear before he began rigging the *Endeavor* down at the wharf.

First thing in the morning each day, Ralph sat in his workshop with his crew, drank coffee, joked around, and discussed plans for the day.

Once everybody settled in and went to work, Ralph moseyed on down to the town dock. He had on his usual working attire—a short-sleeved blue-cotton shirt with white stripes, tan straight-legged khaki pants, boat sneakers, and a light blue brimmed sun hat to keep his ears from getting burned. In his hand he carried two large eyebolts.

Ralph placed the first eyebolt about a foot and a half from the nose of the bowsprit; the other he placed two feet down from the first. He scrutinized the fit of the flying jibstay to the first eyebolt, attached to the mast cleat the day before. Reggie came down to the dock.

"What happened—is it too short?"

"Uum, can't make it fit," replied Ralph, as Reggie watched him tighten the turnbuckle to the stay. Not much was said as the crew worked. They knew each other and their moves all too well.

After careful analysis and adjustment, Ralph connected the turnbuckle of the flying jibstay to the first eyebolt. The attaching of the jibstay to the second eyebolt was done with the same attention.

Reggie, Ralph, and the rest of the crew took off for their lunch break.

When they came back down to the wharf—they carried the boom with them. Together they proceeded to place the boom to the mast just above the mast saddle. Just as a hand clutches around a tall glass, the boom held on to the mast in a fixed grasp. The boom extended from the mast and back a foot and a half past the stern. This allows the mainsail to move.

As Ralph sat on the deck of his boat contemplating his next move, Marion appeared. She needed to consult with Ralph about financial matters concerning the purchase orders she held in her hand. It didn't take long. She stayed down at the wharf awhile to watch the men work.

Although the wharf wasn't surrounded with activity most of the time, it still was the gathering point of local people. The community was tight. Ralph didn't need to greet the fishermen who came to dock, or people arriving on the daily twenty-passenger ferry that ran back and forth from the Cranberry Islands, or other sailsmen who were preparing their boats for another day of sail. He knew them all. They all took

110. Richard and Ralph fit the boom to the mast just above mast saddle.

an interest in Ralph and his boat; they inquired about the progress of the *Endeavor*. Many liked this quiet, soft-spoken man as well as the work he put out.

Most of the time, Ralph had the town dock to himself. He enjoyed his space. Ralph's work space was always organized—the only tools lying around were the ones he was using for his immediate task.

When Ralph decided to attach the jibboom (allows the jib to move), he went up to his workshop to get the boom and the marline he needed to complete the placement of the boom. The jibboom was attached between the bowsprit bits and the second stay turnbuckle.

Ralph returned to his workshop and carried down a spool of Dacron polyester rope. Preparing to splice, braid, and seize rope for a strap (used as support for the stern-line block pulley through which the mainsheet operates), he seated himself on the two foot stools that he situated on the wharf next to his sloop. Straps are usually premade, but Ralph reaped enjoyment from handcrafting the strap in the old self-sufficient method.

"I take one strand and I lay it up into a loop of three strands [Ralph separates the one strand into three]. This is the strap to go around the boom to hold the mainsheet. It's the way to do it—it's the old way."

Ralph first measured the amount of rope needed for the strap. Next he unraveled the one strand of rope so that he could braid it into a.

111. Richard and Reggie watch as Ralph begins to make straps.

112. Sailers' thread and needle are used to sew the strands together.

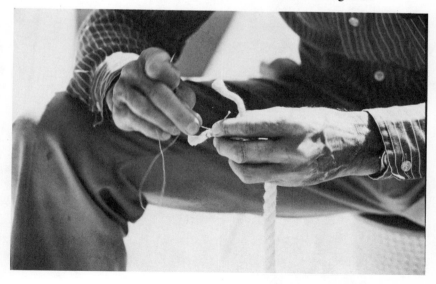

113. Strap hung from boom just above traveler.

114. Rigging the
topping lifts.

three-stranded rope to make the strap stronger. A large sailer's needle and thread were used to sew the strands together.

He then formed a large loop and seized the two overlapping ends together with marline. The very tips of the ends, where the rope was sliced from the spool, were tied off with marline so that the rope wouldn't unravel. Ralph took more marline to tie off a smaller loop to extend below the larger one. Inside this small loop he placed a curved aluminum piece that is called the thimble. The mainsheet lock moves through this without friction. It was hung just above the traveler positioned on the stern deck.

Rigging the topping lifts required Ralph to hoist himself up in the bos'n's chair. Just as a wing-spread seagull lands to rest upon a piling, he poised himself in comfort as he artfully, precisely, and patiently continued the placement of the left topping lift through a block pulley at mast top.

He did the same with a right topping lift through another sheave in the same block. These topping lifts are used to support the boom when there is no wind so the boom will not collapse on the deck of the sloop. The topping lift is slack when the sails fill with wind. The other ends of the topping lifts were cleated just below the mast saddle.

Since more blocks had to be made to complete the rest of the rigging, at 4:00 Ralph called it a day.

Once again, the fog lifted late the next morning. This gave Ralph and his crew time to finish constructing single blocks, double blocks, and cleats for the rest of the rigging. Ralph carried the blocks to the wharf.

To allow the amount of give-and-take needed to control the boom, a double-sheaved block was attached to the strap and then to the trav-

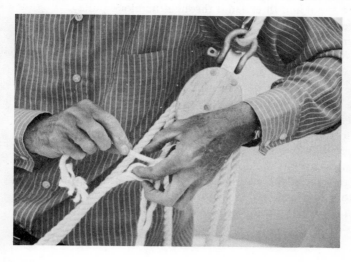

115. Mainsheet is threaded through double block hanging from mainsheet strap.

116. Topping
lifts and strap
secured in
topping
lift-mainsheet bit.

eler. The mainsheet will be rigged through the block. Ralph released
some rope from a spool and threaded it through the block pulley.

Richard cradled the boom at midpoint as Ralph supported the stern
end while they manually carried the boom over to the port side of the
Endeavor. This was done to figure how much rope footage the boom
needed when it was pulled in and let out according to the wind's com-
mands. About a hundred feet of rope was measured and then spliced.
Ralph sewed the severed end to prevent unraveling.

Ralph wanted support for the boom while the rigging continued.

Reggie went to the workshop and brought back two blocks of wood
and a cradle made with two pieces of wood nailed in an X shape. With
him came Renato carrying the topping lift-mainsheet bits. To secure
the cradle, Reggie placed the two blocks of wood, one on either side,
against the bottom legs and nailed them to the deck of the boat. The
boom was put in a resting position between the two top ends.

117. Ralph
threading the
stay halyard.

Reggie also screwed the topping lift-mainsheet securing bits to the boom. These were eight-inch rectangular pieces of wood which hold the mainsheet strap and topping lifts in place. One was placed on the starboard side of the boom and the other the port side of the boom just above the traveler. Holes were drilled from the top to the bottom of the bits to enable the topping lifts to be threaded through and secured.

As Reggie was preparing cleats for the jib sheets, Ralph hoisted himself up in the bos'n's chair to thread the flying jib halyard (which raises the flying jib sail) through a block on the top mast cleat. Once threaded through, the halyard was then cleated below the mast saddle. It is temporarily tied to the stay just above the turnbuckle, as it waits to be tied onto the flying jib sail.

He did the same with the jib halyard. The only difference was that the block for the jib halyard hung from the second mast cleat. The flying jib halyard and jib halyard are both seventy feet long. Ralph only measured through observation—not with exact measuring tools.

Reggie finished securing the jib sheet cleats to the deck of the sloop about fifteen feet down from the bow. This secured the flying jib sheets. (When the sloop turns, pulling in of one sheet and letting out of another will allow the sail to be shifted with the wind.)

LASHING THE SAILS

They were now ready to begin lashing the foresails. Ralph went back to his workshop to get the large red sacks the sails were enclosed in.

The snaps that link the sail onto the stays came with the sails. They were put on the flying jibstay above the turnbuckle just the same way the snap of a dog leash is put on a collar. The clew ring (left bottom of sail) was tied with marline to the bottom of the flying jibstay turnbuckle. The next ring in the sail was linked to the first snap above the turnbuckle. Ralph continued until all the rings and snaps were attached. The top head ring of the sail was knotted with marline to the eye loop of the staysail (flying jib sail) halyard.

Ralph tied the two flying jib sheets to the foot ring. He then measured how much rope was needed to reach from the sail to the cleats and allow wind play with the sail. The flying jib sheets were about fifty feet long.

Lashing the jib sail was done basically the same way. Because this sail was rigged with a boom, it had to be attached through rings along the bottom of the sail. This was done by starting to weave rope through the foot ring, down around the boom, and up through the next ring. By pulling tightly as he went along, Ralph was preventing any gaps between sail and boom.

Ralph arrived at the clew ring, gave the rope a few wraps around the boom and through the ring, and tightly tied the sail down. The jib halyard was knotted to the head ring. On the starboard bow there was a cleat to which the jib sheet (not to be confused with flying jib sheets and cleats) attached. Lashing was finished for the foresails.

Finally, the topping lifts were sewn through the topping lift-mainsheet bit. Reggie quickly moved from doing that to placing a stainless-steel twine (same material as shrouds and stays) over the bowsprit nose. The loop in the twine fit snugly over the nose. On the starboard outside bow hull was a tang (small metal piece attached before launching). This is where the other end of the twine was fastened. Reggie repeated this process on the port side of the *Endeavor*.

118. Richard and Ralph snap the foresail onto the flying jibstay.

119. Ralph securing fairlead.

As he was doing this, Ralph was attaching the fairleads to the bow deck. (They were small horseshoe-shaped pieces of metal which the two jib sheets go through before the sheets are cleated.) This allowed the jib sheets to be controlled closer to the deck of the boat instead of swinging in the air.

After measuring the placement of the oar locks, the crew called it quits on the work day. Although the days at the dock ended at 4 o'clock, Ralph spent nights in the workshop making the parts of the boat necessary for the rigging to be done the following day. Blocks, straps, and cleats were all handmade.

Ralph was down on the wharf before the fog lifted the next morning. He knew the final stages of rigging were going to take place. The gaff was carried down to the wharf before the fog lifted.

Ralph hoisted himself up in the bos'n's chair with the aid of a visiting photographer to begin the rigging of the peak halyards. He had to tie the bitter end (end of a rope that is always secured) to the top mast cleat.

Reggie walked down to the wharf bringing two gaff strap plates with him. While Ralph was in the bos'n's chair, Reggie began to secure the two strap plates on the gaff as it was lying on the wharf. The straps that were placed on the gaff were the same as the mainsheet strap placed on the boom. Reggie secured the straps in place with the wooden plates.

Once the bitter end of the halyard was knotted onto the mast cleat, Ralph lowered himself to the deck to help Reggie place the gaff onto the mast.

They each grabbed an end of the gaff and nursed it onto the deck and attached the jaws of the gaff around the mast just above the saddle and the boom.

As soon as the gaff was in position, Ralph grabbed the excess halyard rope he dropped after he secured the bitter end of the halyard. He carried that up the mast with him and threaded the halyard through the sheave in the top block that was hung from the top mast cleat.

Carrying the halyard rope back down, he threaded it through the first strap on the gaff. Back up the mast he went with the rope and threaded it through the second sheave of the block. He brought it down to the deck and passed it through the second gaff strap. Ralph then took the halyard as far as the second mast cleat and wove the rope through the sheave of the block that was hung from that cleat. Finished rigging the peak halyards, Ralph lowered himself to the deck to cleat the rope at mast saddle.

As it was cleated or uncleated, the peak halyard served to raise the gaff at a perpendicular angle when the gaff was hoisted to lift the mainsail.

120. The gaff jaw.

121. Reggie attaches gaff strap plate.

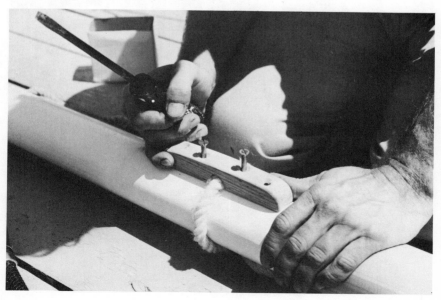

Ralph wore a climactic smile as he experienced the final stages of his dream.

Reggie, preparing to rig the throat halyard, inserted two large eyebolts to the jaw plate, one on the right side and one on the left. A double-sheaved block was attached to these eyebolts by two rings connected to the bottom of the block. There was a ring for each eyebolt.

Ralph, beginning to rig the throat halyard, hoisted himself up to the second set of mast cleats. Richard and Reggie took care of the lazy jacks. Lazy jacks allow the mainsail to rest atop the boom without falling on the deck so that the mainsail doesn't need to be furled manually. Richard tied the lazy jacks onto the midpoint of each topping lift so that they would reach and hang at midboom. Reggie placed two lazy jack cleats on each side of the boom where the lazy jack ropes attach.

With a coil of rope on the deck, one end of it in his hand, Ralph rigged the throat halyard. He took the end, put it through one sheave of the double block, brought it back down to the deck, and put it through one sheave in the double block connected to the jaw of the gaff. He then brought it back up to the double block at the second mast cleat and threaded it through the second block sheave, bringing it back down to thread through the second sheave of the jaw block. Finally, he went back up the mast to the cleat where it went through a becket (an

122. Rigging throat halyard to jaw of gaff.

eye in a small knotted loop) to be seized and tied off. The rope hanging that was connected to the coil on the deck was used to lower and raise the gaff. Cut from the excess coil, the throat halyard was cleated to the mast.

The mainsail was ready to be lashed on. Ralph pulled the sail out of a red bag.

With marline, Ralph began to sew the right head ring of the sail through four holes drilled in the gaff jaw. The holes were drilled just in front of the two eyebolts used for connecting the gaff jaw block. They were sewn together just as a button is sewn on a shirt.

To begin securing the mainsail to the gaff, Ralph knotted the end of a rope to the right head ring. Then from the right to the left, he threaded the rope through the rings along the top of the sail, back up around the gaff, and back down through the next ring. Once Ralph reached the far left and the left head ring, he threaded the rope through a hole drilled in the gaff tip, back through the head ring, pulled the rope tight so no gaps could be left between sail and gaff, and then secured it with a knot.

Richard and Reggie pulled at the peak halyard and the throat halyard to raise the gaff and sail a little at a time. This enabled Ralph

123. The final knot in securing the mainsail to the gaff.

124. Securing the mainsail to mast hoops.

125. The mainsail foot ring is threaded to jaw of the boom.

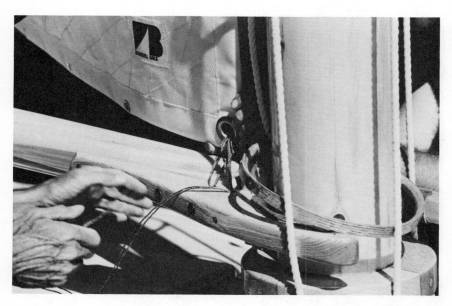

to tie, with marline, the sail to the mast hoops placed on before stepping the mast.

There were nine mast hoops, one extra, to tie to eight sail rings along the side of the mainsail between the right head ring and the foot ring. Ralph did this until he arrived at the foot ring.

After he tied the foot ring to the jaw of the boom, Ralph and Reggie tenaciously threaded the mainsail to the boom in the same way they did with the gaff and sail. The securing was done the same way—only quicker. They knew, except for the final last-minute touches, she was rigged.

Energy electrified the air. Richard ran for the flying jib halyard. Reggie raced for the jib halyard. Ralph, with an open rapturous smile, hoisted on the peak halyard and throat halyard.

All the sails billowed up in thunder like a flock of ducks taking flight.

SAILING

"Did she sail any different than any Friendship you've ever been on?" Renato wondered.

"Yeah, she feels lighter, 'cause she is lighter," answered Ralph proudly.

"You think you're ever gonna build another one like her?"

"Oh, I might. Never can tell. Build one like that only bigger. I like the big open cockpit. You're not up on top in all that wind. I didn't use a metal boom fitting or anything. Too expensive. Simpler. Serves its purpose."

"Gonna take ya awhile to recover from all this sloop business."

"Yeah, I'm really tired. Oh, I've always wanted to build a Friendship Sloop for myself."

Ralph doesn't use sailing as a sport. It's his way of getting away.

"Yep. If I can. I try."

The Seafaring Life

Cecil Kelley

By Andrea Downs and Cynthia Pinkham
Photography by Mark Emerson and Lynn Kippax, Jr.

"I never lied in my life. Sometimes I stretch it a little on one end or the other, try to make it interesting. But it's founded on the truth. Always enough truth in there that you can't call it a damn lie—don't mind my swearing. You know it's part of my vocabulary.

"You can call me Cecil R—R for Rhodes. I happened along at the time General Rhodes had the war with England, and I've been 'General' ever since."

Cecil Kelley is a genial man of seventy-nine years whose watchful blue eyes hold more than a hint of mischief. His pipe is a steady companion which he uses to punctuate an unending flow of outrageous stories. He pauses to puff, tap, tamp, or rekindle while his listeners catch the point, erupt with laughter, or ask the right question so the game can continue.

"I was born right here in Jonesport. I been so many jobs, vocations, I don't know as a book could stand to list them. I don't think there'd be pages enough. I done fourteen years with the Coast Guard. I done twelve years in the old Lighthouse Service. Of course, the Coast Guard was a lifesaving service then, before they changed it over.

"I worked in the lumber woods, in the pulp woods. I've worked with the undertaker, yeah, I've helped plant some of 'em.

"And, oh God, I've been to sea—I've been fishing off and on since I

128. Cecil
Kelley.

was around nine years old, I guess. I've done a little farming, a lot of
cattle stomping—I've had one or two horses. Had a little mink ranch.
I've raised geese, ducks, pigs. You know, I made some starts.

"I was raised on salt water; Mother never had milk. So here I am,
seagoing, you know. I'm going to tell you the truth. I been fishing ever
since I was big enough to drive a motor. I was probably eight or nine
years old. I did that up until we were married.

"I went into the Coast Guard. I was too light—I weighed a hundred
and eighteen pounds. And Commander Sands was the Coast Guard
commander then. I wrote him a very nice letter, and told him if I got
some of that government food I could probably gain the necessary
weight.

"By God, they took me on six months' probation! Now didn't I eat
some bread and molasses. Oh boy! That's what the cooks called number nine—every morning for breakfast we had number nine. Hot biscuits and molasses every morning. By God, when my time was up, I
had gained sufficient amount of weight that they signed me on.

"And after about one hitch, I transferred to the Lighthouse Service.
Then I went under Civil Service and I did twelve years on Thatcher's
Island. That's up off Cape Ann, up Massachusetts. Then I got transferred down here, right back to my home town. And I did eight years
here. And then the government under Roosevelt, for economy reasons,
he dissolved the Lighthouse Service. And, of course, it was an economy
move because it cost twenty-nine times more to operate it after they
took it over.

"They've made it automatic, but, my Christ, they have to go down, two, three times a day. Well, when I was down here, there was just two of us. Twenty-four-hour watch, but you knew you was good for twelve hours every day, and you took care of all the upkeep.

"We had to paint all the buildings and the catwalks, and all of that stuff. Shine all the brass. And course they *love* brass, there's plenty of that. They don't have that now—coat of red paint hides all the brass. In the old Lighthouse Service, you got a drop of paint on the brass, you heard about it! Right quickly, too.

"And all those damn prisms, you know, they was glass—beautiful glass. I don't know but they changed all that when the Coast Guard took 'em over. Like down here—we was so particular. The light had to be extinguished in time for sunrise whether you saw it or not. And she was lit exactly as she dove behind the west. Now it goes all day, all night. They say it's cheaper to operate it that way. Well, I don't know, the way energy is, I think it takes some, don't you?

"We was down on Libby Island. I tell you, it was a long lonesome night. Up every damn night. Why I suppose I've seen the sun rise or set more than any other. Twenty-odd years I never missed one, and I've seen quite a lot of them since. Now I go to bed before the sun does, but later I won't. I'm up before she's [wife] up in the morning.

"I smoke till I get my tonsils burnt out, then I have my breakfast and go to work, ayuh.

"Today it was never a better day ever a man could ask for. Flat, calm, not a ripple on the water. Outside, every bit of sea you could land in a canoe. Right outside on the outshores. Beautiful, but no lobsters.

"I come within two dollars and thirty-three cents of breaking even. I had to reach down for that. I paid it on the tool shed. I mean, I got three little lobsters. I got five harbor perch out in my net.

"I came back and put the nets up down at the piling. You can't leave 'em in the water, so you dry 'em out days and put 'em back nights. But I'm not going to put them back out now till the middle of next week, 'cause they didn't do too much. It's a little early . . . and maybe I rushed it a little. You can't hurry it, you know.

"I hauled, I guess, fifty traps. I got three legal lobsters and two of them had only one claw, and the other one just growing back. It had lost it in a battle. And I came out within two dollars and thirty-three cents of breaking even." He roared, "Now what the hell's the matter with that?"

Regardless of the difficulties, Cecil still likes lobstering. "That's just like Santa Claus coming. You haul those piles of boxes—you don't know whether you're gonna get nothing, but it's fascinating. I like to do it.

"[I've been lobstering] on and off since I was nine years old. Still about the same old thing. Pull your heart and liver out and get nothing for it. And it adds up about the same way, ayuh.

"[Lobsters] travel in cycles, in my belief. Some years are a lot better than others. Now about three years ago I told my wife, 'I think they've reached a peak.' They've been going down ever since. This year's the worst it's been in twenty years now. It's the same way with everything.

"Sardines. Now, I've had three weirs. I knew about every sardine boat, and there was a lot of 'em. Must have been about fifty. Now there's only about a half a dozen left on the coast.

"Sail vessels, I have been in them. They're all gone now. They've been out of the picture for years. But there's schooners, you know, big spars and sails, canvases. Yep! I went on one of them when I was only fourteen years old."

Cecil told a story that explained the flexible approach he takes when dealing with fact and fiction. "I was on Thatcher's [Island as a light-house keeper] after a big northeaster, you know. When you're on Thatcher's, wind comes northeast, you ain't gonna land down unless you got a helicopter, and there was no helicopters when I was there quite a few years ago.

"I was walking around one day, thought I'd cruise around the island. A big gale of wind, storm, raining. I went to the northwest head, looked down, bank goes right down steep to the water.

"Rocks had laid a guy on the beach. I went down and seen he was dead, drifted in there. So I went back and called the crew and we carried him over the bank. Got part way up there and I lost my foot and fell in. He came down right on top of me. I went 'OOOP!' You know that would nerve somebody up—it bothered me a hell of a lot. He had me pinned down. They lifted him up before I could get out from under him and then we dragged him up in the building there.

"Oh! Terribly water soaked, and mouth and ears and eyes full of sand and gravel and seaweed. I went back after we got him up there and I laid him out. Used to work with the undertakers and laid him out the best I know how, washed him up and cleaned him up.

"Of course this storm, nobody could get over there [to the main-land]. The coroner told me to take care of him till the weather broke and we'd get him to shore. Two or three days, the weather smoothin' down, the coroner called me and told me to bring him ashore. Well, I had only the damn little dory with no engine in her. So the Coast Guard came over and they weren't too happy. They was scared of the dead. Now the dead won't hurt you. That's one thing you don't have to worry about. So they said, 'Would you take him ashore?' I said sure. So I took him ashore in the Coast Guard boat. The Coast Guard fellows stayed on the station till I came back with their boat.

"Went up and landed him up there, took him up to the police sta-tion. The doc was there and he's sitting at the desk smoking cigars and talking with the chief. He said, 'Death by accidental drowning.'

"I'd seen him. I knew that right across there, his skull was broke right in, where he'd been hit with a belaying pin. I found out later he was a fisherman, went fishin' drunker than hell, probably disagreeable. When they got out far enough, he didn't get any better, so they bumped his head and threw him the hell overboard.

"Of course, the murder was committed from Gloucester. When I was up there, every night there was a murder committed in Gloucester. Down the docks, wa'nt no trouble in the morning to fish somebody out.

"So Lord, it kinda made me mad [when the doctor said accidental death] 'cause I knew it was murder. So, by God, I went down to the desk and I said, 'Doc, you are crazier than hell. That man was murdered! His skull was broke right in. The print is half round; he was hit by a belaying pin.'

"Doc said, 'Look, you shut your goddamn mouth up. You don't know nothing anyway and never did. You get on that goddamn boat and get back to the station.' And that's it. You can't argue with a doctor. They have too much service.

"So I went to Gloucester after that several times, and I seen him sitting there in the park on a bench. I walked right by the goddamn thing and turn my head the other way. I wouldn't speak to him.

"Passed on about a year, I guess. One day I was going down by the park, and he was sitting on the bench. He hollered, 'Come over here a minute.' [I says] 'Ah, go to hell.' He says, 'Come over here, goddamn you, come over here.' I went over.

"He said, 'Now, won't you sit down?' There's nobody there, just him and I in the park on the bench. He says, 'You're kinda ugly at me, ain't cha?'

" 'Well, Jesus,' I said. 'I thought that you knew something, but you don't know a hell of a lot. That fellow was murdered and you know it.'

" 'I don't know he was murdered,' he said, 'and I didn't see no marks on him or nothing!'

" 'Now,' he said, 'I am going to tell you something. I've been a doctor quite awhile. That day you picked his body up, his wife was in the Danvers Hospital, confined. What kind of goddamn thing would that have been, to break the news to her that her husband had been murdered and thrown the hell overboard out there, eight or nine miles in the ocean? How do you think that would have gone?

" 'Now,' he said, 'they didn't have a thing in the world, they had nothing, but he had one little lousy life insurance policy [that] paid double indemnity for accidental death. Accidental death by drowning.' He said, 'That paid her maternity bills, probably she had a few hundred dollars left over to start life over again.'

"He said, 'You think I did wrong?'

"And I turned right around and bent over and said, 'Doc, you kick me the whole way right across the park and then kick me back again. I think you're a doctor, first-class doctor!'

"And that ended it. When I left there, we were buddies. Don't you think that he didn't know what he was doing?"

The doctor's priorities in fulfilling his official duties seem to have been shared by Cecil, judging from another story he told. In any case, for Cecil Kelley people come before the rules.

"They made me federal warden, you know, when I was down here in the service [Lighthouse Service]. Come down here and made me federal warden.

"They used good judgment, [as] many goddamn friends as I got. They would think I would arrest any person for doing anything! [Not] unless he's murdered somebody that didn't need to be killed. Course, if he needed to be killed, I don't know. So I come up here to the landing. There's two more wardens here, federal wardens.

"The people living down on the island, they was having it hard. There wasn't too much to eat. They had to eat a lot of birds. You know, ducks, seabirds. Sure.

"They [the other wardens] said, 'You got to take us down, we gotta go catch them out there. They're shooting birds out of season.' Vapor was flying. You couldn't see, oh, fifty yards. It was cold, about zero. I said, 'Sure, I'll take you down.'

"So when I reached that point at the island, I just reached down and got that goddamned old crank horn, set her up on the washboard and started cranking her. Them fellas all disappeared up to the house. You could see where they walked up, the frost in the rockweed.

"They [wardens] said, 'What you doing that for?'

" 'Why,' I says, 'you don't suppose I'm going into a harbor as thick as this is without blowing my horn. Jesus, I guess not. Very bad. I might run over something and get into a scrape. I guess you have to blow your horn when you're going into a harbor in thick weather.

" 'Oh, don't you forget that,' I said. 'You may be wardens, but you don't know what in the hell you're doing.'

"And by God we went in and landed and walk in and here these cracks were in the rockweed that was froze in low water. 'What the hell is down there?' they said.

" ' 'Somebody probably just came back from clamming over there,' I said. The wardens didn't know what it was about. I did.

"When they got all through, they went around [the people] and said, 'I hear you fellas is killing the birds.' I said, 'I live down here and a damn funny thing. I don't know nothing about it. I never heard a shot. I guess you got the wrong thing.'

"When I landed them, they said, 'Goddamn you, you got too damn many friends down round there. We don't like you monkeying around down there.'

"I said, 'Some of them will shoot you quicker than hell, too.' They would. I had some boys down there who would shoot a man just as quick as he'd eat.

"Well, if you was hungry and they was trying to stop you from eating, and your family from eating, wouldn't you kill? Damned sure I would," Cecil said, fixing a steady, unblinking eye on his listeners.

There were six children in Cecil's family. "I'm the only one of the six that is what you would call a full-fledged dropout. Never got by the

seventh grade. The rest of the family is all got those goddamn gray strings of letters in back of their name. College degrees that reach from here to that Latter Day Saints Church over there. My brother, he don't know how to live. He couldn't sit down five minutes, he'd be losing interest, he'd be losing money on it.

"Well, I sit down, and I'll stay from here to Christendom. I don't care whether I work or not. 'Cause I've enjoyed life to the full. And I don't worry too much about anything. The rest of them is all having sessions with the Internal Revenue people every year or so.

"And they [IRS] don't bother me any because I don't earn nothing. But I eat good, I live well, and I don't know why I should go on from there.

"Well, my poor mother used to say, 'Blessed be nothing.' And I think she had a point. God, Mother took a chance—that's why I'm here. Now why in hell shouldn't I gamble a little?"

Cecil had an adventurous childhood. "We were bad then, but we didn't do any damage. Now we stole an automobile one night. We was just kids. The first one we went to steal belonged to Ed Plummer . . . the Plummers over there used to run the store.

"Ed had a little dog, and an old Model T Ford. And we thought probably we'd steal Ed's car. He was down where they had the picture show here every night. We was going to steal the car. We raced up, and by God, when I put my hand on the side of that car, that dog took a hold of my wrist, filled his mouth solid full. So I knew we didn't want to steal *that* car.

"So, we got down to Morey Kelley's. [He had] an old Dot. They've since gone out of business . . . like the Edsel. Well, we was gonna drive that one. We got in, turned the key, stepped on the starter, and she caught fire. The whole length of her. So, as luck would have it, an old pyrine gun was hanging right around the dasher. We grabbed it and pumped her out.

"We disappeared. We wasn't around when the show was out. No, we was a long ways away. Weren't our fault she caught fire—the god-damned thing. Probably saved their life. Probably would have gone up around a tree."

Cecil has always kept a safe distance between himself and the churches in Jonesport and Beal's Island.

"Take that church over there. I sat over here and watched them bastards go in there every Saturday, Sunday, and Monday. A fella and me, he used to live here. We chummed together. He was a bad boy, but he was one of the best in the world. He could think of things to do! Gotta laugh sometime.

"We came by there one night and they was screeching and hollering and raving. Windows were up—it was a hot night." Cecil and his friend lighted some firecrackers.

"Going loud as a cannon there, you know. Jesus Christ, they come out through the windows, the doors . . . we was disappeared. But we was far enough so we could see the motion. They thought the Lord had come. Ayuh, yessir! They thought he really had come.

"You know, there used to be an awful lot of religion on Beal's Island. Oh, it was terrible. Oh, they was so goddamn fanatic. Why it would drive you up a tree without a limb on it. I'll tell you, course it's kind of a military secret, but it happened years ago and I guess they can't do away with me now.

"I was just a young fella, you know. Fourteen, fifteen—chasing 'round the girls same's you do about that age. So I used to sneak over there [Beal's Island], and they was solid full of religion. Oh, my God, they was awful religious!

"And they'd have those preachers come down from Canada twice a year. I'd call them house cleaners. They'd come up, you know, their mouths riddled to hell with gold teeth. They'd get up there and screech and bellow and blast, and they'd tell some of them goddamn heart-rending stories. They just made them up. And they'd get them people worked into a, well—crazy. They was just crazy as coots.

"So I went over there one night. I went over there to see the fun go on. And they spouted around and hollered and screeched, and throwed a few hymn books and the pages come out and scattered all over the place. Oh, they was wilder than the Holy Rollers.

"They might be hitting on some useful religion, but it don't make any difference. I don't believe in any of them.

"And so, by and by, this fellow got up and said, 'Now brothers and sisters, we have been under an awful expense coming here. We have saved so many of your souls. We have to leave tomorrow, awful sorry to go.' But they was going somewhere else to clean house, you know? 'And now we'd like a little offering to help us along our way.' So they set this table right in front of the altar, and they said, 'Bring a little donation to help us on our way.'

"Now, they hadn't been under any expense. The railroad hauled them for nothing. Preachers had a pass in them times, to go anywhere on the railroad free. While they'd been there, they'd just visited around among the people, and eat and slept, and it never cost them a nickel. Not a nickel! So they [the congregation] started getting up.

"Well, I guess the first one went down, he prob'ly had a half a dollar, an old silver half a dollar. Now he threw that down. And that fella with the mouth out, saw that goddamned gold glisten, and said, 'Brother, that's going to be too heavy to carry. We'd rather have paper money.'

"So the next one jumped up with a dollar bill and he rushed down—and the next one run down with a two-dollar bill. And all those people, they won't be outdone.

"So, I was sitting right next to the isle, and there was such a stampede. Why, one of them rodeo shows wouldn't have been half so dangerous. They was rushing down by with these bills, you know? But they be so damned crazy. I reached out and snatched that bill, put it into my pocket. So easy, I'd get another one.

"Well, by that time they'd held forth until about two o'clock in the morning, and that table ran right over with the money—right down to the floor. They prob'ly raised about three, four thousand dollars.

"I stuffed that goddamned ol' pocket till it was full. And they'd go down with that empty hand now—and they never knew that they lost their money going down there. Crazier than a flock of sheep.

"I got home right before they decided to break camp. I thought it was time to get out. Well, I come home. Course, Father was always worried about me up all night, ramming around. Most always he'd be setting up sucking on his corncob pipe to see what time I got home. Ask me a few questions—where I'd been, who I'd seen. I always had to lie a little *then*.

"But anyways, I got by. So when I got all straightened 'round, I put my pocket right on the table. 'Good God!' he said, 'where'd you get all that money? You held up a bank or rob somebody?'

"I said, 'I ain't robbed a soul, ain't held up a bank. That is honest pickings. Earned every cent of it.'

"He said, 'How?' I said, 'Picking it out of people's hands—going out to the damned altar over at that Beal's Island Church.' He said, 'Amen, brother, you done just right.' "

"I never ran away from home. I worked in the woods cutting pulp wood, logs, and stuff like that—winters. That was a nice job, too. First winter I cut lumber, long lumber for a fella named Robinson. They had mills in Sherman Mills. The first electric light I ever saw.

"That cookie job I had was a doozy, I'll tell you that. If you're traveling one camp to another—mealtime, you stop right there. You get your meal, get one free. Course, you stay and get two, you've got to pay a day's board. There was enough for them stragglers, those poachers, and there was trappers. And they weren't all woods people.

"The main diet was baked beans. That was on the table three times a day. There was prunes all the time. Stewed prunes. Old Henry [Nichols] came in one night, and you know his mouth was shaped just like a shark. And he could eat just like a shark. And he sat down at the table and all he ate was prunes, see? And biscuits—prob'ly twenty-five biscuits. And the prune seeds, my God! Got so high you couldn't see no way around.

"So when they were finished, Worchester [one of the bosses] come along for me. I was cooking. He said, 'Don't touch this table now. All around, but don't touch this here.' I went, 'What the hell is the trouble?' He said, 'Oh, I wanted to count the prune seeds, just for fun. We'll see how many prunes that Henry Nichols et tonight.'

"I think there was a half a million—that's how high he could count. Yessir, by Godfrey.

"But I got a lot of them [stories] I wouldn't tell in mixed crowds, I can tell you that! I have one story I can tell you though. They came pretty damn near landing me in Atlanta.

"Mr. Roosevelt went down 'round through here, Franklin Delano, on his trip when he was President. Down the lower end of Bar Harbor, going out of the harbor, there's two little islands. One is entitled the Virgin's Breast, the other one the Nipple.

"Well, this morning in the paper came out [that] if you made a progress report to the Bangor *Daily* [*News*] on the President's trip, and you was the first one in—why, you'd get a dollar!

"So I watched the old President go down, and when I thought he was about in, I called the Bangor *Daily*. Told 'em I had a progress report. Told 'em that President Roosevelt had just passed the Virgin's Breast and was now approaching the Nipple.

"Jesus Christ, so help me! That night every FBI man in the United States, and some from Canada was on this doorstep. Thought I'd slandered the damn thing. I hadn't done no such thing. Coulda put me in Atlanta for my life.

"Well, happened to be the cameraman that was with Mr. Roosevelt, a couple years previous to that, had been with me on Thatcher's Island —making a motion picture. *Lady From Hell* was the title of it. And course my wife and I pinch hit for some of those expensive actors and actresses.

"So that night the FBI was lined up here, and all ready to take me, when this government man showed up to see me. He was with the President, helpin'. When he showed up, by God, them FBI men took off like they'd run into a hornet's nest. Yeah, sure as hell.

"But I never got the dollar! No, sir. And I shouldn't have signed for the damn paper anymore, but I did. I sure was entitled to the dollar, wasn't I?" Cecil allowed one of his two sharp eyes to laugh as he took a puff from his pipe.

"I never was drunk in my life. Come awful near it once or twice. I crawled in from that wharf one night, 'bout eleven o'clock, on my hands and knees and . . . made it right to the door, and never needed a bit of help. That's the nearest I've come to being drunk.

"Had an old doctor up here. Used to take him down [when] some of the crew would get sick—pneumonia or so forth. I had to come take him down there.

"One night after he got done waiting on them—came into the house to have a cup of coffee with me and [to also] drink a round. He says, 'Let me tell you something, sonny.' He said, 'I'm gonna teach you how to drink rum so you'll live to be eighty-five.'

"I'm doing all right on it. I think his directions was good. His prescription for drink was 'moderate, well diluted.' Take a little in a glass and then put in a spoonful of sugar and pour in boiling water. Fill the glass right up and give it the Rocky Mountain Spin and take an hour and a half or two hours to drink it. And that once a day—it won't hurt ya a bit. Most of it, you won't get drunk and it's all right. I highly approve of it.

"All through Prohibition I had rum. On that damn station I had a lot of friends running rum. I had rum all the time. And never had any at home, you know. Father wouldn't have it in the house. I got brothers that never touched a drop. But I smoke and I drink a little. Always friendly with the ladies—but damned old. Now they know it. Don't *they* rub it in. Yes, don't they rub it in. Goddamn 'em.

"And grandmother drank a barrel of rum a day. When my grandfather passed on—he was seventy-six years old when my father was born. Well, he was the father of roughly, let's say, seventy-five children. And when one wife would die today, from childbirth, before dark he was married to another one.

"When he died, well, of course, she was left the whole thing. He owned a lot of vessel property, you know. Owned shares in all the vessels. They was paying money, too.

"So Grandmother would order a barrel of rum when the vessel went to Boston. Well, when they come, they'd throw it in the boat and row it right down to her. So when they rowed it down, all the neighbors and friends and the whole goddamned other town—Beal's Island.

"They'd arrive down there, and they'd stay until they'd drink that rum up, see? And then she'd have a barn moving. They'd take the barn down and move it about ten feet and put it up. This goddarn great big barn holds thirty, forty head of cattle. They'd drink up the barrel of rum, they'd stay a week or ten days—clean up two bushels of potatoes and everything that went with it. Chicken and lamb and stuff.

"And the next vessel would arrive, and another barrel, and they'd move the barn back again. And they wore the barn out till it got so damn old you couldn't stand a cow in it. And the money got gone, and the vessel couldn't come. She lost everything—mortgaged everything. She lost the whole damned island [Head Harbor Island]."

Cecil's father managed to buy back seven hundred acres of the thousand that were lost in his grandmother's time. Cecil recalled with pleasure the role he played as a young man in helping his father gain vengeance from an unscrupulous lawyer.

"Then one time, the old man, sometimes he's disagreeable. So we had a little law scrape, and this goddamn lawyer over to Millbridge wrongly advised him, but took a retaining fee and a little more money. Every while he called up for a little more money. The case never came to court. He drained the old man. So the old man told me, he said, 'I wish there was some way to get even with that bird.' I said, 'So do I, but we'll see.'

"Prohibition was on, you know. I was coming home on leave from Cape Ann—'cause we had thirty days a year off. I got aboard the train,

changed trains in Bangor . . . started down the coast. And this lawyer
was aboard then, and here I was in that goddamn monkey suit and all
those brass buttons fully set. He thought probably I was an admiral.

"So every once in a while I'd see him go down in the little place
where the conductor took care of his tickets. I knew what he was up to.
By and by, he come up and he said, 'Hey, wouldn't want a drink would
ya?' I said, 'I heard you the first time, my friend. Yessir, I'm just about
choked to death.' So he took me up there, he turned me out a big one
and him a small one.

"He'd been drinking quite a lot, so I put that in me, and by and by I
said, 'Chummy, don't you think we should have another one?' So I
turned him a long one and me a short one. And after we got that down
the holding, he refused to drink anymore.

"He passed out. He had these two great suitcases. Twenty-four bottles or more in each one of them—bootleg stuff. So I shacked them
right up, and sat right up there. So we got down to Columbia Falls.
They rolled him off, and I said, 'Them is my suitcases, don't bother
them.' Topcoat hanging, I said, 'My topcoat, don't bother that.'

"When I arrived out on the platform, Father was there, my other
brother was up to meet me. Course, I'd drunk a little too much. When

I stepped off the platform—just the flight of stairs went down there. I went down, suitcases and all, but never broke a bottle.

"Next day I sold enough to pay off all of the goddamned bills that lawyer had stoled from him, and I got his suitcases and his topcoat. And he don't know who the hell I was and never found out. Just an honest deal, I called it.

"I think I'm doing *real* well. I haven't earned twenty cents in ten years, but I've been around, aggravating people. I got more friends than you can shake a stick at.

"Well, that ain't too bad. I would say I've been very fortunate. I've had a lot of sickness. I've spent six years in hospitals. And here I am, sitting here under this damned apple tree now, with no other ache or pain in the world."

133. Dan, Bob, and Dave.

Cripes! That's Bad Luck!

By Greg Violette
Photography by Mark Emerson
Illustrations by Greg Violette

> *"They care as little what becomes*
> *of them as any set of people*
> *under the sun, and yet no one is*
> *so apprehensive of omens and*
> *signs as are sailors and fishermen."*

This quote from Brand's *Antiquities* interested us so much that we visited the fishermen around Cape Porpoise and Kennebunkport, Maine, to find out what superstitions they knew and maybe (a little clearing of the throat) even believed.

Now, imagine a weather-grayed, low-roofed, little chicken coop of a building. The kind of building you can expect to find a fisherman in on a day as gray and rainy as this particular day we decided to visit the fishermen. (Actually, it's the only kind of day you can find a fisherman around. They're always out in their boats on good days.)

Let's go inside. Through the door we see a group of them, sitting and standing about the buoy-hung room—feeling warm by the wood stove —joking and laughing and sometimes arguing.

In the room are Arthur Gott, Dave Reynolds, Bob Schmidt, and Dan Wentworth. We're going to add to the group Smokey Coyle, Stilly Griffin, and Ken Hutchins, fishermen we caught at separate interviews, but since they're talking about the same things, we figured we'd put them in the same imaginary workroom together.

One of the first questions we asked was if they knew where superstitions started. Arthur Gott, a big fellow with curly hair and a wide grin, said, "I don't know where the hell they originated."

Leaning back in an old office chair with a beer in his hand and a

134. Arthur.

battered beach hat on his head was Bob Schmidt (who is known as the Dutchman). He said, "Jesus! I don't know. I'll tell ya one thing. The fellas that really do believe in it, you'll never hear a word out of them. If you ask 'em anything about it, they'd tell ya nothin'. They don't want you to know that they do."

Dave Reynolds, the huskiest of them, said, "I think they dreamed them all up. Don't you?"

Stilly Griffin, who has been interviewed in *The Salt Book* (pages 110–19), declared, "Superstitious. Yeah, there's a lot of people that way."

"Well, I'll tell ya. Most of these . . . the blue and the pig. Damn old. You know?" Bob said.

"Oh yeah, been around a long time," said Arthur.

"Christ. Years ago, the sailing vessels [would] take the pigs right on board with 'em," pointed out Bob. "You know? Keep 'em alive as long as they could and, you know, pigs and chickens . . ."

Smokey Coyle is a long, lean, soft-spoken man who said, "A superstition is something worked up to be . . . you know, don't walk under a ladder. Same idea as that. It's common sense. I keep my mouth shut and go out. That's the best to do. I bet you, right now, in this present, modern age . . . I betcha there's somethin' those astronauts gonna do before they take off to the moon."

Unlucky Days

"Are there any lucky or unlucky days?" we asked.

Stilly was the first to answer. "Good Friday's one. You wanna wait for Good Friday, and that'll rule the weather for forty days and forty nights. He rules the weather for forty days. Oh, that don't mean . . . you'll get some good days in between. That still goes along for forty days. Friday the thirteenth is another one you wanna look out for. You get up Friday the thirteenth, you don't wanna push it too hard, 'cause it'll come right back at ya. They always claim that Friday the thirteenth was bad luck."

"All seems the same to me," said Dave.

"I never know what day it is," laughed Arthur. "Deb's [his wife] mother won't even get out of bed Friday the thirteenth. Sure as shit somethin's gonna fall on her."

"It don't make no difference [to me but] I been waitin' all these years for my birthday to fall on the thirteenth," Bob said. "Can't do it. I was born on the tenth! Sonavabitch! I think I finally figured that out, you know. Waiting for my ship to come in on Friday the thirteenth and just come till 'bout a year ago, I was born on number ten."

Then Stilly told us this little predicting poem concerning the weather.

> *Rainbow in the mornin'*
> *the sailors' warnin',*
> *Rainbow at night,*
> *the sailors' delight.*

135. Stilly.

136. Smokey.

Signs

Smokey said, "It's a sign. There's a difference between signs and superstitions. A sun dog [rings around the sun], that's more or less a sign. Like clouds forming or things like that."

"Ayuh. You gitta thundershower in the mornin', most generally early, and the tides come in," said Stilly. "That thundershower will probably hang around the biggest part of the day. I've been got in a goddamned thundershower! I know what them bastards are!"

Alewives

Dan Wentworth spoke up: He's been in *The Salt Book* (pages 51–56), in a story about lobstering written by his bait girl, Anne Pierter. Dan brought forth a new topic, "Then there's the alewives."

Stilly: "Oh, them goddamned things!"

Arthur: "Yep. That brings a storm."

Bob: "Well, I believe that. It really does! Spring of the year."

Stilly: "We'll have some beautiful weather . . . they bring them goddamned alewives down there in the spring [for] lobster bait. They haul 'em in the traps. By Jesus Christ! They get them in, and the very next day or for a week you won't go out lobsterin'. The wind blows all the time! The gale winds! Them bastards!"

137. Ken.

Bob: "Makes sense if nature and the alewives . . . maybe that storm has somethin' to do with the alewives runnin'."

Arthur: "I'll bet it drives them up in there [up the river]. Good place . . ."

Bob: "Well, I don't know how much you'll have in there. Every year you have them spring breezes. You gonna have 'em."

Dan: "They was usin' alewives for a month to six weeks anyways. Well, you're bound to get a breeze in between there somewheres."

Ken Hutchins, the oldest of the group, who was featured in a *Salt* story about tuna fishing, said, "The only thing I know. They brought a lot of lobster bait to us."

Stilly (angrily): "They ain't no good! Ain't worth a damn! Might as well put a shingle on your lobster trap. Catch as many lobsters as a goddamned alewife."

Frogs Peeping

Ken: "That's good luck. Any kind of fish, when you catch 'em [is] good luck. When you catch 'em to make a livin'. I've been lobsterin' forty-three years and in the spring of the year . . . why, when the lobsters come out, that's when the frogs peep."

Arthur and Bob simultaneously said, "That's when you're supposed to set your trap!"

Ken (laughing): "That's what I used to tell them guys over there [pier], and they usta get a big kick out of it. So when they see me now in the spring they say, 'Well, 'bout time for the lobsters to come, the frogs are peepin'.'"

But Stilly had entirely different feelings about frogs. "Oh, goddamn those things! When [they] come out at the spring of the year, that's when all the ice goes all outta the ponds. Bullfrogs start singin'. Christ! One fella told a guy, 'Now's the time to set your traps out for lobsters.' Right when the bullfrogs start asingin'. And Christ! He set out a whole lotta traps. Some of 'em, I don't think he's seen 'em yet. They're still gone! Ayuh. That's bad luck, them damn things."

Birds

Ken: "Birds is always good luck. Any kind of bird is good luck."

Stilly: "'Cept seagulls. They shit all over."

Arthur: "Yep. Pain in the ass, 'bout all they are."

Dan: "What's that old superstition of the albatross there . . . following . . ."

Dave: "The Ancient Mariner."

Bob: "The Ancient Mariner, yeah."

Dan: "Follow him around."

Arthur: "Put the whammy on him."

After fish, amphibians, and birds, the next natural thing for the fishermen to talk about was mammals.

Pigs

Smokey: "Well, they [fishermen] always talk about the queer fellow. The pig. Everytime you mention that, you're in trouble."

Bob: "That's all they'd say, 'quare animals,' but they wouldn't say 'pig.'"

Smokey: "They always call it 'queer fellow' when they mention it aboard a boat."

Stilly: "Oh geez! Don't mention them goddamned things in the boat! Bad luck! Wicked bad luck! Christ! You mention that to any lobster catcherman, hear that . . . he won't stay around where they are. He'll walk right the hell off, and I don't know'f I blame him. Goddamn! They're bad luck!"

Smokey: "You don't know what could happen. You're li'ble to sink right in it [the water]. One time, we's watchin' a school of fish come in down to where we were staying down easterly, and Alvin Fisher was with us that time. He mentioned the word and away the fish went. They backed right up and wouldn't come near us. They never came back."

Then Bob started a story, "Years ago when we was mackerel draggin', there was old George Nunan . . . we took a magic marker and drew a picture of a pig on the landing board. George Nunan, when he sees it, he jumped on that thing and he stove the sonavabitch to smithereens. If you coulda made sawdust out of anything by jumpin' at it, he did it."

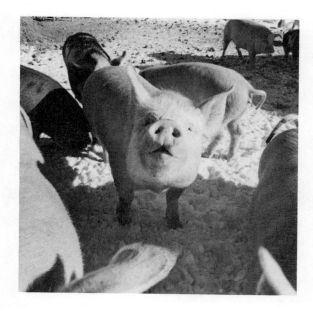

139. Pigs.

Arthur spoke, "Remember when they threw that pig overboard that was down the Pig and Saddle [a local shop that uses the figure of a pig to identify it]? Remember that? Foggy for twenty, thirty days, and they threw it overboard. It cleared up! We had a hellavah fog, you know. Nobody could get out and bring nothin' in. One night we figured that goddamned pig was doin' it!"

Bob joined in, "Christ! That bastard weighed two, three hundred pounds, I guess. Coupla fellas, they went confiscated it, and took 'er up to Port bridge and thrown 'er right the hell overboard. It floated back."

Then Stilly told us, "Jesus! The boys over the river there. One time they's tryin' to play with me there. I went in. They says, 'Why don't ya come in the bait shed?' I says, 'I seen what you had in the boxes.' But I said, 'You wait till the end the year and you won't end up with nothin'!'

"And it ended up at the end of the year, they said they didn't do so good. Lot of 'em admitted it, too. After that year was up. I said, 'Well, there you are right there, ya sonavabitch! That animal you talked about is the one's that caused it!'"

Bob: "That's what Kenny said that day . . . 'member we was saying that. Kenny got so mad, turned around and walked off. You [Arthur] brought down alongside and put bait aboard and you just said, 'Pig, pig, pig, pig . . .'"

Arthur: "Damn plank fell off!"

140. More pigs.

"[Kenny] turn right around and walked away. 'Those goddamned fellas is gonna get in trouble doin' that shit.' Yeah. He believed it."

"She goddamn near sank."

"Arthur was goin' 'Pig, pig, pig, pig . . .'"

"Yeah. Plank came off it. Almost lost it. Goin' down quick!"

Ken Hutchins had his own story. "The only episode of that superstition stuff was when the vessel blew up down Cape Porpoise. I kept tellin' someone . . . They'd get up in the mornin'. Before they got through one subject to another, we'd all wind up talkin' 'bout pigs. I says, 'Boy, you fellas. Keep right at it. Have that for breakfast every mornin', that ol' pig. You've had it. You wait and see somethin' happen.' And it did!

"See the vessel I was in there . . . well a lot of them vessels was just gettin' electric lights, and she had kerosene lamps. It was in the spring of the year and we was after them haddock. See, when they come to spawn. So we set down there, and there come a breeze and cripes! We never got out for three or four days. It's stormy in the spring. When we got out we lost a lot of gear.

"So we was in the Cape, laying there, bringing in new gear. It was after dinner and I had ate my dinner. I had all my trawls all rigged and baited. I was coming home and I got down here on the hill down here. It's called Crow Hill. Come up around the turn there, I heard this explosion and I looked down the harbor. You could see down the harbor there and I said, 'Cripes! That must be the vessel that must've blew up!'

"So I started to run and I run and when I got down to the Cape there, down the square, down where the stores was, I met somebody and I said, 'What happened?' They said, 'Ship just blew up and they was spillin' gas.' Cripes! I had stopped for a few minutes, got my wind and started to run. I run from there down to the Cape.

"By the time I got down there, they put so much water in her. They put pumps right in and everything. Sunk her. Right long side the wharf. Cripes! I had a nice camera and a nice double-barrel shotgun. Cripes! Lost my gun. I lost my clothes. I lost everything.

"They had 'er sunk, and I says to them guys I saw there, 'Well, talkin' 'bout that old dentist.' I never called him pig then. They called them dentists. I said, 'I told you something would happen!' And what had happened, they filled the tanks too full and it run over and went down on that kerosene lamp, and that's what made it explode."

Arthur said later, "We brought our pigs to market one time. We went down around the pier. Christ! You should have seen everybody scatter! Stilly almost broke his neck gettin' out of there! Hogs are oinkin' away."

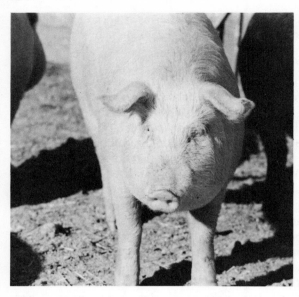

141. And more
pigs.

"We paraded them all over the place," laughed Bob.
"They wouldn't come near us."
"Hot. Was it hot out there."
"Then we stuck an ear in Smokey's bait barrel. Well, a tail."
"You know when we slaughtered the hogs. Then we cut an ear off
and a tail. Took it down and threw it in Smokey's punt. He went down
there and grumbled. Well, I'll tell ya. He got it outta his punt, but he
wouldn't pick it up with his hands. He didn't want to do that. That was
too close."

Cats

Pigs bring bad luck—in the form of bad fishing weather—but on
land the·offending animal is the black cat, for fishermen no less than
landlubbers, if they happen to believe the superstition.

Ken: "Yah. A black cat is always superstitious."

Stilly: "When you go along in the car, and you see a cat cross ya by.
You want to turn around and go back the other way. If you don't,
you'll have a flat tire."

Dave: "I kinda half believe that, but I'm not gonna go forty, fifty
miles to go around it."

Arthur: "They say if you run the sonavabitch over, it ain't bad.
Remember that day whatchamacallit was hot? He chased the sonava-

bitch through the woods with his truck. Yeah. Wasn't gonna let the cat cross in front of him!"

Colors

Ken: "I don't know if it's true or not, but there's . . . I worked on a vessel. They had plenty of superstitions, you know. They didn't want nothing to do with anything black. The boots didn't matter. That was about the only thing. Black boots was all right, but when you take the black mittens and black ambrilla [umbrella] or a thing like that. Yeah. That was superstitious. If you had a pair of black mittens or anything like . . . You wouldn't've wore 'em else they'd come . . . That'd be the end of 'em. They'd throw 'em overboard there.

"One time I had an ambrilla. This girl used to teach school up there [Portland], and I got acquainted with her. I went out there one night. It was rainin' and got off the electric car. I had to walk from Congress Square, Portland, down toward the vessel, so she lent me an ambrilla, so I sneaked aboard the vessel and I went down and underneath my bunk was a locker. Underneath it, there was a pigeon hole there, and I put the ambrilla into the hole.

"So the next trip when I got in, I was goin' out to see her, so I went to get her ambrilla and I reached in to the thing. It was gone! Somebody watched me prob'ly when I come down with the ambrilla and watched me when I put it in there, and [he] took it out and threw it away and that was the end of it. Just disappeared."

Black was a superstitious color. Was there any other color? That's when we heard about blue boats.

Smokey: "I don't know where that came from. I think that came from Nova Scotia, the blue boat [superstition]."

Arthur: "Bad luck. I don't believe it. I have enough hassles."

Stilly (with disgust): "I don't care for them. They're bad luck. I can prove that one. There was a guy lived right across the street here. Painted his boat blue and some hellava storm down here and she washed up on the road here. Within the year they took him down Augusta and put him in the nuthouse and that's where he lived till he died. So I don't want a boat painted blue.

"I don't want nuthin' in the color blue. Ayuh. I had a blue motor. Ayuh. She was blue when she came through, and I got the mechanic come down and painted her gray. Color her over gray. Ayuh. Get ridda that blue.

"Bad luck! Engine trouble and everything else. That blue. Christ! I wouldn't even own a lobster pot blue or goddamned boat blue. You tell everybody, and they just look at ya and laugh and still keep paintin' the boats blue. I either like a gray boat or dark green."

Ken: "The only thing I ever heard superstitious aboard the vessel was anything black. A lot of fellows now paintin' their boats blue. Years ago, a lot of vessels was painted blue, too. Blue was never a bad color. There's a lot of blue boats now."

Winches and Hatches

Dave (with a laugh): "There's another thing. Harley was superstitious about goin' in my boat there, and he wouldn't go in it 'cause it's left-handed." (The winch for hauling traps was on the left side, rather than right.)

It seems that left-handed boats bring people heart attacks, but Arthur says, "Yeah. That's what they told me when I had my left-handed one. If I had a new one, I'd have a left-handed one."

Bob gave a reason why this superstition may have started. "Always pullin' with your left arm. Course, your heart, I guess, is s'pposed to be on the left side."

Since we were on the subject of boats, Smokey mentioned something concerning a certain part of the boat. "There's an old sayin' about a hatch cover bein' upside down."

Arthur: "You're not supposed to. Don't really want to chance it."

Stilly explains, "A cover that goes over your rudder, your shaft. So you can get at it. Never tip that upside down when you take that out. That's bad luck. Make sure it lays down the right side, the way it's supposed to."

Ken exclaimed, "Oh, cripes! Boy! That's superstitious! I forgot about that one. Take a vessel there. They usta have great, big hatches and they had ringbolts in'em. They hadda take two guys to lift 'em off. Course, that's how big they was and . . . cripes! If you took one off and layed it upside down. Boy! You've had it!

"You're 'llowed to turn to shore. When they got in, they'd say, 'Pack your bag and get off.' If you turned it upside down."

Smokey explained how this particular superstition may have started. "Naturally, if you're out in the ocean and you got your hatch off upside down and you get a sea [wave] or something. Naturally, you're askin' for it. So things like that . . . that's what superstitions derive from.

"What I mean, you're gonna get in trouble if you get a sea break across the deck and your hatch cover's off and upside down. How you gonna get that on and bolt it down?"

Stilly, who is sort of the acting general of Government Wharf in Kennebunkport, where the fishermen's bait barrels and gear are stored, said, "Never turn a bait barrel upside down in the boat. That's bad luck. Somethin's liable to happen.

"That could cause a leakin' or it . . . Christ! could cause all . . . kinds of . . . lot could happen that way."

Ken: "Upside-down bait barrel? Don't consider that much . . . I never did."

Smokey: "I don't know about the bait barrel. How'd that get mixed up with that? I know the old-timers over the river there, they're dead set against the bushel baskets [which are used to bring their catch to market] being upside down. It coulda been bait barrels, but that's what I heard it was."

Bob: "Well, you ain't supposed to turn hatches and bait barrels or buckets or nothin' like that . . . your boat's supposed to roll over. Be careful you step 'board my boat. I don't believe in this shit now, but as the fella said, 'I don't believe in it, but I don't do it.' ".

Whistling

Then they started talking about a superstition that sometimes brought good luck in the days of sailing vessels and now brings bad luck in these days of motorized propulsion. It depended on whether a fisherman wanted wind or not.

143. Ken tells a
tale about
whistling.

Smokey: "Tap a mast and whistle; get a gale of wind. Years ago,
they used to do that. Old fishing with wind. My father used to, when he
had a Friendship Sloop. He used to tap the mast and whistle."

Stilly: "Never whistle on a boat. That's bad luck. Christ! That'll
come up a squall and blow you right the heck upside down! When you
whistle, you're callin' for wind."

Arthur: "Yap. Callin' for wind."

Dan: "Singin' and whistlin'."

Bob: "Whistle up a breeze."

Arthur: "Teddy Wildes gave Jim hell one day. Jim's always whistlin'. He's leanin' up against his traps down the pier whistlin'. Ted said,
'Get the hell away from those traps if ya gonna whistle. After I put 'em
in, there'll be a breeze.'"

Everyone laughed, and then Ken started a story of his whistling experience. "When I was a kid I usta go on the big vessels there. I was a
flunkie. Usta help the cook with things. And in 1916 well, this guy
come over and asked my father if I could . . . he wanted me to go
swordfishing. They was goin' out to Block Island.

"My father said, 'He can go if you don't go any further than Block
Island.' I was a great hand for whistlin'. I was whistlin' one tune. I
whistled all day long.

"Up around seven o'clock, this guy George Nunan says, 'For God's
sake, Ken!' he says, 'if you don't stop whistlin' that same tune. Cripe!

We'll all be lost!' That night we got blown into the Gulf Stream. We was in there three days!

"I think the tune I was whistlin' . . . 'Westwinds.' That's what it was. That was the time we saw a submarine. German submarine. The Germans was around then in 1916. World War I. We's layin' there. It was after the breeze. We had a lot of stuff out ahead of her.

"We drogued her, you know, to hold her in the wind. A barrel of cylinder oil outside lashed to the riggin'. This George Nunan. T'weren't for him we'd all been lost. He took a little bit, drilled a hole in the bottom of the oil barrel so a little trickle of oil would run down over the side and make it smoother around the vessel.

"That night . . . this Billy Mitchell, an ol' fella, he was the cook. He's settin' down there watchin' the seas, and he estimated about seventy feet high, the seas. Happened to look astern and he saw this periscope.

"This periscope comin' through the water, and he hollered to everybody, 'Come up!' and George Nunan come up and she come right up. Come right along side of us. They'd been torpedoing vessels on Georges [Bank] and everywhere around. Up around the light ship [ship that served as a floating lighthouse].

"Cripes! Soon as they got up there, they stopped. Stayed right there. When the seas . . . you could see the whole middle of her, and then we'd in a trough at sea. They're so deep, see the whole submarine and then the seas would raise the ship up, all you could see was the conning tower. In them seas there you could see the whole belly of 'er.

"Then George Nunan says, 'Boy, that ain't one of our submarines.' He says, 'That's a German submarine,' and George says, 'They'll prob'ly hang around here and in the mornin', they'll prob'ly torpedo us,' and George says, 'We won't be here in the mornin'.'

"As soon as it was dark, why we cut all the stuff away we had out, all but the big anchor rope and the anchor we had strapped on a plank. We cut everything away and let it go adrift, all but the anchor and the rope, and we hauled that in.

"Then in the middle of the night, and it shut in thick-a-fog, and George said, 'This is good. Don't start the engine or anythin'. 'Cause,' he said, 'we start the engine they'll know we're gone, but we'll just turn around and just let her go.' Drift off.

"The next mornin', course we started the engine then. Thick-a-fog and everything. We didn't see no more of her. Took us three days to get inta the south shore light ship off New York. Took us three days. Steamin' and sailin' and everything."

"My mother-in-law was tellin' me a story last night about the old fella bought some wind," said Smokey. "It'd be calm somewhere. I

guess they was runnin' lumber or somethin'. Old fella looks up and says, 'I'd like to buy a quarter's worth of wind.' I guess he threw a quarter overboard or somethin' and along came a screechin', howlin' gale. I guess it about blew the sails off her. So when he got through it, he said, 'If I knew it come so cheap, I only woulda bought a nickel's worth.' "

Tobacco Juice

After we all had a good laugh, Bob started to reminisce, "My ol' man. I went with him. Christ, I'se about knee high, you know. Years ago. And he never told me why, but when he'd go set traps in spring . . . Christ! When he'd set, he'd spit a gob a tabacca juice on that first buoy. First trap he set in spring, he'd spit 'bout a quart a that friggin' tabacca juice. You know how he chewed."

"Right. Always chewed tobacco," agreed Smokey.

"Never spit on another one. First trap he'd set in the spring, he'd spit on."

"Yup," Smokey said. "Used to be, you know, twenty, thirty years ago they always did. Spit on the first buoy. It didn't have to be the first day of spring either. Every day pick up a string and spit on the first one for some reason."

"Don't know, he never told me why."

While thinking about traps, Arthur said, "I don't like to put thirteen traps on a string. I don't like that damn number thirteen! I don't! When I get thirteen, I know the trap's empty. I know damn well it's gonna be empty! That's why I get from twelve to fourteen real quick."

Women Aboard

Then we asked the fishermen about bringing women aboard the boats, and Bob said, "We don't mind." But Stilly and Arthur thought otherwise. "Oh, Jesus Christ! That's a bad one!" "Yeah. That's bad luck."

"No. Cripe no!" Ken protested. "Why years ago, them guys, when they usta go in them sailing vessels, they all would take their wife with 'em. Lots of guys usta get married on them boats, usta go to China and around Cape Horn and them places there."

To which Bob said, "Well, I wouldn't bring my wife!" Then, "Danny over there," pointing to Dan Wentworth, "he's had bait girls for how many years?"

"Eight," said Dan.

"Well, Anne Pierter was one of 'em," said Arthur. "Deb was my bait girl. I married her for Christ's sake!"

Bob: "Jesus Christ! That's a choker right there!"

Dave (to Arthur): "Wouldn't you like to have that to do all over again?"

Drinking

Then there was one final question we asked. "Is there any bad luck connected with drinking?" and Arthur Gott replied, "Not that I know of. Just when you go home or when you don't go home!"

145. Arthur has the last word.

146. Maggie Griffin.

When You're Married to a Fisherman

By Rachel Brochu
Photography by Mark Emerson

Maggie Griffin of Kennebunkport

"I was born a farmer's daughter. What I miss is that rooster, the smell of the hay, the spring, the fields, and the gardens. But I wouldn't go back. I wouldn't change it for the ocean. I love the ocean."

Maggie Griffin was born on a farm fifty-eight years ago. The past forty-one years she has been married to Stilly Griffin, a lobster fisherman. They live in Turbots Creek in Kennebunkport, Maine.

"His step-grandfather brought Stilly up to meet me. I was still in high school. He told me that Stilly was a hard worker and had lots of money. I figured that I ought to grab onto him, so I did.

"We went together for a short time before we were married. A matter of months. I don't remember any proposal—I think that we both just took it for granted. I think that we just figured that we were going to get married. That was it.

"We were married in North Berwick. It was a small wedding. My brother and my girl friend stood up for us. Stilly was so nervous that he got the rings mixed up. He was going to put his big ring on my finger!

"Then we forgot to pay the minister. We started out, got in the car, and he said, 'Oh! We forgot to pay the minister!' We had to go back and pay him.

"I loved being married. And I loved housework; truly I did. Really! We had a ritual, the other wives, the neighborhood wives. You did your washing on Mondays, the ironing on Tuesdays. You baked your beans on Saturdays. Everything was done like a schedule. You always knew what you were going to do that day.

"It was great when the kids were small. I remember that we had a collie dog when young Stilly was just a little fella. That dog was so smart! He wouldn't let young Stilly out in the road. That dog would walk right out in front of him and push him back. Young Stilly would go to get underneath the sun porch. The collie would grab him by the seat of the pants and pull on him! He'd get so mad, but he was just a little fella then.

"I used to love to cook. I didn't like baking so well. You see, Stilly doesn't like fruits in his sweets. He likes them plain.

"My favorite to make is stuffed baked lobsters. Stilly cleans the lobsters and splits them for me. Then I take the tomalley from the lobsters and mix it in with the cracker crumbs, some melted butter, salt and pepper, and a little salad dressing.

"Mix it all together and stuff it back in the lobsters. I bake it for forty-five minutes. I start out with a hot oven and slow it down. We eat a lot of lobster in the summer. It's so damned cheap you may as well!

"When I was younger I used to spend hours at the stove stirring something to keep it warm until he got home. After a while you learn that you don't do that."

By far the most difficult times in the life of a fisherman's wife are the hours spent waiting for the men to come home.

"When he doesn't show up I keep myself busy. He's been overboard more than once, that fella.

"I was up painting one night. Up painting the kitchen and waiting for Stilly to come home. He was out. His boat had come up on a rock. I thought that he'd never get home. Finally he showed. It was a rough night. It got so that for a while after that, when the gong rang, and Stilly was out, I was petrified until he got home.

"It's that water. You never know it. It can be as calm as can be and then storm up pretty fast. The only one I would go out on a boat with is Stilly. Even though he can't swim, I don't think that it makes a difference out there if you can swim or not."

Maggie continued. "I know a lot of the summer people that want me to go out on a boat with them. But I won't go. Stilly knows that water."

"There's more water out there than I can drink," joked Stilly.

"There was that time that he fell overboard when he was out sardining with Ray White. Bobby Schmidt dove overboard and helped him.

When he came home he was blue. We had whiskey in the house. I don't know how much he drank, but you'd never know he'd had a drink, he was so cold.

"Stilly doesn't drink. But he used to. We both did. I remember one time he didn't come home for supper. His parents were over. They're death on drinking.

"Well, in comes Stilly. He still had his rubber boots on. He'd been out with Chink McKay. I saw his father coming and I says to Stilly, 'Here comes your father.'

"Well, he ran and hid under the crib in the room. His father come in and asked me if I knew where Stilly was. I said, 'No, Dad. He's probably down to the beach or something.'

"My little daughter Loraine came in, cute as a button, and said, 'I want my Daddy Stilly to come out from under my crib bed!' And there he was with his rubber boots sticking out! I was always hiding him on his folks, always!"

Looking back on their younger days, Maggie admits, "It's hard to be a fisherman's wife. Especially when you're young. They're home bodies. Mine is, anyway. He loves his home and that's it. When you're young, you want to go to parties, go dancing.

"I would have liked to change his makeup. He had an insanely jealous makeup. I just couldn't make him see that his suspicions were crazy. I couldn't for years. But he's outgrown that now. That was very hard for me—very hard. I love people and I love to be with people.

"But he's honest. And he pays his bills! Boy does he! He can't wait until they come in so he can pay up. He waits for the mail to come in, the light bill, the telephone bill. And I have to sit right down and write them up.

"God, but we've had some hard times. We'd wonder where the next meal would come from. We really did. We did stick together, but it was rough. We've had some damned rough times. Damned rough. No money coming in. But we always had enough such as it was.

"Even now I can tell when something bothers him. Or if it was a good day. He's not all smiles when he comes in the door. I can see it on his face. He's quiet. I have to ask him, 'What's the matter, Stilly?' He tells me.

"It was the little things that bothered me. The laundry. If ever I get a load of laundry to do that doesn't have one thing in it that smells of bait! And where he puts his hands when he drives the car! I get out and they smell like fish. That really gets me mad.

"I used to hate all that. His old fish clothes, the smelly rubber boots. I used to hate all that terribly. But you get used to it. You may as well.

"That's the way it is when you're married to a fisherman."

Betty Hammond of Harrington

By Sandra Morin
Photography by Lynn Kippax, Jr.

"Anyone who's married to a fisherman has to be disciplined." This is the no-nonsense way that Betty Hammond looks at her job as the wife of a lobster fisherman in the small seacoast village of Harrington, Maine. Betty is a strong-voiced, sturdy-looking woman who stands "four feet eleven inches from the floor."

148. Betty Hammond.

"I do as much as I can to help him. I try to paint the buoys for him, which has to be done each year. This year he taught me how to mend the bait bags, which I weren't too swift at it, but I did the best I could.

"When he has something go wrong with the boat, I'll try to go down and help him with that. Keep him company when he goes after his baits and stuff. I take a lot of phone calls when people want lobsters or crabs. I'm quite busy right here just doing that.

"But we work together. We always paint the boat together. We always spend at least three weeks with the old boat around April.

"Every now and then I have to clear off the buoys because they get all grassed up [with barnacles]. So I have to take a day or so and go down with Clorox and rub and scrub them. Why I even brought blood to my fingertips, 'cause the Clorox is so strong," she says as she displays her calloused hands.

"I do all the business end of the work. So if there's any complaints, they all look at me," she chuckles. "I try to be nice because when you got to do business with people, you got to meet the public.

"If you don't have the gumption to stand up for yourself, they'll walk all over you. I try to be nice and easy going, but the minute I think I'm being pushed around or rolled around, I come to a screeching halt and

I stand my ground, and they know I'm there. I might be little but they know I'm there."

Betty and her husband, Francis Hammond, have a family of five children that are "his, mine, and ours. He lost his wife of leukemia back in sixty-three. I had two little girls and I was working at a restaurant in Bangor." Members of their family knew each other and Betty came once to baby-sit. "I've been baby-sitting ever since, but I wouldn't give it up for nothing! I love all the kids.

"We all get along good. We have two grandchildren, a grand-daughter, and a grandson."

One of the first times that Betty was ever on a boat with her husband, she had a shocking experience. "A long time ago," says Betty, "we were fishing and the dogfish [small sharks] were quite thick around here. I was sitting at the foot of the boat, this was when I was first learning about lobster fishing.

"My husband brought up a trap and there were some dogfish in it.

149. Betty and Francis Hammond.

I'm sitting down at the stern of the boat, and I asked him if I was in his way and he said, 'Oh no, not at all!' The next thing I know down he comes right beside me with a big dogfish. I jumped right up through them just as fast as I could go. I was petrified! I told him the next time to let me know!

"I like the ocean. I'm scared of it, but I like it. I'd like to be out there right now with him, but I feel that I should be right here with the kids so there is at least one home supervisor in case of emergencies.

"The boy goes with him now. My daughter went last year. They split three days apiece. One would go three days, then the other one would go three days.

"So they all have a good idea of what their father does for a living, and how he brings in the money.

"I do like the water and I like working with it, but I know it tires you out. Ya spend all day in this fairly cool breeze, then you come inland and the hot air hits ya. And there's nothin' left. Ya all gone."

"Every day he's gone, till he's back again, there isn't a minute of my time that I'm not wondering where he is or if he's all right.

"One night he was down the road talking to one of the fellas and I had my son gulp down his supper. I couldn't eat. I told him to get on his boots and go out to find his father. He was just down the road. I think you worry from the time they leave home in the morning till the time they come home at night.

"So many things can go wrong. It doesn't take long if you're not paying attention, to get the rope around your leg, and when that trap goes over, there's a lot of weight behind it and it can pull ya over.

"You can lose power on the boat at the wrong place and the wrong time, and one of those big waves will come in and make ya drift over to the rocks.

"He's gotten hit in the head I don't know how many times, and it could have knocked him out, left the boat out of control. That's why I don't like him out there alone."

Betty is just as aware of the good side to her husband's work as she is of the hard work and dangers. "I consider he's free. He does what he wants to do, and he works for himself year round.

"I feel that if a man does what he wants to do and his wife backs him, not nags him, but backs him and helps him, that makes him feel more independent. I think a man works happier when he does what he wants to do, not made to do what someone else thinks is better for him. And I feel as though when he's happy, that makes me happy.

"I like to go out on the boat with him. Matter of fact when the kids are all grown up that's what I intend to do. I intend to go with him. I like the water!"

Dot Ridlon of Cape Porpoise

By Debbie Bereshny

"I'll never go out again.

"Well, let me see. I went lobstering with him a good many years ago in a rowboat. It was foggy and he had left me on this rock. I couldn't see anything. He was only gone a few minutes. Went to haul a trap.

"Anyway the waves were splashing up around my feet. Honestly. The rock didn't seem any bigger than a foot round and wide! He swears I was on an island, but I never did believe him.

"Well, I could have been. There are rocks before you get to the island," Dot Ridlon admitted. "I just went out with him for fun that day. I'll never go out again."

Dot and Fremont Ridlon have been married fifty-four years now. They live in Cape Porpoise, Maine. Dot has many hobbies: cooking, knitting, and spending some of her time wondering what Fremont's going to do next!

"Once Fremont was hanging some fishnets at the top of the garage when the rungs of his ladder gave way. He went down, down, and hung there about three feet from the ground yelling for me.

"The lady across the street heard him hollering and got help from the man next door. By the time the doctor got there he was back on his feet, thank God!"

150. Dot Ridlon.
(*Photo by E. J. Blake*)

Close calls are an everyday occurrence in the life of a fisherman's wife. Dot has had a good life. She and Fremont have three sons, Gary, Richard, and Robert. Like their father, all her sons enlisted in a branch of the service. Today she has had "all but a Marine in my family."

"When Fremont's out fishing," Dot is usually busy in her kitchen. "I love recipes. I collect them. Here's one that's easy to remember.

"Take two cups of clams, two cups of milk, two cups of cracker crumbs, a dash of salt and pepper, and a little butter.

"Mix them all together, and add the butter on the top. Bake at 350° until it begins to puff up. Sometimes I add half milk and mushroom soup."

Would she offer any advice to someone about to marry a fisherman? "Just don't be waiting for him to come home for dinner."

Debbie Gott of Kennebunk

By Rosanne Beauvirage
Photography by Mark Emerson

The morning rush is over. The small restaurant on Route One in Kennebunk, Maine, is nearly empty—for now. Off to the side of the dining room is a cramped kitchen occupied by two large refrigerators, a gas stove, and an oven. There are shelves of food. Work counters and a mix and match assortment of pots and pans fill up the remainder of the space.

Debbie Gott is preparing the noon dinner special. The spicy aroma of spaghetti sauce fills the hot kitchen. But the heat from the stove and the din of the refrigerators and dishwasher does little to slow Debbie down or supress her laughter.

She is a strong, energetic twenty-eight-year-old, happy with her life as both a businesswoman and fisherman's wife.

Debbie enjoys waitressing with the day crowd when she can be her unpredictable self. She can run her own show. She has always been independent. She knows what she wants.

"I decided to marry a fisherman when I was a little girl." She slices a piece of raisin bread for an order. "Did I know what I was in for? No!"

Soon after Debbie met Arthur Gott, she was hired as his bait girl.

151. Debbie Gott.

Her duties included pegging the lobsters' crusher claws, assisting Arthur in baiting the traps, and repairing the buoys.

She loved working on the ocean, although it was not always such smooth sailing.

"What a cheap bastard! I was the lowest-paid bait girl in the entire county of York! Really! Low pay! I was doing five traps. [The lobstermen give traps to the bait person and the bait person keeps the money made on the lobsters from these traps.]

"The other bait boys had ten to twenty-five. I had five. Now that's cheap! He was giving me all the bait barrels filled with maggots [rotting redfish and herring was used for bait]. He used to give me the job under the steering wheel where all the maggots and all the [stuff] would be hanging.

"But nothing bothered me.

"One time he got mad at me because he thought I said something I didn't. I took all the previous day's catch and threw it overboard. He told me to swim to shore!

"I don't think I ever dared to say too much, but things change after you're married for a while."

More than communications changed after their marriage. One was Debbie's relationship with her mother-in-law, Mary Gott.

"Since I've been married, my mother-in-law is the best you could have. I mean, she's absolutely wonderful! She'll take my side before Arthur's.

"Before we were married, she sent the cops after me! His mother's Irish—right off the boat! Hey, I was taking her baby away!

"Irishmen don't get married before they're thirty-five, and Arthur was only thirty-two when we got married. I was twenty.

"Really, she sent the cops after me. I was so upset. Everybody in town was laughing. They thought it was a riot 'cause they knew Mary. And then she wouldn't come to our wedding. But since we've been married, she's the best mother-in-law you could have."

Although life as a former bait girl and present fisherman's wife can be troublesome, Debbie's experience enables her to paint a seldom-understood picture of these men and their relationship with the sea.

"There's some times when you're watching someone do a job that they're a part of, and it's like watching someone dance. It's really beautiful. And if he reads this, he's going to think it's ridiculous.

"But it's true. You watch these guys doing it and they're fantastic!

"Arthur will admit that he enjoys the ocean. But I think a lot of the fishermen don't even realize that they are even aware of it. They don't intellectualize things. And they know the ocean. A good fisherman will admit when they're not familiar with things."

She knows Arthur is sure of what he's doing. She has no cause to worry about him when he's out. She sets a spoon down and leans against the refrigerator.

"I think that fishermen are a little gullible to a certain extent. They'd do anything for you. They're almost innocent, and they can't help it. They get screwed all the time.

"Like people coming down and hauling over their traps, and stealing the traps and everything else. If you went up to one and asked him if you could have one of his old traps, he'd give it to you. If you ask, he'll give you anything in the world.

"So they're always going around feeling cheated. They really are a nice bunch of people.

"But together they can be awful. There's a lot of competition around. Like—not help the guy who caught more lobsters than the other guy. Or never tell anybody that you're making money. That's the fisherman's motto.

"They're always poor because [if they're rich] then everybody and his brother is going to want to be a lobsterman."

Debbie laughs. "It's always bad. Always. Funny how the mortgage

gets paid and the kids go to school . . . but my experience is that when they buy a new pick-up truck is ALWAYS when they can't afford it. It's in the spring—when they're piss-ass broke. That's when they buy 'em. It's like a pacifier.

"Unfortunately having enough money is an important factor when a couple has a family to care for." The job of a restaurant owner, cook, and waitress is a result of this often meager income from lobstering or fishing. Fishermen's wives have to be flexible enough to adjust to such hardships.

"My knowledge of fishermen's wives is pretty limited in this area. They all seem to work, and that definitely seems to be an improvement. You don't have money in the winter. You never know, something always happens.

"Being a lobsterman's wife is an everyday job. It's like farming. You can't predict anything. You can't put in more hours and expect to get more money. If the lobsters don't go into the trap, there's nothing you can do about it. It can be very frustrating.

"It really does a number on you when we get a big storm or a hurricane and he's just set his gear and you know it's gonna be wiped out.

"Every winter we go through the midwinter blues. All the fishermen go through a depression. We get drunk for weeks! And they're all going

to sell out. They've had it. They can't take it anymore. There's no god-damned money in it.

"Last winter I thought he was really going to do it. The thought of not having any contact with the ocean was like losing a child.

"When we were first married and we were so poor, if we didn't have the ocean we would have starved to death. You steal the kids' money out of the piggy bank and go buy a pack of cigarettes. You know you shouldn't be smoking anyway—you feel twice as guilty.

"Life with the ocean is like a character of Thomas Hardy. You have to go daily down to the ocean to see if it's still there and drive around. The waves' still coming in. That's part of the ritual. We eat lobster, crabs, and fish, and we always have our trip to the island.

"Our big event is going to the island. I call it Gott's Isle. There were people out there one time we went out. We always go out really early. They were on our spot! They were out eating breakfast.

"I told them that this was Gott's Isle, and I stood there and tapped my foot. They left. I was so mad! Arthur said I was very rude, but that's my big event."

Living by means of the ocean is a hard way of life. But the good times are worth the bad times for those who live by it. It's food, income, and recreation.

"When you work something, it's not the same as just using it. You work to get it. Then to have it work against you, it's a relationship you've gotta have in order to appreciate the good. You've got to go through the bad a little."

She pulls four or five loaves' worth of bread dough from a large mixer. It's evident she's a hard worker. She doesn't seem to mind.

"I've never been sorry. Most wives that I know are married kinda happily. It's difficult to tell. They're really proud of what their husbands do. I think that's one thing fishermen's wives have in common.

"So if someone was lucky enough to marry a fisherman, I think that's great. 'Cause I think it's a wonderful life!"

Sam Polk

By Andrea Downs and Cynthia Pinkham
Photography by Lynn Kippax, Jr.

Sam Polk, a gentle, soft-spoken man, sits in the open doorway of his barn, where he whittles laths for his lobster traps. His small, wizened face, topped by a shock of white hair, glows with an artless spirit. He wears a checkered farm shirt and work boots, instead of the green shirt and hip boots worn by most fishermen around Jonesport, Maine. Sam gestures with his right hand as he gets involved in his stories.

"I love fishing. It's all I ever done in my life." Sam, now eighty-nine years old, retired from fishing only a few years ago. The landmarks in his life, both personal and geographical, are fishing landmarks.

"My first experience came when I was 'bout seven years old, first time I ever hauled a lobster trap over the stern of a skiff. I had 'bout

154. Sam Polk.

five traps, 'course those traps were good. Pulled them all out by hand, see? No engines. Got ten cents for our lobsters, no matter what size they were.

"After I grew up, age twelve, why I used to lobster in a rowboat. And my father and I used to do a little trawling in the spring, hand-lining . . . get up at two o'clock in the morning, catch a few fish, in the afternoon get back . . . take the southwest wind, get back home.

"Well, course I been a lobster fisherman, and a codfish fisherman, and I've been seining mackerel, red herring, pollock . . .

"When I first went lobstering offshore . . . I was between fifteen and sixteen years of age . . . and there used to be the old coasters sailing the Maine coast, anywheres from New York to Philadelphia, loaded with bark, lumber.

"Lots of mornings, we was going out to haul, you could count anywheres from six, seven, and I have counted as high as twelve ships, some light, some loaded. Some would be going east with coal, some, most of them, going west loaded with lumber and laths.

"Them days were a lot better than they are today . . . most generally you had a job and you could go in the boats, and you could travel along anywheres: the shore from Southwest Harbor through Portland, 'long the coast, Mt. Desert Rock, 'Tinicus [Matinicus] Rock, up in the way between 'Tinicus and Vinalhaven, back to Rockland Bay.

"We used to go to Portland. I loved Portland, and I liked Boothbay. Went to Boothbay a lot. And I was in Boothbay the first time that they ever sold Bailey's popcorn . . . Bailey's popcorn was the first popcorn ever sold in bags. That's quite a record, eh?

"I never was west of Portland Light [lighthouse]. I fished east of Portland Light. I guess I've been in all those harbors, but them's all built up now.

"When I was seventeen, my uncle, he spoke for a sloop boat, and he said, 'I'm going to have a new sloop boat.' And he says, 'Do you want to go in with me?' 'Well,' I says, 'what am I going to go in with you with?' 'Well,' he says, 'same as I do . . . pay it as we earn it.' 'Well,' I says, 'if that's the way, why yes.' Well, I left my father and went with my uncle. We went together for four years, and we done good.

"We went mostly wintertime together. In the fall of the year, he went down to the Island [Beal's Island], we called it. He camped on the Island, see? And I stayed to home, I lobstered up inside [in the harbor]. And he fished down 'round the Island. But we went fifty-fifty just the same, see? Then, when we got blowy weather, then we doubled up and went in the sloop boat. You know, it's like anything, if you got a business, money coming in, it's good.

"My people was poor. Course, there was a lot of poor people. You never heard tell of poverty. Where they ever got this poverty from, I don't know. It's horrid, instead of telling someone, 'You're poor' to tell them they're [in] poverty. Well, everybody wasn't rich, same as 'tis today."

Sam's mother knitted and made garments for the family out of worn clothing. "When I was a kid, I wore pants up here, above the knee. And I remember the first pair of long pants I wore . . . I must've been thirteen."

In Sam's time it was legal to leave school at age fifteen. So after completing seventh grade, Sam quit in order to fish full time. "We walked to school, no matter how the weather, rain or shine, snow or ice, walk. No rides, no automobiles . . . you walked or you didn't get to school. If you stayed home, somebody would come take you to school . . . and if he [truant officer] come three times, he'd take you to jail.

"When I was a boy, you couldn't do anything; if you did, you went to jail. They'd give your parents a warning, see? They know what the rules was, what the law was. If you broke a window out there, you put it back. You didn't leave it."

However, ". . . one time [in the fifth grade] there was a boy named Orange Cummings, and he sat right next to me. And he always wanted my berth on the settee in the anteroom where we had our class. It was late in the fall, cold, and they had one of these oil burners, pot stoves, you know, burning in this room. When I went in, he pushed me and I pushed him, and upset the stove.

"Set the school on fire. Well, the teacher drove us all outdoors, and hollered for help. Well, at the time some people happened to be right handy, men, and they come up and put the fire out. That's how near we come to burning up, see? We didn't get into trouble, you know. It was just as much my fault as it was his, and his aunt was our teacher, so they hushed it up.

"But my best life was when I was nineteen, and up till I got married. 'Cause when I was a boy . . . when I got to the age of nineteen, I could look for good times, know what I mean? I went away, I didn't stay around home. I went away and went aboard the vessels and going into different places, you know, and 'round, seeing different things. That's what I like the most.

"Course, I've had it good since I got married, but I mean, when you get married you get tied down." He laughed, "And you don't have the liberty you do when you're single. Here we been married sixty-three years, and hope to go a few more, you know.

"I had been twenty-six in October. My wife had been not eighteen in January. She had to write to her mother and ask her if she could get

155. "I went away, went aboard the vessels, going into different places, see-ing different things. That's what I like the most."

married, to marry me. She wrote back and said she didn't care, she could make her own bed, so we got married. Well, I come in from seining [fishing with a long net]. It was kind of foggy, and late in the afternoon.

"And I went home, changed my clothes, took a bath, and fixed up and said, 'I'm going to get married.' I says to my mother and my older sister, I says, 'Would you like to go along and be witness?' And they says, 'No,' and I says, 'Thank-you.' She says, 'I'd rather see you going out through there in a box, than get married.' Well, I was going to get married, so off I went.

"Three weeks later, when I come back, I went down to get my clothes, and my mother throwed me a pillow, and she says, 'Here's your pillow.' So that's what I had for a home, my pillow."

Sam moved into rented homes, eventually buying a house for the two of them, and later, his two children. He liked living on solid ground, but spent most of his time afloat.

"I love the sea. You know, I get seasick just as quick laid down in a boat's cabin today as I would first time I ever went in a boat. But 'long

as I was on deck, it never was big enough. Long as I was working . . .
but if I was in the cabin and she's rolling me that way, and then by and
by your stomach got a little upset, and it's an awful feeling.

"I've been in some bad places. Didn't know enough, probably," Sam
chuckled. "Well, I got broke [a wave broke on his boat] once, in my
thirty-foot boat. I had a cloth cabin on her, a little cabin. I had some
traps on my boat and there was awful good lobstering to the rocks . . .
there was no lobsters in the bay. And when they set off we'd had calm,
but there it was awful rough. The flood tide had made the sea come
with it, but there was no wind." Then he started to haul in his lobster
traps.

"Boy, I looked, and he [the wave] was coming, ayuh, two, three
come in there, 'twas a little farther than that window [forty feet]. Boy,
I dropped it [the line]. I let go the line, and jumped . . . and put myself in that little cabin, that way. Well, I could feel her going at that
point.

"I had a 'make and break' engine in her [one of the earlier gasoline
engines which, to reverse, had to be turned off and started again at just
the right time]. If I'd had another one, 'lectric one, that would probably have stopped her. But she kept pounding. Well, when I got out
where smooth water was, water was on the floor, 'bout that much water
[three feet]. Then I had to turn around, stop the engine, and bail out.

"The ocean is good.

"And, you know people, the way they got it now, in those boats they
got. Before we had a sloop boat, no engine. If there was a little wind, we
was lucky. If it was calm, we had to row or tow. You go out in the
morning, early, get back in the afternoon. 'How many traps you get?'
'Oh, we never got any, never got out there.'

"But now, why it's all power, and all they got to do is reach up, grab
a toggle [the marker put on the lobster trap's line], haul a little bit in,
tow it on that, and just watch the boat and go 'round. Nothin' to it.

"[But] I like sails.

"When I was here lobstering, I had a home here. And I'd leave anywheres before daylight . . . right around four. I'd be down to the
shore, quarter to five. I'd leave, well, when all the rest leave. If I was
half an hour late, and everybody's gone, seems as though the day was
gone. I wanted to be there when the rest went."

However, they did not all go to similar places. "I was a bay fisherman. I was no rock fisherman. I liked the ocean. Well, there was plenty
of room. And I never liked the rocks, 'cause rocks is all right calm and
pretty, but when it was blowing on, it was a hard job, to get in, 'cause
if you got fouled up, you was in trouble.

156. "I love fishing. It's all I ever done in my life." (*Photo by Mark Emerson*)

"And I learnt the bottom. I knew it as good as it was. I figgered it pretty good.

"I've gone with my father, when it blowed hard, when we went to sea, lobstering. If she spit water up, or spray up over our bow, if it come toward us, we took it. We never had no place to dodge it.

"And I seen my father . . . he used to have a moustache . . . and I've seen him when it's been so cold, the water'd run down, and it would freeze on his moustache, and he'd have to reach up and pull it off.

"We used to clam, too. I never dug no worms [seaworms]. I don't think I'd like it. Now that's like my grandson up here. He goes nights. He, last year he used to go all night. When he lived home, he'd get up one o'clock at night. With a light on his head, go out worming. I said to him, I says, 'You're going to be an old man when you're a young one, Warren,' and I said, 'You're going to kill yourself.' 'Well,' he said, 'money's good.'

"I said, 'Yes, but it's nothin' like health, though, money.'"

Sam has enjoyed good health most of his life. "I never had a headache. Didn't know what a headache was till I got up into my fifties. I could work, if I didn't get tired so easy, as good as I could when I was eighteen."

157. "If it come toward us, we took it. We never had no place to dodge it."

A few years ago, Sam went to the doctor. "[Doctor] asked me what I was doing, told me not to. He says, 'Can't go [fishing] anymore.' He didn't tell me why, or anything. He called my son-in-law up, and he says, 'If he comes down, don't take him. Course, I could have gone. . . .

"You know, I get tired, but I keep on, 'cause I like to work. I always did, from a baby up. I always have, I always will, till I drop over.

"I like to sit down in the rocker and look out the window, but I still like to be out[side]. And when it rains, I go out, just the same.

"I like any kind of work—I'll bar haying—[but] I like to farm a little. I wouldn't make no big farmer. I don't want to go to no farm to work, but I like to have a nice piece of land.

"And I'll tell you another thing I like an awful lot. Well, I used to make a lot of traps, lobster traps, big ones. I never made no little ones [miniature traps], till I come up here [Indian River] and started in to it. Something for me to do [since he stopped fishing].

"That's all I ever built in my life, is traps, since I was big enough to drive a nail. I give 'em all [the little traps] away. Now I've gone into the coffee-table business." Sam makes square traps for glass-topped coffee tables; lawn chairs; rocking chairs; chicken pens; swallow houses; and rabbit hutches.

"I built one out here for the rabbits. I had some wild rabbits." Sam and his daughter-in-law, Iona, have a long-standing joke about animals. "Every winter she calls up and says, 'What we going to have?' 'Well,' I says, 'what do you want?' 'Well,' she says, 'I want a pig.'

"First she wanted a cow. I said, 'Look, you can have all the cows you want, and I'll do everything I can, but,' I said, 'I'm not milkin' no cows.' Because I've never milked. When I was to home, I never learnt, 'cause if I did I'd have to. 'And,' I says, 'I'm not going to learn now.'

"Then she says, 'Well then, what're we goin' to have?' I says, 'I don't know.' She says, 'Let's get a pig,' and I said, 'All right.' So we got a pig, raised him up for November, last November, had him killed.

"I went, 'Now. What's coming up now?' She says, 'I'd like to have a calf.' So we got this calf. And I kept him.

"Then last winter, I says, 'Now what you goin' to have?' She says, 'I'd like to have some hens, chickens.' Sam chortled. 'Well,' I says, 'I want some turkeys.' She says, 'We don't want no turkeys.' 'No,' I says, 'you want hens, but don't want me to have no turkeys.' I says, 'I'll get my turkeys; you get your chickens.'"

Sam thought the story about the ram they once had was the funniest of all the animal stories. "He was death on Iona and I. We was too good to him, I guess. She took these peelings out this day. He come and bucked up and boy, he butted her down. He knocked her down," laughed Sam. "Hurt her hand and, when she went through that door, he was right at her tail.

"She come upstairs a-raving. She says, 'You're gonna kill that thing.' I said, 'What's that now?' She said, 'Didn't you see that?' I said, 'No, what was it?' 'Well,' she said, 'that ram has butted me down and hurt me.'" Sam laughed. "She said, 'How about you get rid of him.' She's the one who builds 'em up, see, and I'm the one who takes care of 'em." Sam chuckled. "No, she's good . . . Iona's just as good as gold."

All his life, Sam has been independent and hard working. He spent over seventy years fishing from and living in Jonesport and is satisfied with this life. As Sam sums up his experience, he says, "I've had a pretty good life. I've had hardships and things." Although he'd like to see some of the places he visited as a young man, Sam is content to stay near Jonesport. It's home.

159. A bark. (*Sketch by Robin McGahey*)

Grandfather's Golden Earring

By Robin McGahey
Interviewing by Nat Bailey, Robin McGahey, and Greg Violette

One small, thin, gold earring. What does it symbolize today? Well, just about whatever the wearer chooses it to mean—a different meaning to each person who wears the ring.

But it did have a specific meaning at one time. It was a tradition in the 1800s that anyone who sailed around Cape Horn, on the southernmost tip of South America, received a small, thin, gold earring.

We got this story from two unique women, the Furbish twins, Edith and Ethel, of Kennebunk, Maine, who are ninety-two years old. The lively twins were willing to share with us their memories about their grandfather, Franklin Efrim Furbish.

When we went to their home, Edie brought out some pictures. "This was my grandfather, Franklin Efrim Furbish. His people came from Ibenes, Scotland, something like that."

We asked how long their grandfather had been a sailor. "I suppose he was from the time he was a little boy. He went to sea when he was a cabin boy. Then he became a first mate on the ship that Captain Bragdon sailed on, Captain Bragdon from over Cape Neddick way.

"They went down around the Horn in a bark with a load of paving blocks," Ethel explained. "Wooden paving blocks for the streets of San Francisco."

"Yah, it took six months! I don't wonder it took so long in a bark. They weren't very big vessels, ya know," said Edie.

"Course, sailing around Cape Horn was dangerous," added Ethel, her face serious. "It was a graveyard of ships and, uh, it still is!"

We asked the name of the bark. Edie answered slowly, after thinking awhile, "We don't know. I wish I'd asked Mr. William Barry. I worked for him, and he told me about Grandfather. He and Grandfather talked a lot."

160. Edie, left, and Ethel look at old family photos. (*Photo by Robin McGahey*)

"They went down around South America," Ethel continued to explain. "Yah, down around South America, and they didn't go through the Straits of Magellan, because there were pirates!" It seemed to us quite remarkable to hear someone talk about pirates. We were all very amazed as we sat in Edie and Ethel's living room listening to them talk.

We asked if sailors were given a reward for going around Cape Horn. They answered simultaneously.

"No, no." And Edie added, "The only reward was they got a gold earring." Had their grandfather been given a gold earring?

"Yes, it was on his left ear. He used to set in his chair—nobody took his chair. He always sat in his rocking chair by the stove and we could see this ring, a thin . . . gold . . . earring in his left ear.

"The earring was a good luck sign for going around the Horn. After he passed away, it was given to one of his daughters, but nobody seemed to find it afterwards."

"And I wonder why he never had one in the other ear," said Ethel, with a hint of laughter in her voice. We laughed with her. The Furbish twins have a way of making something simple into a happy and interesting thing.

"They landed in California to unload some barrels of apples," Ethel continued. "By the time they got there, the apples were all rotten, ya know. They wanted them for seeds so they could plant apple trees over there. Grandfather said they got big money for 'em."

"They had to also go to shore for water, when he got to California," Edie said.

"Yah, there was a little peninsula; he put up in there."

"They had to go for water, fresh water, 'cause they couldn't carry enough like that. They had to choose, to get one of 'em to go ashore. Course, it was pretty wild then, big snakes, they could see 'em crawlin'! Great big ones in the rocks. Course, where there's rocks, there's usually a mountain stream where they could get fresh water, I suppose."

"A fellow on board stabbed Grandfather," Ethel told us. "Grandfather was a first mate at the time. Course, there were fortune hunters at the time, ya know, some riffraff. They left the traitor on a deserted island off San Francisco somewheres."

"Yes, an uninhabited island."

"In 1849."

"Grandfather was out there and he went to Sutter's Gap, where they was digging gold in forty-nine," said Edie. "He had about fourteen hundred dollars in gold dust when he came into New York, where they assay it, ya know."

"They went with these little burros," added Ethel. "Of course small donkeys are burros. And they went across the Panama and come across to the Atlantic Ocean side. When they got to the station, these burros, they belonged on the Pacific side. They'd just take off and send 'em home alone."

"Yah, it cost five hundred dollars to have a burro, you know."

Then we asked the twins what their grandfather did with the gold he brought back from California. Ethel said the claim didn't prove very rich.

"He didn't have much left after they'd took out what they call a 'tare,' ya know what I mean?" Edie said. "I suppose he turned it into American money, what there was, but there wasn't much left, from what I understand. He had some gold quartz he got, and it stayed on his mantelpiece for a long time to show people, but someone swiped it! We never dared to touch it. We just looked at it."

Edie left the kitchen and went into the next room. She rummaged around for a few minutes, then brought out a painting.

"This is Grandfather's house."

"It used to be in the woods," said Ethel, "and it had a barn across the street. Years ago, we had a horse called Bob. We used to use him to go out to the woods to pick up dead wood, ya know, pine limbs. There were some apple trees there," she said pointing at the painting. "They were russets. And there were bee hives there. You had to go slow by there so's you wouldn't 'wild' the bees."

"1872 that was, the original house. It was a little house and it was built on and built on. Grandfather had it built on like that. Course, they took boarders. It said on one end of it, 'Furbish House' and you could see [the words] through the paint for quite some time, but you can't see it now."

"The date is on the barn across the road," said Ethel, after Edie finished speaking. "The road went across between the house and the barn."

"Yah, he used to drive the cows across the street right to the well house to a great big trough, and the cows would go in there to drink. There was kinda an open place in there [the barn] where they'd hang the corn, and they used to dry it out on wire so the squirrels, rats, and things couldn't get it. And he kept plenty of cats to watch out for them."

Ethel had a small twinkle in her eyes as she confessed what she and her sister had done. "He had a yellow cat he liked very well and she had a kitten, ya know, that he thought a lot of. We had an eye on him, and we stole it!"

"We took it, yah!"

"We stole both of them!"

We all laughed at this as we tried to picture Edie and Ethel stealing the two cats. "Did he ever find out who took his cats?"

"He didn't find out for a long, long time, after we had named the kitten 'Cricket.'"

"We used to go out on Sundays to pick berries. Grandfather owned a pasture and he used to charge a dollar per season for anyone to pick blueberries. Course, we didn't have to pay."

"We used to go down on Sundays for dinner at Grandfather's house, ya know."

"We used to set at the table and he always served and he'd always say some sort of prayer before we ate," said Edie.

"He was good at it, too. There would be about ten of us," added Ethel. "We used to sit at the table and we wouldn't speak. I was kinda scared."

"Children should be seen and not heard, ya know. We didn't say

161. "He had a yellow cat he liked very well and she had a kitten, ya know, that he thought a lot of. We had an eye on him and we stole it!" (*Sketch by Greg Violette*)

much. He used to say, 'I don't know what it is about kids. You children don't seem to bother, or say anything.' Ya know, we were quiet. Mother told us to watch our manners and do what we were supposed to do. We never spoke until we were spoken to." Ethel's face had turned serious.

"He never said anything to us at all," said Ethel. "He never made of us at all. We were kinda afraid of him. We weren't made of much. He

162. Ethel, left, and Edie hold up an old photo of their Grandfather and Grandmother Furbish. (*Photo by Lynn Kippax, Jr.*)

wasn't a man that made of much, but," she paused and smiled, "we were lucky for a piece of pumpkin pie or a cookie or anything that Grandmother gave us."

"Grandfather would go to church, and he took religion always aboard ship."

"Mother said he used to swear like everything . . . well, he didn't swear, but he could say anything quite sharp without swearing."

"Course, Grandfather, he was a selectman and road commissioner and he never missed a town meeting. If there was any kind of business with people and they didn't know how to do it, well they all came over and Grandfather would straighten it out. He was just like a lawyer."

"He was quite well educated in business. He came here from the Atlantic Shoreline [Railroad]. He showed them how to motorize."

"He wasn't married then. He later married somebody from Springvale."

We wondered how long a life Grandfather Furbish had lived. "He was ninety, and Grandmother was seventy-five, thereabouts," answered Edie.

After the Furbish twins finished their story, we stayed and talked with them about themselves and their life. They brought out remnant after remnant from their past. When the time came to go, we left with more than we had when we came, carrying with us the shared memories of the Furbish twins.

163. (*Sketch by Kenneth H. Smith*)

The Wreck of the Schooner Charles

By Dorothy O'Keefe with Patricia Shearman and Pamela Wood

We are fascinated with tales of a bygone era when great-masted, wooden sailing vessels ruled the vast oceans and the lives of the men who sailed them.

Shipwreck. The sight of an ailing ship struggling with the rising tide, unable to right herself, as onlookers from the shores of the coastal settlements were left powerless to do anything except witness the death and destruction.

Almost every coastal village along Maine's Atlantic seaboard has visible reminders of the great ships that went down. Gravestones tell of those who perished at sea, markers commemorate the lost ships, and living residents recount stories of shipwreck told by their grandparents.

Newspaper accounts of the time carry vivid descriptions of the floundering ships and their doomed passengers. Journalists spared no words in trying to capture the sense of loss and grief that surrounded such an event.

Yellowing pages from the early 1800s tell of broken masts held by tattered rigging; of fragments of the ship and cargo swept into sight, only to be sucked away by the riptide; of cries for help from the victims. It was, we are told, a sight that weakened the strongest.

Words that might seem extravagant today were used in the days of the great sailing vessels to tell of shipwreck. To us, these dramatic accounts more nearly reflected the tragedy than today's more tame and unimpassioned news stories.

The shipwreck of the schooner *Charles* in 1807 off Cape Elizabeth, Maine, illustrates how such events were treated and how they continue to live in the minds of local people almost two hundred years later. It also holds particular interest because of some of the details we have uncovered.

Our attention was first drawn to the shipwreck by a headstone overlooking the site where the schooner ran aground. It is the headstone of a young unmarried woman who was traveling with her trousseau from Boston to her home in Maine, according to local people.

The headstone reads: "SACRED to the memory of MISS LYDIA CARVER, DAUR. OF MR. AMOS CARVER of Freeport aet. 24: Who with 15 other unfortunate passengers male and female, perished in the merciless waves, by the shipwreck of the schooner *Charles,* Captain Jacob Adams, bound from Boston to Portland, on a reef of rocks near the shore of Richmond's Island on Sunday night, July 12, 1807."

Stirred by this account of a young woman who drowned on the eve of her marriage, we sought more information about the shipwreck. A broadside preserved by the Massachusetts Historical Society told of the wreck (Maine was then a part of the state of Massachusetts) and two Portland newspapers published eloquent stories.

An interesting fact emerged. The ship struck the rocks at about midnight. The wreck of the *Charles* occurred, ironically, less than fifty feet from an island off the shore of Cape Elizabeth, Richmond's Island. It was July and the water was warm. One wonders why most of the passengers stayed aboard as she sank, when land was so close. Was the night so dark that they knew nothing of the nearby island?

By morning the hull of the *Charles* was completely bilged and sixteen of the twenty-two people aboard had drowned, including the captain, Jacob Adams, and his wife. Thomas Phillips, the cabin boy, drowned the following morning in his attempt to board a rescue boat.

Just as remarkable was the behavior of the captain, according to accounts in the Portland *Gazette.* Four men, including the captain, left the ship, gained temporary safety on some rocks, and decided to swim to shore. But Captain Adams, "hearing the shrieks of his wife and the people on board," decided to turn back and try to help them. He drowned while trying to get back to the ship.

We have pieced together the following story of the shipwreck from old newspaper accounts. (Note: All italicized passages are taken from the Portland *Gazette* dated July 20, 1807, except the final paragraph, which is taken from the *Eastern Argus* dated July 16, 1807.)

The morning of July 12, 1807, dawned bright and clear, a brisk and steady northwest wind ensuring Captain Jacob Adams "a fair prospect of having a safe and speedy passage." At promptly seven o'clock that morning, the schooner *Charles* set sail from Boston en route to Portland, a part of the Commonwealth of Massachusetts.

The number of passengers, coupled with the crewmembers, totaled twenty-two persons on board. A valuable cargo estimated at twenty-five thousand dollars constituted the remainder of the hold.

Charles, her sails billowing as they harnessed the wind, must have been a magnificent sight as she made her way up the coast. Spirits were high in anticipation of a short, uneventful trip. Conversations most likely ranged from weather to past voyages, and the impending war with Great Britain.

By sunset the seas were high and the air blanketed in a soft fog. At the passing of Boon Island, only a few hours had lapsed when Captain Adams estimated their location as being four or five miles south of Cape Elizabeth, and a short distance west of Portland Light.

Tho the mate was forward, he was not apprized that danger was near 'til he discovered brakers [sic] at the distance of about four times the length of the vessel, which proved to be on a ledge near the shore of Richmond's Island.

The alarm was instantly given, and the vessel, going at the rate of 7 or 8 knots, before the wind, an attempt was immediately made to haul off, but before this could be affected, the stern struck on the ledge, when she broached to; and there being a very heavy sea going, threw her nearly on her beam ends.

One man (Sidney Thaxter) leapt into the water, and got upon some rocks that were near (and bare at this time), by the means of a plank run out from the vessel, the captain and two others got on the same rock; but finding the water between them and the island too deep to ford, by swimming about 30 feet, three gained the shore and urged Captain Adams to follow them; but hearing the shrieks of his wife and the people on board, he said he would endeavor to return to their assistance or perish in the attempt.

He again reached the rock he first got upon, but all his efforts to regain the vessel were unavailing, the tide rising fast remained in this hopeless fixation for about an hour, till a sea washed him off and he was seen no more!

It is not in the power of language to describe what were the feelings of those unfortunate persons who were at this time clinging to the vessel which was now bilged, her deck nearly perpindicular and under water except the weather gunnel—a violent sea constantly making a breach over them. In this fixation, and expecting every moment would be the last, were a husband, a father, a brother, and a friend, striving to preserve each other from a watery grave, exhibiting a scene of distress beyond the power of conception!

Before any aid could be afforded (which was about eight o'clock the following morning) 14 persons were washed from the wreck, or perished through fatigue occasioned by the violence of the sea.

Saved—Mr. Sidney Thaxter, Mr. Moonie, and Mr. Cook by getting on Richmond's Island soon after the vessel struck; taken from the wreck Monday morning, between 8 and 9 o'clock, by the assistance of boats, Mr. Williams (the mate), Mr. Samuel Richards, and Mr. Pote, passengers, who were in a very weak and exhausted condition.

For those drowned was written, "May the greeting of angels welcome them to that blessed haven, which is vexed not by storms, nor troubled with disasters, and their souls be harboured in peace."

Sails in a Bottle

By E. J. Blake and Pamela Wood
Photography by Lynn Kippax, Jr.

"That's where I get my pride. It's not in making money. It's—when I'm gone, these will always be around. I got ships in probably at least ten different countries. That makes you feel good."

As he speaks, Winson Morrill of South Hamilton, Massachusetts, leans intently over a long-necked wine bottle while his left hand maneuvers a billowing sail into place with almost imperceptible motion.

He is performing a piece of magic that has bewitched children and sailors, kings and captains for two hundred years: putting a tiny ship model into a bottle.

Part of the magic lies in the wonder of it all. How does the ship with its tall masts and furled sails get through the narrow neck of the bottle? And part of the magic lies in the beauty of the object. Within the gleaming glass contours of the bottle rests a handsome little ship, complete in all its exquisite detail, a pleasure for the eye to see and the hand to hold.

For Win Morrill, putting ships in bottles is more than a hobby. It is a passion that has consumed him for almost fifteen years.

"Just as soon as my wife clears away the supper table, I start right in," he says, explaining how he finds time for the hours and hours of intricate work that go into each bottle. "I make time. That is just it. Make time when I get home.

"It's amazing how the hobby grew," he said, grinning. "I've done over four thousand now.

"Of those four thousand ships, I bet I gave at least 98 per cent away. I do not attempt to commercialize on this craft, only that I am thrilled seeing my work on prominent mantels throughout the country. I have given them to historical societies, museums, civic groups, and in exchange for historic woods."

164. Winson
Morrill working
at his kitchen
table.

Around him as he works lie his handmade tools, so carefully designed, each for its own task, that he can put whole fleets of ships in
bottles, rather than the usual single ship of most hobbyists.

He is in a characteristic pose, working at his kitchen table in his
stocking feet, chain smoking, glasses pushed back on his forehead. He
gets extra height to perch above the top of the bottle by haunching on
one leg in his chair.

"You see the way I sit," he says, laughing, "and I'm comfortable. Sit
on my legs, you know. For a fifty-three-year-old man, that ain't bad!"

It is not only the extraordinary zeal with which he pursues his craft
that sets Win aside as an unusual craftsman. His work is distinguished
for two other reasons.

First, his ships are linked with history, their hulls carved from the
remains of historic ships and buildings for which they are named. In

Buckingham Palace is displayed his model of the *Endeavour,* Captain Cook's famous ship, which Win carved from wood taken from the wreck of the ship recovered in America.

Many of the ships are carved from landmark structures in Win's native New England. He has made one ship from wood taken from the House of Seven Gables when it was remodeled, and another from the old Salem Custom House.

Another will be made from Beverly Farms, the house where six generations of Win's own family were born and lived, from the 1600s until 1910. "My father was born there, my grandfather, my great-grandfather, my great-great-grandfather, right down the line."

A second distinguishing mark about Win's ships in bottles is that he has developed his own particular techniques for the craft.

"I don't use the conventional way of building the whole ship, then putting it inside [with masts and yards folded down] and pulling the thread and everything goes up.

"Even that's pretty hard—to do it right. No matter which way you do it, it's a lot of work to it."

Win does much of his construction within the bottle itself, working with sixteen long-handled tools he has fashioned from coat hangers. Some are flat at the end, some round, square, hooked, and pointed; some are straight from top to bottom, some curved at various angles for working within the bottle.

The hull and individual masts, along with part of the rigging are constructed outside the bottle. Then the ship is put into the bottle in sections, hull first, masts one by one into the holes drilled for them. Much of the rigging is done within the bottle.

The work within the bottle calls for small, tight strokes with his tools, which Win controls with the precision of a surgeon. "It looks hard," he admits, "but if you keep working at it and working at it, you can do it.

"The way I do it, I can do a lot more. Like I can put all these masts in a bottle," he says, pointing to a seven-masted ship. He can also put more than one ship in a bottle—three ships or even a fleet of ships. Several of his models are ships within a bottle within another bottle, and he has even put ships in light bulbs.

One of the advantages of Win's method is that he can position his ships anywhere he wants in the bottle, bottom or side. When the ship is constructed outside entirely, the bottle must be turned on its side as the ship passes through the neck and is lodged in the side. Bottles done by this method are always exhibited lying on their sides.

Win developed his own method and his own tools to fit his particular needs as a craftsman. His right hand and arm are limited in the tasks they can perform because he had polio years ago.

165. Win can put a fleet of ships in a bottle.

166. Maneuvering a ship into a large light bulb.

His method has since been learned and practiced by craftsmen who have the use of both hands because it allows far more complex construction within the bottle.

While Win refuses to acknowledge that his arm is an impediment to doing what he sets his mind to do, he does admit that it may have some bearing on why he works so hard at it.

"I'm the kind of guy who's always got to prove he's better than someone else at something—where I got this stupid handicap. I mean, I built this house from scratch. I was just about the only one out here [South Hamilton] when I came here.

"So I'm always doing something. I mean if I wasn't doing this [putting ships in bottles], I might go out and shoot a President or something," he says, laughing.

Before he began to put ships in bottles, Win was making ship models. One model in his living room has a crew of 115 men. "Then I was over to the Salem Museum once with my daughter and wife.

"I happened to see a ship in a bottle over there, so I thought I'd try it. I made about three of them before I had any luck.

"The first time something went wrong, I was down in the cellar with my daughter. The ship was all finished and I was just putting the pennant on. Every time I touched the strand of the ship, she'd sink a little. Finally the whole half of the ship sank in the putty there. So I just took it and smashed it against the wall.

"Well, the next one I worked on it until late, and about three o'clock I just reached for an aspirin. The aspirin bottle slipped out of my hand and hit the neck of the bottle and broke it. That was ship number two.

"Couple nights later, I tried again. I forget now, the third didn't work out too good.

"But the fourth one turned out remarkably well. I've got that right around the corner [in his living room]. I mean it's really one of the best I've ever done. I wouldn't sell it for a million dollars!

"In about four thousand ships, I haven't had any problems since then!"

To demonstrate his craft, Win begins to make "just a simple little three-masted ship.

"These are my tools over here. These are all made out of coat hangers. Each tool has its own special job," and each is about a foot long. He has sixteen tools made from coat hangers in a variety of shapes with a variety of ends (see Plate 168). "Throughout all these years, I can make them talk, more or less," Win says.

He also uses a utility knife, two hand drills, a common clamp, a long spring-release tool, a gouger, and scissors.

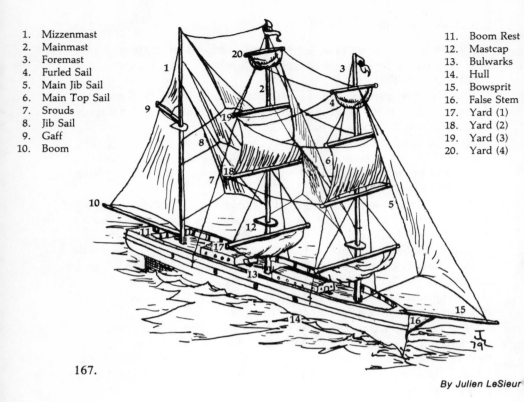

1. Mizzenmast
2. Mainmast
3. Foremast
4. Furled Sail
5. Main Jib Sail
6. Main Top Sail
7. Srouds
8. Jib Sail
9. Gaff
10. Boom

11. Boom Rest
12. Mastcap
13. Bulwarks
14. Hull
15. Bowsprit
16. False Stem
17. Yard (1)
18. Yard (2)
19. Yard (3)
20. Yard (4)

167.

By Julien LeSieur

168. "Each tool has its own purpose."

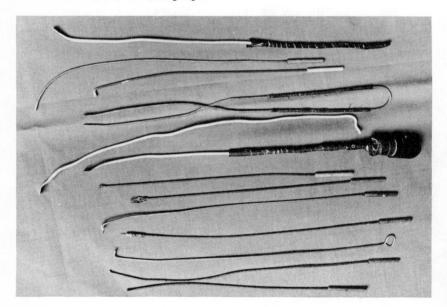

Win begins the hull with a small piece of soft pine wood free of knots measuring about 3½ inches long and ½ inch in width and depth.

For his first step, he selects his utility knife. "This is my basic tool here, the best tool I have. This is the one I do all my carving, cutting, and everything else." With the utility knife, he whittles the hull, shaping the bow and stern. He is careful to be sure that the shaped hull fits through the neck of the bottle.

Using a medium-fine sandpaper, he sands the rough exterior sides and bottom of the hull. At this point, he puts his trademark on the ship, turning it over to write "Morrill" on the bottom of the hull.

Win attaches a common clamp to the hull and, using his thumb as a guide, runs the knife lightly ⅟₁₆ inch within the top side of the hull all the way around.

Following the line he has marked with his blade, he makes a cut ⅟₁₆ inch deep around the hull, forming the bulwarks (railing).

Next he uses a small gouging tool to scoop out the deck within the area of the cut. Then he sands the deck area.

Now Win makes the bowsprit. With his utility knife he notches the bow. From the stockpile of hospital applicators which he uses for bowsprit, masts, yards, and boom, he snips 1¼ inches for the bowsprit. He sands a point on one end and, with his utility knife, tapers the other end. He inserts the tapered end into the notched bow and glues it in place with Elmer's glue.

169. Carefully carving the hull.

170. Attaching a common clamp to the hull.

171. Cutting the bulwarks.

172. Gouging out the deck.

173. Gluing on the bowsprit.

174. Drilling three holes for the mast.
175. Rounding off the ends.

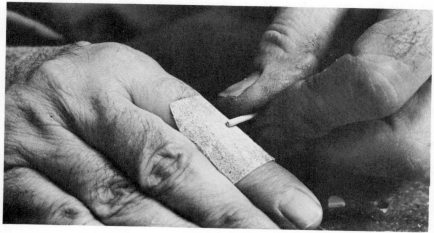

176. Gluing the boom onto the boom rest.

Next he makes the cutwater (or false stem), which fits against the bow under the bowsprit. He cuts this piece from thin wood, about $\frac{1}{16}$ inch in depth (see Plate 167). Then he attaches it to the bow and bowsprit with glue.

With a 16-millimeter drill, Win bores three holes in the hull for the masts. The hole for the mainmast is drilled in the center of the hull and holes for the other masts are spaced about an inch fore and aft from the mainmast.

He shapes a ¾-inch piece of applicator into a boom for the ship, rounding each end by sanding it. Placing an applicator in the aft hole where the mizzenmast will go, he lines the boom up so that it will touch the mizzenmast. Then he levels the boom by bolstering it with a small sliver of wood. He glues this boom rest into place, then glues the boom to the boom rest and to the stern.

Now Win paints the hull with white wrought-iron Dekorator's enamel. While the hull dries, he proudly displays a boxful of preconstructed cabins. These are made from tiny blocks of wood, each painted white with a flat black roof, dwarfish windows and doors.

Two of the tiny cabins are glued to the deck, centered between the holes drilled for the masts. With a black Magic Marker, Win lightly outlines the bulwarks and portholes. He also writes the name of the ship on the bow and its home port on the stern.

177. Painting the hull with white enamel.

178. Attaching the cabins to the deck.

179. Lightly outlining the bulwarks.

Now Win makes the mast caps. These are cut from a flat wooden stick about 4 inches long and ¼ inch wide, which resembles a doctor's tongue depressor or wooden coffee stirrer. In the stick he drills a series of holes ⅛ inch apart that are large enough to insert an applicator (about 1/16 inch in diameter).

He cuts this stick into sections, each section containing one hole. These sections will serve as mast caps for each of the masts he constructs.

Next he makes the masts and yards from applicators. For this ship, Win cuts three masts, each 4 inches long. Then he cuts the yards from the applicators, making four yards for each mast. The bottom yards are cut about 1¼ inches long. The other three yards for each mast are cut progressively smaller by ¼ inch so that the top yard is ½ inch long.

With a number 71 or 72 drill, Win drills four holes in the center of the mainmast and the foremast, starting about ¾ inch from the bottom of the mast. The second and third holes he drills are about an inch apart and the fourth hole is about ¼ inch from the top of the mast.

He threads the mast caps on the mainmast and the foremast about ¼ inch above the bottom yard hole and slightly above the center of the mizzenmast. He daubs Elmer's glue around the three mast caps to hold them in place.

180. Marking the portholes.

181. Slicing the mast caps off.

182. Cutting the masts.

183. Gluing the mast cap to the mast.

184. Connecting the yard to the mast.

185. Making the "lifts."

Now he attaches the yards. Using tweezers, he pushes a common pin through the yards in the center and then through the holes he has drilled on the masts, so that there are four yards on the mainmast and foremast. He snips off the pins close to the masts.

He paints the masts and yards, using the same white Dekorator's enamel he used for the hull. "Oddly enough, that's the only paint I've ever been satisfied with," he explains. Then he stands the masts in slots he has made on his working board to let them dry.

The next step for Win is to begin the rigging by cutting the "lifts" which connect the yards. With a 4-inch piece of polyester sewing thread, he connects the bottom yard of the foremast with the yard above it, wrapping the thread around one end of the bottom yard (1, see Plate 167), pulling it up to the yard above (2) and down again to the other side of the bottom yard, making a triangle. He wraps the thread around the ends of the yards, dabs it with glue and cuts off the extra thread.

Then he connects the two top yards (3 and 4) in the same way. He repeats these steps with the mainmast.

To make the sails, Win uses a white, fibrous ✕20 ribbon like that used in a florist shop. "I can paint that and get a nice sail, make it look like any sail I want. I use this because it's pliable. I can work with it, and it'll take a beating going through the neck of the bottle."

186. Connecting the yards.

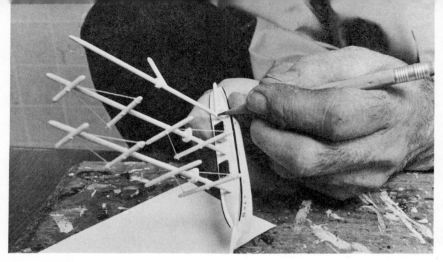

187. Measuring the mizzenmast sail.

188. Marking the size of the sail.

189. Cutting the sails.

Win coats the ribbon with the same white paint used for the ship. After the paint has dried, he cuts the jib sails, main topsails, and furled sails for the ship with scissors.

Now he works on the mizzenmast. First he makes the gaff, slicing off a piece of applicator about ¼ inch long. He attaches the gaff at a 45-degree angle at the center of the mizzenmast just below the mast cap.

To mark the pattern for making the mizzenmast sails, Win places the mizzenmast on the ribbon, drawing the two sails to fit above and below the gaff (see Plate 188).

After cutting the mizzenmast sails, he runs glue up the side of the mast and on the gaff, then holds each sail in place with tweezers for a few seconds until it adheres to mast and gaff.

He attaches the main topsail and furled sails to the yards of the mainmast and foremast with glue (see Plate 190). Each of the main topsails is attached only at the top.

Now he cuts and glues on five jib sails, three running between the mainmast and the mizzenmast, and two between the foremast and mainmast. The jib sails are permanently attached at the top, but temporarily glued at the bottom with only a speck of glue. (When the masts go in the bottle, the jib sails must hang loose at the bottom.)

190. The bottom mizzenmast sail.

191. Gluing furled sail of foremast.

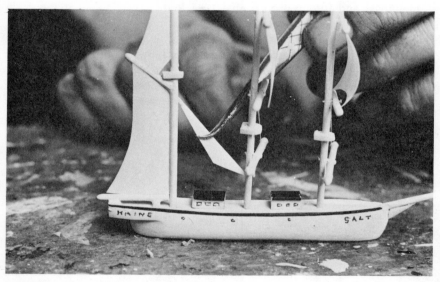

192. Attaching a jib sail.
193. Positioning the main jib sail.

194. Attaching the rigging.

He attaches the jib sail to the top yard of the foremast at its center with a small dot of glue, then attaches this triangular sail at its base to the bow with a small piece of string. The third corner of the jib sail is attached with glue temporarily to the bowsprit.

Next Win makes the shrouds (rigging which goes from the top of the mast to the sides). He cuts off two pieces of thread twice the length of the mast. Taking the middle of each thread, he ties one with a square knot at the top of the mainmast and the other at the top of the foremast. He lets the threads hang down until he's ready to attach the ends.

Win is now ready to put the three-masted ship into the bottle. All steps that can be done outside the bottle have been completed, and the remaining steps must be done within the bottle, manipulating with delicate movements the long-handled tools he has created just for this purpose.

First he removes the masts from the hull, standing each of them in the holes he has drilled in his work board. (He must detach all the jib sails at the bottom where they have been temporarily glued.)

195. Removing the mast from the hull.

196. "One small lump at a time."

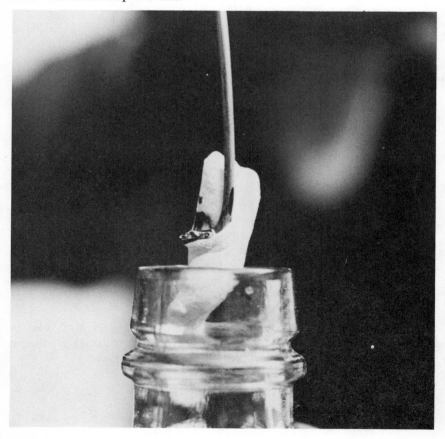

He spreads Prussian blue oil paint on the bottom of the bottle with a flat-ended tool. The paint bonds the bottom of the bottle with the putty (used to simulate the ocean) he is going to put in next.

He puts the putty in, one small lump at a time, until he has enough to cover the bottom of the bottle. He shapes the putty, pushing it down with a tool that has a flat foot on the end.

As he shapes a bed of cresting waves from the putty, he adds dabs of blue paint to color the ocean. "You can make the ocean as big as you want," Win says.

Before he puts the hull through the bottle neck, Win carefully removes bits of putty and paint from it. "I don't get too much on the neck. When I'm through, I just wipe it off."

Using a long tool with a spring release, which Win says can be bought in any hardware store, he picks up the hull by the bow. Turning the bottle on its side, he takes the hull through the neck stern first, releasing it on the bottom of the side. He takes a new hold on the hull at its center and, turning the bottle upright, positions it in the putty. With a flat-bottomed tool, he pushes waves (putty) against the bottom of the hull, securing it firmly.

197. Placing the hull into the putty.

198. Pushing the putty up against the hull.

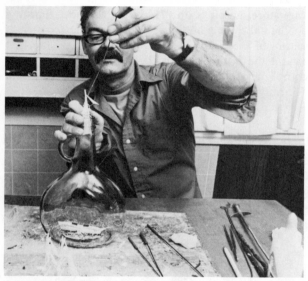

199. Lowering the mizzenmast into the bottle.

200. Placing the mast firmly in the hole.

201. Slipping in one yard at a time.

Now he puts the mizzenmast into the bottle. First he slips it partially into the bottle with his fingers, until all but half of the topsail is through. Using a tool, he pricks the topsail to gain a hold on it, then lowers the mizzenmast to the hull and maneuvers it gently into the hole drilled for it in the stern.

"I put the foremast in next," explains Win. First he turns the yards flat against the mast, "or as flat as I can get them," by folding down the sails. Then he tilts the mast, guiding it with his thumb. When the topsail is half in the neck of the bottle, he hooks it with a tool that has a common pin on the end and lowers it into the hull.

"You can actually feel that when it goes into the hole," he says as he lowers the mast into place, then pushes until it stands firm. He dabs glue around the base of the two masts to keep them permanently stable.

Now he straightens the yards, using a hook tool.

At this point, the main topsail of the foremast is attached only at the top (yard three). To billow out the sail, Win moves the ends of the sail to the stern side of yard two and then pushes at the center with a small tool to puff it out.

"In time, that sail right there, I'll get that so it billows out from the yard," he says. After a few more gentle pokes, he attaches the sail with glue to the ends of yard two.

The rigging tied around the top of the foremast is now attached on each side. He dabs glue on each side of the hull about halfway between the foremast and mainmast.

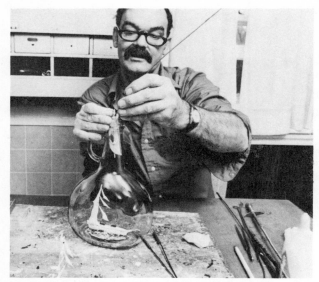

202. Hooking the sail with a pin tool.

203. Piercing the sail with a pin tool.

204. Maneuvering the mainmast through the neck of the bottle by folding the yards down against the mast.

"I'll wait a few seconds for that to get tacky. Then I'll draw down on that to make it tight." He pulls the lines down against the side of the hull until his tool slides off the end of the thread, leaving the lines firmly anchored.

"I'm about ready to put the mainmast in. Do the same thing [as with the foremast]. Tilt it, now that's hard to tilt." Carefully he maneuvers the sails into the neck of the bottle, letting his fingers gently bunch the yards and sails so that nothing obtrudes.

As with the foremast, he straightens the yards on the mainmast, billows the main topsails, and attaches the top rigging to the hull on each side.

Win stops to make a point about using glue. He emphasizes that he uses a fresh dab for each application, lining the blobs up on a small glue board.

He then reglues the jib sails at the bottom, this time permanently.

It is time to attach the rigging that runs from yard to yard between the mainmast and foremast. He cuts eight pieces of thread, each about an inch long. Then he dabs glue on the starboard ends of each of the bottom yards (yard one) of the mainmast and foremast. A piece of thread is attached to the glue, connecting the two yards.

He repeats this step between yards two, three, and four on the star-

205. Win lowers the mainmast into place. Using the pin tool enables him to lower the mainmast gently into its proper hole.

board side, and then between the yard ends on the port side, until all eight threads have been glued into place.

The final triumphant step is to cut from bond paper three pennants to identify the ship. In the case of the three-masted vessel he has just made, Win writes "Salt" on the center flag, "Maine" on a flanking pennant, and "1978" on the third.

He accordion pleats them and attaches one to the top of each mast, making sure they blow out in the direction the sails billow.

The ship is complete, each part securely in place. "Once these are all done, I can really pound the bottle, and the bottle will break before anything on the ship will come apart."

Win taps the bottle, turns it upside down, and nothing inside it moves. He makes his ships in bottles "to last a hundred years."

206. Win pulls the shrouds down firmly against the side of the ship. The glue is slightly tacky so that the shrouds will hold tight.

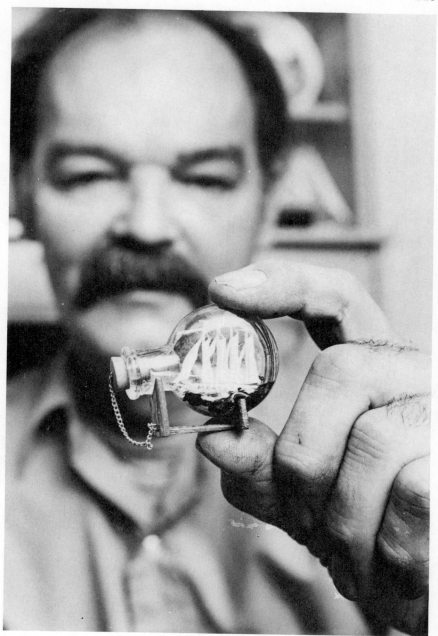

207. Win holds the smallest bottle he has filled with a ship.

208. (*Photo by Lynn Kippax, Jr.*)

Island People

Swan's Island is a jagged promontory rising off the northern coast of Maine, whose wooded hills shelter a plethora of deer (no hunting allowed), a sprinkling of houses, three white-frame churches, a general store, about four hundred year-round people, and several times that many in the summer.

The five miles of churning sea that separate the island people from the mainland have insulated them against the ticking time frame and bustling commercial centers across the water. Changes that have come so rapidly to the mainland in this century have crossed the water slowly. Not until the beginning of regular daily ferry service in recent years did significant change begin on the island, but even that is muted by the nature and history of the people.

Swan's Island people still have many of the values and practice many of the courtesies that we associate with people who lived a hundred years ago.

On Swan's Island, people wave to each other as they pass on the road, whether they are traveling by foot, by bicycle, or by car. They also wave to strangers ("to make them feel to home"). Older people address young people as "dear," and this includes older men talking to young men. Levi Moulden, as he talked to young *Salt* interviewer Herbert Baum, called him "dear" as naturally as his wife addressed the young women by the same word.

Sense of community is stronger on Swan's Island than on the mainland, rigorously guarded by the boundaries of the limited land that rises above sea level. There is an absolute sense of "they" and "we" on the island: "We" are the islanders and "they" are the people who are not.

Pleasures are simple and hard-won; life has never been a bed of roses for the island people. Despite their isolation from mainland commerce and activities, the lives of Swan's Island people do not have the idle, luxuriant drift that we associate with the lives of South Sea island people.

For the men and women of the island, life has been a ceaseless round of hard work. The provision of food, warmth, shelter—the most basic needs of life—has called for daily struggles.

Each day by dawn, the men are off the island fishing, work that most of them have been doing since they were nine or ten years old. In earlier days, many of the men also worked in one of the two fish-packing plants or in the quarry, fishing before or after they had done a day's work. Now that refrigeration and concrete have ended the need for salt fish and granite, the fish plants and quarry have closed, the island population has shrunk, and fishing is the principal work of the men.

For the women, doing the family wash by hand, with its inevitable pile of fishermen's garments stiff with grease and fish bait brine, was not the least of their struggles. Of the days prior to washing machines, Ruth Moulden recalls, "I'd get through [wash day] with my hands all bruised and bleeding."

For most of the women, the work hasn't ended with household tasks. Like Ruth Moulden, many women have done the heavy outdoor chores on the island, and they have done this heavy work for the same reason Ruth did. " 'Cause Levi [her husband] couldn't," she explains. "He was out there [in his boat] every day working and tired to death and worn out when he got in.

"We was burning wood, and I used to go out and cut his kindling wood on the chopping block right out there. I'd cut his kindling so he'd have it until the morning. He got up at three o'clock, for gracious sake." Ruth dragged all the rocks from the shore up the hill to build the foundation and chimney for their house.

Like Ruth, many women help their fisherman husbands earn a living. Ruth baited trawl lines on the wharf for Levi for twenty-two years. Some of the women even fish with their menfolk. Emily Sprague fished with her husband, Austin, right up until she died.

What have been the pleasures of these hardy people? The dances that were frequently held on the island, the informal "neighboring" among friends and family, and the small extras that work brought: "Go down here to the store and buy some gingham and a little hamburg, and my land! I'd come out the nicest time of it!" says Ruth.

There is more. Islanders take concrete pleasure from their particular sense of history, from their very real knowledge of owning a time and a place in the turning world because they have spent the time and occupied the place.

It is a common thread of identity that runs through the five personal-

209. The ferry
Everett Libby at
Bass Harbor,
Maine.

210. Ruth
Moulden of
Swan's Island,
Maine.

ity sketches of island people in this section: through a major article about Ruth Moulden, and shorter articles about her husband, Levi, and three other island men, Walter Stinson, Edwin Gott, and Basil Joyce.

Ruth defined this sense of time and place—of history—for herself and for the others. Has she ever wished to live anywhere else? she was asked. Has she ever wanted more than Swan's Island?

"I never had any desire," she replied. "No. This is my life." She paused to search for words. "After all, this is . . . this is my life. This is what I'm used to. This is what I've made. I've made this, see. My life here and my home that we've made together. And I'm happy here."

As Ruth leaned back in her chair, relieved that she had found the words for her thoughts, it was clear that she was right. Her home, her life, her island do indeed belong to Ruth Moulden. She has earned every inch of what is hers.—PW

211. Abandoned lobster vessel on Swan's Island.

Levi Moulden

By Herbert Baum III and Dorothy O'Keefe

Levi Moulden, an islander for all of his eighty-five years once told an inquisitive visitor the difference between those that live on Swan's Island and those that don't: "There ain't no difference. But we're foolish and know it, and you're foolish and don't know it."

Mainlanders who ask foolish questions about the island figure heavily in Levi's stories, which are repeated and remembered well by all the island people. Levi seems to serve as the principal island spokesman to the outside world.

One of his stories about Swan's Island involves a nurse.

"She wanted to know how we got by on this island with so many storms washing up over the top of it. I told her, 'Oh, we had holes bored all around the island. Fast as the water came in, it went out and went overboard.' She came back that afternoon and said, 'You're a damn liar.'"

As quick as he is to defend his home from the "foolishness" of hundreds of visitors in the warmer summer months, Levi is often the first friendly islander people meet. Every morning he is at the ferry terminal awaiting the arrival of the first crowd.

"I enjoy it here. I started lobstering when I was nine years old at twenty-five cents a day. That was before they had a gasoline engine. We had a sloop, a Friendship Sloop. Same as they got today."

Like many of the other men on Swan's Island, Levi began to set his own lobster traps at an early age. He continued to catch lobsters every morning before heading out to the other jobs he worked at on the island as a young man.

Born in 1894, Levi recalled stories from his early childhood on Swan's Island. "I'll tell ya, this island was inhabited by Indians. I'm going by what somebody told me. Some white men came on here and drove them off. The Indians named this island Hockamock.

212. Levi Moulden of Swan's Island, Maine, with his cat, Mike.

"So this bunch of white men . . . one of them took his coat off and laid it on a stump. The Indians was watchin' 'em, and they went and burned it [the coat].

"The Indians commenced to dance and say, 'Burn coat! Burn coat!' The white men after that named this island Burn Coat. That went on 'til a man from Massachusetts named Swan come here and bought all these islands.

"He found out there was good wood lots on here and all that stuff. He bought it and they named the island Swan's Island. They built vessels to come here and lug the lumber off. They had a grist mill and all that business. That was before I was born.

"From there on a man named Crabtree came from Massachusetts.

He ran a quarry on here—a stone quarry. He built houses for his workers to live in and stores . . . everything.

"Those quarries, they only paid a dollar twenty-five a day. You got paid once a month, so the stores would write down what you got for groceries. Then you would pay them once a month.

"You had a dollar twenty-five for living! How would you like that? God, no, dear, we never had nothin'.

"I worked in the quarry for one dollar a day, ten hours. Then I worked a while for two dollars, eight hours. Then one year for four dollars and forty cents a day, eight hours.

"I weighed 'bout ninety pounds. You ought to been there and you'd see. We was draggin' them dogs to hold the stone on. See, a dog is a hook that you put into the stone. There would be four of us on there. The dogs weighed one hundred pounds a piece. It was hard work. Then I went into the salt-fish business.

"There was a man named Sylvester Moss from Long Island. That wasn't a good location for him. He put up a fish stand here. They kept building them on and on just like that. The salt-fish business was good.

"They used to ship them into foreign countries. That's where they shipped them salt fish. They used to salt them here and ship them away. Well, they started to get them Frigidaire trucks, and that spoiled the salt-fish business. That's how it happened."

While Levi was talking about the salt-fish business, his wife, Ruth, returned from doing her morning errands. "Here comes the old ground hog now!" Levi greeted her with a big smile on his face, the same smile that has greeted Ruth for the sixty years they have been married.

"I found her on the clam flats," he laughed. "No, she came here with her father, and she got snarled up with me somehow. I don't know how."

Levi and Ruth reminisced about their life together . . . the hard times they had lived through. "We had stewed peas, baked beans, and chowders," Ruth said, "but we never went hungry."

"We've seen some hard times," Levi added. "We've had some awful good times.

"I used to drink when I was a young fella. I used to drink when I was working, although I never lost no time with it. She wanted a car, that was in forty-eight. I said all right, but she wouldn't have one while I was drinkin'. So I went twenty-two years without one drop. She'd bake a cake with vanilla in it, I wouldn't eat it!"

"I never drank and I never smoked," Ruth added. "Half of the time, you don't know what you're doing, and what's the sense of being alive if you don't know what you're doing."

"I have this arthritis," Levi went on. "I went to the doctor and he took the pills away from me and told me to take four or five big spoon-

fuls of whiskey every morning and night. Well, I feel better and I don't take no pills no more. I got me a funnel now!" he laughed.

Levi was full of stories. Often he smiled, looked around the room at each one of us, and told a story about something that he had done or heard.

"This insurance agent went out to the country, and he run around all day and he got lost and run out of gas come dark. And he looked and he sees a little light and there was an old farmhouse. A young couple just got into it and they didn't have no telephone, no nothin', and they told him that he couldn't telephone and that they was five miles from town. So he said, 'Can I stay here all night?'

" 'Well, yes,' they replied, 'but we only got one bed and we ain't got nothing to eat hardly.' 'Well as long as I can stay, I don't care.' 'Well, you got to sleep with me and my wife.' 'Well that is all right.'

"So they had supper and all that they had was apple pie, and after they'd all had one piece, he wanted more and the farmer said, 'You can't have it. You can't have no more apple pie.' And he put it away, the apple pie.

"Well, they went to bed and along towards twelve o'clock, the old horse got kickin' out in the barn and the farmer had to get up and go out. So, the girl rolled down alongside the insurance agent and said, 'Now's your chance!' So the insurance agent got up and finished the rest of the apple pie!

"I got a lot of good stories. I can't say 'em. I got some good ones."

"I don't allow him to tell no dirty stories," Ruth countered.

214. The *Everett Libby* leaving Swan's Island.

Many changes have come to Swan's Island in Levi's lifetime. Electricity is fairly new. "That's the best thing that ever happened to us when we got electric power. I had a power plant of my own before we got that one [electricity]. A generator. Had awful good luck with it."

Television, however, is not highly thought of in Ruth and Levi's home. "It raised the devil with everything," Levi complained. "Couldn't speak to nobody and they wouldn't speak to you. People would watch television instead of going to dances and stuff. They'd turn the TV on and look at that thing."

Ruth came out of the kitchen with a fresh batch of cookies and added, "It spoiled the neighboring."

The ferry, too, has caused many changes on the island. "Oh yah, it raised hell with the summer people. They were driving us off the island, or trying to. There are some good people and there are some damn fools."

Even though the ferry has brought a lot of new people to the island, it has been a big help to almost everyone there. When someone is sick in the night, the ferry is right there to take him to the mainland. Levi had one experience with that and he was taken to the hospital in the middle of the night. But he had a good time teasing the nurses.

"I had a hemorrhage for a whole week. I had to take Milk of Magnesia and milk too. A whole week mind you. And one night, they always kept me awake, and so at 2:00 on Sunday morning they took it away from me and everything. They said I was to go into the X-ray room that day around six. I commenced to have awful pains through me. Well, milk caused a stoppage. So the doctors they was all downstairs, and they couldn't give me an enema.

"So when they come up, the nurse was ready to give me one. She gave me oil enemas and it didn't work. And she was all nerved up. I said, 'Look, dear, go get some Drāno.' I said, 'We use it to home all the time.' She was mad. She went out and she got me some stuff and it was all right. It worked. She said to me, 'What do you mean you use Drāno to home?' I said, 'Yeah, in the sink to clean it out everytime.' "

Levi knew so much about the island that it seemed his family must have lived there for many years. But this was not so. "All my people come from Bermuda. My father was born on Mt. Desert Island, but his father come from Bermuda. He [his father] was a mason and everything. She [his mother] stayed home and had the babies. There's nine. Five girls and four boys. They all lived here, but all moved away.

"I didn't want to chase them. I was a fisherman. I liked it here. I couldn't see any sense of going away.

"They are all friendly here."

Ruth Moulden

By Anne Pierter
Photography by Lynn Kippax, Jr.

Ruth Moulden is a strong-minded woman; she has clear-cut beliefs and values, and she lives by them. She also enjoys life. Her laughter brings warmth to the Moulden home on Swan's Island, blending continuously with her husband Levi's chortlings. Ruth married Levi when she was sixteen, and now, more than sixty years later, Ruth and Levi are still going strong.

Looking back through the years, Ruth began to recall some of the struggles and hardships of her life that began when she was twelve with the death of her mother. The only child of a traveling blacksmith and his wife, she grew close to her mother in her younger years and remembers those days as protective but carefree. After her mother died, she went to live with relatives before joining her father two years later on Swan's Island.

Ruth was thrown into the world of household chores and hard work that she had never known. She met that challenge the same way she has met all the challenges in her life—with courage and determination. Ruth's memories also reflect the good times her cheerful outlook has given her.

"I always had plenty of dresses to wear, and I had long hair then and plenty of hair ribbons when I lived off [off the island on the mainland]. When I was going to school, oh they had a lovely place to skate right across from the schoolhouse. And it was sort of a meadow, and they flooded it.

"Course, Mama was awful careful of me, with one child. Now I never went barefooted in my life. I could wear sandals, but I couldn't go barefooted. But she'd let me go on that ice because, if something happened, I'd only go till probably my ankles or something, see. But if it had been in a pond, she wouldn't have let me gone. But, oh I used to skate and skate and skate and have such a good time.

"But Mama never taught me anything. I couldn't wash dishes. She never taught me to do a thing, and that's an awful mistake. She did everything, see. I couldn't do anything when she died.

"And then when I went to live with my relatives, they wanted to get what work they could out of me, and I didn't know how to do it. The two years before I came down here [to Swan's Island] with Papa, was a miserable two years. Course, I had nice times in with it, I had friends and like that. But what I mean, where I lived, my aunt wasn't good to me, just disagreeable.

"I'd wash dishes and she'd go over them with her hand to see if she could feel anything, you know. And then she'd want me to dust with a dry mop. I didn't know anything about dry mopping, but I done the best I could. Then of course, after a while, I found out how to do it to suit her.

"I can't tell you a lot about the island because I didn't come here until I was fourteen. My father was a blacksmith when the quarries was running here. We rented a house over in Minturn [one of the three towns on Swan's Island]. Now my father was a good cook. When I came down here, Papa taught me biscuits and molasses cakes, and things like that, that he could make, see.

"I got married when I was sixteen, when Levi come home from the war." Levi recalled, "I went in the service, and after I came out we were married in Rockland. When we got married, when I got through, we went home, and we had three dollars to split between us. We've had some awful hard times, but we've never been hungry."

"When Levi asked me [to marry him], course we went and told Papa. And he didn't have any objections. Now that I think it over, I can see why. You see I was the only child, and my father couldn't take a little girl with him going around to different jobs. And he couldn't leave me around.

"He knew Levi's father and mother, and he just hoped that Levi would be good to me. He didn't know his daughter very well, you see, because he was away. Mama and I lived together most you see, so he didn't know that I would stick up for myself, regardless of what. Papa didn't know that because Papa never laid a hand on me in his life. And he didn't like to have Mama do it. So he didn't know me as well as my mother did.

"See, Mama would've known that I wouldn't have taken anything from anyone, but Papa didn't know it. Course, he knew me better after he lived with me." After Levi and Ruth married, her father came to live with them in their rented house.

"So that's how Levi got me, or that's how I got him, whichever way you want to put it. But Levi and I always got along all right.

"But when I got married, I was just as green as grass. You see, when I was little in my own home, there never was anything talked about. There was never any dirty talk or never a word ever said in my house, 'cause Mama and Papa never did it, see? And I don't allow it in my house.

"But I didn't know anything. And children now, why—oh the difference. I was too young, dear, to be afraid [when they were first married]. Well I thought it was fun. With Levi it *was* fun, you see. I never thought about the awful things that could happen.

"Oh yes, we had a good time. And of course Swan's Island is an awful place for dances. Always dances here. I've been to as many as five dances a week here. We had our own music, and oh, such a good orchestra, such good music. But you see we danced ballroom dancing, we didn't do the same as they do now, you see.

"And the stores, they used to have traveling men come, and then they'd order what they wanted. And they'd ship it on the steamboat— we had a steamboat then [before the ferry]. Well of course the traveling men always planned on being on Swan's Island dance night.

"Of course I never sat out a dance in the world. I always had partners. And I think I must've been a good dancer 'cause otherwise they wouldn't have bothered with me. But I think I was a good dancer. I know I was. Because I would have to say, 'I'm sorry, I've got this one,' and, 'I'm sorry, but you'll have to wait,' and you know, but that's the way it used to be.

"Levi was never jealous of me. I could dance with anybody in the hall, but I never left the hall. That's one thing I never did, when I went in the hall, I stayed there.

"And he never had any reason to be jealous 'cause I always laughed and talked with the whole of 'em, just the same as I do today. And I never had any chance of being jealous of Levi. So that way we got along all right. Lots of people are jealous-minded to start with, and I never was. And I know Levi wasn't.

"Oh, I think it must be awful to be envious. I never envied anyone. I was always so tickled when anyone would have a new car or something. Now we used to go up here to the dances and they all had long dresses. Course, I made all my dresses. Go down here to the store and buy some gingham and a little hamburg, and my land, I'd come out the nicest time of it. But when I saw someone wear a boughten dress we called them, I mean the ones they sent away to get, oh I thought, 'Isn't that pretty.' But I never felt jealous, 'cause I knew I couldn't afford it.

"I done the best I could. And we lived and we got along. We'd have loved to have had some children, but I couldn't have 'em. I got pregnant once [when Ruth was seventeen], and in six weeks I started in throwing up. And I throwed up and I was in the hospital thirteen weeks, then they took the baby. They wanted me to go seven months, but you see, I couldn't have lived, so they took the baby. He [the doctor] said, 'Don't try this again or you'll lose your wife.' So that's all there is to that.

"At that time, Levi's mother and father lived in Rockland. Then Grammy [Levi's mother] died, and Clara [Levi's sister] was having her house built, so Levi's father come and lived with us. So I had both the old men here with me. Course, Levi was working like a dog, and I always did. I cleaned house and I sewed and I took in washings, and I did everything there was to earn a penny. Because lobsters was twelve cents a pound—here they are three dollars now.

"I've had an awful good life. I've had a happy life. I've worked hard, but hard work will never hurt anybody. I used to do an awful lot of work for the summer people, and I had a lot of trouble with them. I know one man, he used to have a lot of shirts, white shirts, and they had to be folded just right. And if there was the littlest tiny bit of a wrinkle—it wasn't his wife, it was a woman he was living with—she would be awful nasty about the whole thing.

"And I did them three summers I think, and then I thought now, 'Next summer if she gives me any trouble, that's it.' The first time she said anything, I said, 'Look, I've done this for you three summers, and you've growled every summer, so just don't bring them anymore. I'm all through with you.' So.

"And another one, you know, they'd have eight and ten sheets. And I was doing it this ways [by hand]. I didn't have any washing machine. But the rest was all nice about it.

"We used Fels Naptha soap, you don't see it now. They come in bars about so long [six inches], just like a brick. You'd find the dirty spots and rub it on that. And then you'd scrub for dear life, and my hands, oh the skin would be all—oh, you don't know. I had a washing board, but then I had a boiler, and my white things, my sheets and things, I'd put in there and boil 'em. I used to cut up that soap and put it in, and boil 'em on the stove. And then after, rinse them by hand. My hands wasn't very big anyway, and you get that great big sheet in my little hands, oh.

"So one day at the Ladies' Aid—course, I've been going to the Ladies' Aid [the women's church group] since I was seventeen—one day
I said, 'Well I've got my cream-colored clothes on the line, but I'm
going to do my colored ones tomorrow. But I couldn't say white, I
couldn't say white clothes, 'cause they were far from being white clothes,
I'll tell you. But they didn't have bleaches, and they didn't have deter-
gents and things like they have now. You had your soap and you did
the best you could with it.

"Some people were stronger than I was, for gracious sakes, some
people could do an awful better job than I could. But I done as well as
I could and let it go. Of course Levi's clothes were awful hard, bait and
grease. Herring grease is the worst kind of stuff to get out. Course, I
was baitin' on trawls on the wharf." Ruth did this for Levi for twenty-
two years.

"I baited his trawls, but I never went out with him. Lord I wouldn't
think of it. I went in the boat when I had to. Before we got the ferry,
I'd have to go in his little boat. I have been so sick that I laid in the
bottom of the boat and vomited, till I vomited blood. He can tell you

the same thing. Oh, I've been so sick! You wanted to die, and hoped you would, you see. Oh, you're awful sick when you're seasick. Awful sick.

"And, oh one time we went over in his little boat, and coming back he landed me at Atlantic, 'cause he didn't dare to bring me around [to the Swan's Island Village wharf]. A man was with us, and he pulled up his boots and he took me in his arms and set me ashore, he came with me. And we came home and Levi went around. He said he didn't know if he was going to make it or not, that's how rough it was.

"Oh it's awful rough with the wind and the tide just such a way going around there—oh it's out of this world! And he knew I'd be so frightened, and I was sick, see, so he wouldn't bring me."

Ruth sat back in her favorite chair, gazed around the living room, and began to recall how she bought their home. "When I bought this house, I was renting that house down there [across the road from their present home]. I paid for that house down there in rent. And I said, 'Levi, I'm all through paying rent and then not having anything.'

"So this house was down to the shore, and Levi knew the man who owned it. His name was Stanley. I can't think of his first name, it don't make any difference, but his name was Stanley. And I said, 'Levi, I'm going over to Rockland [where he lived], and I am going to ask that man if he would sell me that house.' I think I had a little over three hundred dollars in the bank, but that was a lot of money then.

"We had the steamboat going, and I went over to see the man, and I said, 'I want to know if you'd sell me your cottage down to the shore.' And he said, 'We never use it, and we're getting older, we'll probably never be down there again.' He said, 'I don't see any reason why not.'

"And I told him why I wanted it. I said, 'I have paid Gus Oliver for his house, and I want a house of my own now.' He thought that all over, and he said, 'Yes, I'll sell you that house. How are you going to get it up [from the beach]?' I said, 'I don't know, that's up to Levi, how he gets it up.'

"He said, 'I'll sell you that house and the shed for two hundred fifty dollars. Course, there aren't any rooms or anything in it.' 'That's all right, I'll take it.' I went up to the bank, got the money and paid him.

"Then I bought this piece of land here for fifty dollars from Fred Morse, about an acre I'd say. And it wasn't two weeks before the Bank Holiday. Do you remember the Bank Holiday? Well, they closed the banks. And an awful lot of people lost an awful lot of money. And I guess I might have had seventy-five cents left. But the house was mine and paid for.

"And then Levi and the man that lived next door [Carlton Joyce] went into the woods, and cut trees down and blocked 'em out about

eight inches square. And then they fastened them together with big bolts. They got the house on there, and they had an engine that would pull the house up the length of one of them [bolted logs], and then they'd take 'em apart and put them on again, and pull 'em up so much.

"They was a month from the time they left the shore till the time they put it on this foundation. Levi already had the beach rocks down to the shore that he was going to have put under the house, you know. And I lugged all those rocks up from way down to the shore up for that foundation and that chimney.

"Yes, sir, 'cause Levi couldn't. He was out there every day working, and tired to death and worn out when he got in. We was burning wood, and I used to go out and cut his kindling wood on the chopping block right out there. I'd cut his kindling so he'd have it until the morning, he got up three o'clock, for gracious sakes.

"We lived in the shed [that was purchased along with the house]. They brought it up first. My father was with me, we lived in the shed for all that time, it must have been a year. And Levi would earn enough money, and I'd put it into the house. And then he'd earn some more money and I'd put it into the house. That's how we got our house.

"We came in the twenty-third day of December, in thirty-two. We had our Christmas dinner here. We had a round table then, and we had this little black kitty. We set him down in the chair and he had this little red bow around his neck. So there were four of us around the table for Christmas dinner.

"Levi's father had gone with his sister, she had her house built then, so he had gone to live with Clara, so I only had one of them. My father died with me.

"Levi was awful good to Papa, and that made things easier for me. Now if Levi had growled because my father was with us, that would have been awful hard for me.

"You know some people will growl if they have to have an old man around. But I had had his father around and I was good to his father, but Levi would have been good to Papa anyway, see. 'Cause Levi's good to everybody. And everybody likes Levi.

"And Levi's known by fishermen all over. He was in New York, just him and one of his sister's boys. 'Well, Levi, what you doin' up here?' And it was a man from Deer Isle. You think of it, in New York. He was up there fishing. Levi said, 'I couldn't get away with anything if I am to go away. I couldn't get away with anything if everybody knew me.' Oh, comical.

"And we stopped over here to the ferry dock the other morning. A man come up, shook hands with Levi, 'Levi, how are you, how you been?' Levi said, 'Dandy,' you know, talked, and he went off. Levi went and asked Louise [the ferry terminal ticket taker], 'Louise, who was that man?' Didn't even know him. Well, Louise says, 'That was Bradley Joyce's daughter's husband.'"

Even though Ruth and Levi owned their own home now, they were still faced with more lean years to come. "We had our bad times, and like everybody we went through the Depression, and I hope nobody ever has to go through another one. Now we didn't go hungry, but we didn't have what we wanted. Course, you don't go hungry here [on the island], 'cause you have plenty of fish and plenty of clams. You don't go hungry, but you don't have any luxuries.

"Oh, the cities were beastly [in the Depression]. They couldn't go out and catch a fish anytime they wanted it. They couldn't go down to the beach and get a mess of clams, have hot clam chowders and things like that. A lot were around the restaurants in the garbage pails in back.

"The Depression was an awful time. There wasn't any work. It

wasn't that the men wouldn't work, they couldn't find any work. There wasn't any work for them.

"Two weeks right in this house, I didn't have a shoe or a rubber to put on my foot. Levi had some rubber boots and they was all patched. He could get out and go fishing to go in his boat. But he had wet feet all the time.

"But I couldn't get outdoors, 'cause I didn't have any shoe or rubber. And I didn't have any money to buy one with. And I wouldn't get trusted. So I couldn't pay for anything without it. Well, I do that now. I do that today and I've done it all my married life. If I can pay for something, I have it. If I can't pay for it, I don't have it. Now I don't say that's the right way because people have everything they want.

"But I've felt lots of times, 'Do you suppose they'll ever pay for it?' I've thought like that. I mean I've seen people go over their heads. And Levi said, 'What do you let that bother you for? It's their business.' Course, I know that wouldn't be me, 'cause I wouldn't do it. I just couldn't do it. I can't imagine anyone going over their head.

"It's like I've had two of those credit cards come in the mail. And I was in the hospital one time, and there was one come in the mail, and the nurse come in and I said, 'Have you got some scissors?' And she said, 'Yes.' And I just cut it right up and put it in the basket. 'Cause someone else got my name, see? And that would never do, so I've never used one. I mean I wouldn't know how to use it. I wouldn't know what to do with it, if I had one.

"I was into Britts the other day, oh they had that sidewalk sale, and I bought me a winter sweater, they had them on sale. Oh it's a lovely thing and I'm so pleased with it, and I bought a blouse. I went up to pay for it and she [the salesclerk] said, 'Charge or cash?' I said, '*Cash.*' She said, 'Well we have to ask. That's the rules, I have to ask if you want to charge it.' Now I could've charged that if I wanted to, and they didn't know me from a hole in the ground. Now how would they know if they would ever get their money? I said, 'No, I'll never get attached to these things.'

"I've always paid for everything or went without. But I don't say that's the right way. It's right for me. Has been.

"Levi was talking to the man where we bought our car. Well, I went to the restroom and he saw Levi in the car so he came out. And Levi says, 'Pat, how are you doin'?' And he says, 'Levi, I never saw so much money going in my life since I've had this garage.'

"It's a big garage over there to Ellsworth, one of the biggest ones. We bought four cars from him. But we don't keep our cars very long. The longest we ever kept a car was three years. I tell you, you get a better trade-in, and it doesn't come to repairs, and I think it's better for you all around.

"Now you know, we had our first car in forty-eight, and you know how many flat tires we've had? One. On our way to Boston. Levi had never changed a tire in his life, and it was comical. I said, 'Levi, do you suppose you can do it?' He said, 'Well, I can try.' And he got it up on the jack and then he didn't know how to get it down. Well after a while we fumbled around and got the car down and got going. But that's the only flat tire we've ever had, since forty-eight.

"But he can't change a tire. Course, he goes to the garage and gets his changed, you know, the winter ones and the summer ones, and whatever you do. Course, he don't know anything about it. He's a lobster fisherman, that's all he knows. That's all he ever knew.

"He can't paint. When we come into this house, I did every bit, the painting. Ceilings, the walls, the whole shooting match. I did everything. This spring I did those windows out in the porch. I did them, two coats. Now that's no fooling job around all those windows. It's a

job to paint all those windows. But I'm a good painter, I've had enough experience."

Ruth also laid the bricks behind and the slate underneath her Franklin stove. "You see, I didn't know how to point up very good 'cause that's the first I ever did. Now if I did it again, I would know more about it. You see what I mean? And I would have better bricks. If my bricks had been better and I could have known how to cut them off shorter, then I could have made better joinings, you see.

"But I wanted it [a stove], and it was long before the oil business come. I wanted one of them and I kept saying, 'I'd like to have me a Franklin stove, Levi.' 'Well, we'll have you one, we'll have you one.' Well, after a while, one day we was up to Sears and Roebuck and there were three, four lookin' us right in the face.

"Well, Levi says, 'If you want your Franklin stove, now here's your chance.' So we brought it home. And then I got it home and I thought, 'Well I can't put it up against the wall like that,' and I didn't want it this way, so I thought, 'Well, I'll put it into the corner.' So we got that.

"And then I didn't like to burn my carpet so I went over to a place in Ellsworth and I said, 'What have you got that I can put in front of my Franklin stove?' They said, 'We got some brick.' And I said, 'Well with the brick, I'll be sleeping up in a dustpan [Ruth's bedroom is above the stove], walking on it all the time.' They said, 'I've got some slate.' And I said, 'All right, I'll take the slate.' So I got the slate, got it home and put it down. Well I got it done, and I didn't have to pay anybody for it, see. That's the best part of it, right there."

There are other ways that Ruth is frugal. "Oh I used to do an awful lot of canning and preserving. And I do an awful lot of pickling now, we like pickles awful well. And, oh that zucchini relish is out of this world. And that zucchini bread, oh I put some up with coconut and walnuts, and some of it I make just plain. It's so moist, and it stays so beautifully in the freezer. I've got two cakes and three loaves of rolled oat bread out in the freezer now, and I'll keep adding. And it's nice to have something a little different, if you think, 'Oh what am I going to have?' you know. You just run out and get it."

Before the days of the freezer and its convenience, there were some meals that were as much a part of the weekly work schedule as the washing, like the traditional Saturday night supper of beans. "People don't know how to bake beans now. The younger crowd never had to. You see, I've baked beans all my life. Saturday night you had baked beans and brown bread. That was your Saturday night supper.

"Put 'em in to soak Friday night, soak 'em overnight, and I make a good pot of beans, 'cause I've done it all my life. I don't put in my molasses till about two o'clock Saturday afternoon, 'cause it hardens your beans.

"And I always had my brown bread, four hours in a Crisco can. Have that brown bread and beans to go with it. That was the standard thing. As a rule, when it come Friday night, you put your beans on. Just the same as Monday, you'd start in washing. I mean it was just one of those things. As the years went on, you had your beans, and you wash Monday and you iron Tuesday, and that's the way you went, see. On Wednesday you'd recover mostly. I'd get through with my hands all bruised and bleeding."

Another common island meal is corned hake. Levi explained the cooking process. "It's hake, corned. Salted a little and cooked. You salt it, dear, it's just salted a little." Ruth added, "And you have sliced onions with it, and you fry up a little pork fat and put that over the top. You have turnip or squash to go with it. But you always have onions, slice them with vinegar in it. Now that's an island dinner, hake."

Cod is another fish frequently eaten on the island. "Salt cod," Levi says, "they call 'em Cape Cod turkey. Yup, ever hear tell of that?"

There are plenty of berries to be found on the island. According to

Ruth, "There are blueberries now, and there's quite a few raspberries. But I'm afraid of snakes, and I don't like to go after raspberries. Now blueberries, I don't mind. But the raspberries and blackberries, I don't get many of them unless I buy them. And they cost so much, I don't buy many.

"Yah, I'm sort of niggardly with my money. But it's something I don't have to have. If it was something I had to have, I'd buy it. But I mean, that is my way and I can't help it. When you start in, when you're sixteen, and if that's your nature and you had to go through the Depression, if you had to do it, you just do it.

"I've never made any piece of work—now I've never asked Levi to go off this island. I'll wait until he says, 'Ma, don't you want to go?' or 'Don't you think we ought to go?' or 'Don't you think it's about time . . . ?' But I've never yet asked him to go, to take me. Because there isn't anything that I have to have. I always have plenty of cloth in the house. I've got cloth upstairs, you'd be surprised at the cloth I've got upstairs. If something goes on and I think, 'I ought to have a new suit, I ought to have a new dress,' I just go and pick out what I want and make it.

"Well, I make all my own clothes and everything, you know. Yes, make these shirts and everything. And love to do it. Well, I'll tell you now, course I make suits mostly because I don't want anything very flossy, very fancy, or anything like that. And I wouldn't dare tell you how many suits I've made. They're all up there.

"Now I know I'm a good sewer 'cause I go into the stores and see about the styles. Now right now, everything is floppy and sloppy looking, yes, sack looking. Levi usually turns up my hem. He'll mark it off where it's about right. He'll put a pin in and I'll go from there."

Ruth also does a lot of sewing for the Ladies' Aid. She has helped to make many quilts to raise money for her church [the Methodist Church, one of the three on the island]. "I don't think our church could keep going without what the Ladies' Aid earns. We do everything, quilts and all kinds of fancy work, and we have our suppers, and we do everything we can to earn money.

"You see, I've been at it so long, and I sew. And there's so many of them that can't run a sewing machine. Now when they tack out quilts, then you have to go around them, you see, then you have to baste them. I bring them home on my sewing machine, and sew right near the edge, as near as I possibly can, you see. Levi says I'm too old to do that now. The young ones should be doing it. And of course they should.

"So many women say, 'Oh, I can't do this.' And I say, 'Why don't you start in sewing on that machine.' 'I can't.' That's something I've never said, 'I can't.' I'm gonna try. Now I can't paint a picture, but if worse come to worse, I would try. I don't know what in the world it would ever look like, but I mean I wouldn't set back and say, 'Oh no, I can't.' I'd be darned if I wouldn't try. I'd try it. So many of these people say, 'Oh, I can't do this, and I can't do that.' It's because they're too lazy to try.

" 'Cause you take a king-size quilt, and you've got a lot to handle. It's a lot of work. There's one now that they're making that I'm making with them. It's awful pretty. We sold it at this last fair for a hundred dollars. But it isn't finished.

"Now I can't lift my sewing machine, so I told them the other day, 'If you get a sewing machine up here, Lois will pin them together and I'll stitch 'em.' I said, 'I'll sew it together, but I can't take it home. I'll have to do it up here.' Because doing the work and him growling at me is too much for me.

"I was up there yesterday [at the Ladies' Aid], and I went in last and I said, 'Louella, aren't you freezing?' And she said, 'Yes, but I can't do anything about it. There's three of them sitting here roasting and puffing and blowing.' 'Well, I'm going to turn the heat up.' So I turned it up, 'cause I'm not going to sit there and sew and freeze. Then they puffed and blowed, so I turned it down a ways. But one thing I'm not going to do is sit around and work shivering and shaking."

The island churches also have contact with the Seacoast Missionary. "Well they helped us pay our minister. They used to come here a lot, but now they don't come here so much. But when we have our hymn sings, they bring the man who plays, and oh, can he ever play! Christmas they always send gifts to the older people. The minister brings them or you go over. They have a little party, and you go over and get your Christmas presents.

"So the last hymn sing he [the organ player] was here, and we had a supper, it just happened the Aid was having a supper. They came on and had the evening's service and the hymn sing, see. So I got talking to him. I said, 'Look, now next Christmas I don't want mittens, I don't want any little foolish things. I don't want any socks. I want me an afghan. Tan and brown.' 'All right, Ruth, we'll see.' I said, 'Remember, remember.' He wrote it right down, 'Ruth Moulden.' I think that was just to keep me quiet, you see. But no one knows what they'll send me next Christmas.

"The people connected with the mission make the gifts. Just the same as the Ladies' Aid would be doing. Now that man that lost his boat, we gave him a hundred dollars, the Ladies' Aid.

"Course, the Aid sends gifts to the hospital, and they give an awful lot. And I wish people would think more about religion. I wish people

would think more about what's coming. We don't thank Him. We're thoughtless.

"I think wherever I go, there'll be an awful lot of friends." Levi added, "I've got friends in both places."

"You can't make up your mind, Levi. No, that's one thing you can't make up your mind about. Unless you do it right here on earth before you start out."

Ruth had some private thoughts to share—thoughts about living on the island and about her life as a woman on the island—one afternoon as she sat alone in her living room, curled up in her favorite chair, her fingers busy knitting a wool cap.

Her thoughts, as they often are, were preluded by a funny story about Levi. "He tickles me," she concluded, "always has." Then she began another tale, this time about a trip Levi had made to Sears, Roebuck to pick up some things. A couple of clerks asked him, "What do you do, living on that island?" Ruth chortled, "Levi told 'em we had airlifts to the island that dropped frozen clam juice for the children.

"'What do you do living on that island,'" she repeated, laughing. "If you gonna chase me around for my seventy-six years, if you gonna chase me around, you wouldn't ask. The days aren't long enough to do what we have to do!"

Ruth began to talk about a friend who had traveled all over the world. This was fine for her friend, but nothing she wanted for herself. "I never had any desire to live anywhere else. I thought I'd like to go down one day to Florida. I told Levi. I said, 'I'd like to go down and stay with Betty about three or four days and see what it's like and come home.' I wouldn't like to go down there for a season, or go down there every winter, or go down.

"No. This is my home. This is what I'm used to. This is what I've made. I've made this, see, this is something I've made. My life here and my home that we've made together. And I'm happy here," she said.

Later Ruth's thoughts drifted to fear and courage—to plunging into life without being afraid. "I'm not afraid of anything but a snake. Man nor beast. And he said, 'I'm awful glad you don't live in the city.' 'Cause I wouldn't know what to be afraid of, you see. I wouldn't know what to be afraid of.

"Women, dear, women are tougher material. Take it by and large, women are tougher material than men. Look at it any way you want to.

"Now that's why I want Levi to die first. 'Cause I can stand Levi's death better than he can stand my death. Without me here in this house, I don't know what Levi would do. Now when I'm in the hospital, he won't even turn on the television, he won't eat. He just sets here and worries and mourns and frets until I get home. So you see, he can't take what I can, or what any woman—not me in particular—but any woman can take. Men can't take what women do. They can't stand the pain.

"Levi couldn't have gone through the operations. Course, I've had operations since I was seventeen, since I had the baby. You don't know, I'm all cut to pieces. I've even had cancer. I didn't have any pain, I was just feeling logey, just feeling out of sorts. Dr. Field was coming one Saturday morning, so I thought, 'I'm going over to Dr. Field's to see if he can give me perhaps a little tonic or something to spruce me up.' That's what went through my mind. So I went over and he said, 'How long since you had a physical?' 'Oh,' I said, 'gracious sakes, I can't remember. It's been years.' 'Well, what do you say?' So he gave me a physical. A thorough one and I come home.

"About two weeks later I had a letter come and he said, 'I'm coming on this island and I want you to be in my office.' So I went over, and I said, 'What do you want to see me for?' He said, 'I've got some bad news for you, Ruth. I sent your things away and they've come back. You've got cancer.'

"I thought, 'Well if I've got cancer, so I've got cancer.' And I was going to a jewelry party up to the captain's wife's [the captain of the ferry], so I went up to the jewelry party, and had the best kind of time. Laughed and talked, come home and didn't say anything.

"And the doctor said, 'As soon as I get a bed for you, I want you to come over.' So I didn't say anything, and I thought, 'I'm not going to say anything to Levi.' And then he said, 'You come on such and such a day.' I began to think, 'Now how am I going to get over there and not say anything to Levi?' So I told Harriet and Norman [Burns, close friends of the Mouldens] what he told me, but that's the only two that knew it.

"And then I said, 'Levi, Dr. Field has sent for me to come over, and they want to take some more iron and liver in me. And they'll probably do it oftener than once a week.' When I was younger, I always had to have liver and iron injected, you know. And my behind was sore most of the time 'cause they used to give me 2cc.'s instead of 1cc., because I was down. Course, I was working hard.

"Well, he said, 'All right,' and he took me over, kissed me good-bye, and went. I had the operation and I never made any piece of work at all. And I only cried once, and then I was all alone, nobody to see me. Of course I wondered how things was coming out, prayed a lot.

"Then there came a day that Norman and Harriet brought Levi over. And Levi didn't even know I had had an operation. They was setting around and I said, 'Norman, take Levi down to Dr. MacIntyre.' 'Well, what do I want to go down and see Dr. MacIntyre for?' I said, 'Just go down and see Dr. MacIntyre for me.' So he went down and Dr. MacIntyre told him what happened.

"And now when I go to the hospital, he thinks I'm keeping something from him. And he'll say, 'Norman, do you think it could be cancer?' And I think that's why he can't eat, that's the reason why, you see. He said, 'You lied to me, Ruth.' I said, 'I didn't lie to you. I just didn't tell you.'

"Well, don't you think that was the best way? Why, it kept him from worrying. And when he come over to see me, and sees me sitting up and laughing and having the best kind of time, it made him feel that much better, see?"

Levi, who had been down the road visiting, came into the house singing, "The rich get rich," with Ruth joining in, "And the poor get children." Then they began to laugh.

Walter Stinson

By Dorothy O'Keefe

He is not a large man. His face is deeply tanned, leathery in appearance. He looks much older than his sixty-five years. His hair is in the beginning stages of graying. Meeting this man, you are immediately drawn into his gaze. He possesses the most shocking blue eyes imaginable.

As he sits in his rocker, you have the impression that this man was robbed of his productive years much too early in life. You might want to tell him to get out of his rocker—he doesn't belong there yet. It isn't until much later, as he tells you about his life, that you realize why this is so.

Walter Stinson's house sits a short distance off the main road. It's rather small and painted yellow. The outside is weathered, with a sense of having been there for some time now, solid, as if to say, "I'll be here a while longer." Several old lobster traps are stacked on a side lawn. They've long since retired from their use at sea, but look as though they still have a few good years left.

"I was born up Deer Isle. I've been down here since I was four years old. I come down here with my mother. My mother married a fellow by the name of Fred Turner. I always called him 'Pa,' 'cause he brought me up. I been here ever since."

In Walter's house, feelings of warmth and satisfaction take over. The old treadle sewing machine, wringer washer, and oil lamps lend a sense of timelessness, as Walter remembers the days of growing up on Swan's Island.

While one talks to Walter, his wife sits in the other room knitting lobster heads. "She come from Vinalhaven. She knit heads for different other fishermen around here. She'll knit mine, too. I don't know how many she's knit. She's knit thousands! She keeps knitting."

It's been forty-two years now since Hilda Lawry married Walter Stinson. They have a daughter teaching school in New York. One of

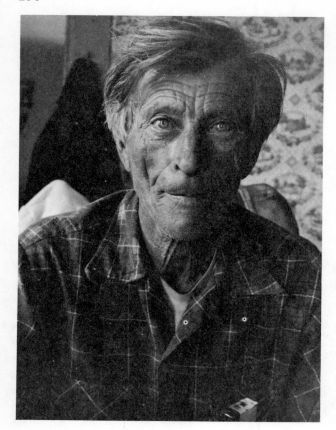

222. Walter
Stinson of Swan's
Island, Maine.
(*Photo by Mark
Emerson*)

their sons has taken over his trap-building business. "You can see him
up the side of the road here, building traps. He took over my business.
Course, anybody wants traps, I'll build 'em."

Walter has a photograph of John Kennedy on the wall. "I tell you, I
go on record as a Democrat. I always vote for who I think is best. I always vote to see who will make the best President or senator, but even
though I'm a Democrat, one woman I always voted for was Margaret
Chase Smith. I always thought she was all right."

It is surprising to discover that out of the four hundred people who
are year-round natives of Swan's Island, none are medical doctors.
"Doctors have lived on the Island, awful long ago, though. Now they
live off. Too bad we didn't have one here now. There's one that comes
once a month.

"My most trouble is with my lungs. Can't breathe. Cold weather lung
trouble. I can always hear my doctor saying, 'Don't be smoking no cig-

arettes.' Then he says, 'You still smokin' them cigarettes, I can smell it on ya. You're just killing yourself.' Well, I just tell him that if I don't have it, I was going to die anyway, so I still smoke 'em. Man killers, I call 'em."

His most vivid memories of his youth are the good times, the baseball games. "I was great in baseball, still am today, of course. We had two teams. Minturn's and Swan's Island's. We'd win one day, they'd win the next.

"I don't like this softball they play now. Call it a kid's game myself. I like the old baseball when I used to play. Stealing bases. I was quite a hand at stealing bases.

"Oh yeah, we'd have dances, picnics, and movie pictures sometimes. Still have dances once in a while. I ain't been for years."

Swan's Island is dry—the sale of beer and wine is prohibited. "It was called dry. Beer was home brew. I don't drink much. I figure that if there was beer on the Island I could go and buy a bottle or a case. Then the money would be right here on the Island. I never made any of it, no. Feller up there in the trailer used to make it. Now when they do it, they use dandelions or something. Tasted pretty good."

He attended school here on the Island. When asked about the subjects taught and what he learned, he sits back and thinks a minute. "Well, can't exactly remember, now. Well, about the same's they do today, except some new stuff come in, you know, and we didn't get 'em." Walter left school at the age of fifteen to work at the fish plant in Minturn.

"I guess you could say I was one of the youngest. I still had a good time, though. Francis Johnson started same time as me. Another one of the old ball players."

Many of the men Walter started out working with remained there until the plant closed down. One of these men was his older brother, Cecil. "Yeah, he was three years older than me. He looked after me. Course, one brother knows more than another's bound to start something. Never come to blows, though!"

Other men that Walter came to know at the fish plant were the owners of the boats that brought the fish in. "Different men owned different boats. They're all gone but one. Everyone's dead but Edwin Gott. He's still living, but he's in his eighties.

"It used to be Edwin Gott, Charles Loy, and Ab Schlagler. Between them all, they had eleven or twelve boats. It used to be quite a place, quite a place."

Inside the factory, Walter worked with a dozen or so men. Together they made up a fast, hard-working team in the salt-fish business.

"We had sixty thousand fish laying one day, and started at seven

o'clock and about eleven o'clock they was all taken care of. We used to
have to take care of sixty thousand fish a day, and a lot of people don't
believe that. Well, we started at seven o'clock and were most generally
done at five or six. It's quite long hours standing on your feet." He explains the process used at the fish plant including his responsibilities
there.

"Well, you probably don't know about it. You take the bone out of
the fish. We call it splitting. Splitting fish. That was my main job at the
plant. The motion was out and back. When you come down, go back
and take the bone out.

"Ever see one of them knives? The knife you use for cutting heads
off is different. Called it a heading knife. You use a special knife for
the bigger cod fish. That knife had lead on it. Made it heavier.

"But this one here's used for hake. The curve is for the backbone.
We called it a splitting knife. You had to use separate knives. Each
man had his own knife. You wouldn't use my knife. If you've got my
knife, look out!

"We used to make our own knives. Took the lead and melted it
down ourselves. Hardly any handle was alike. Some had the handles
long. Course, they had big hands. Mine was small. I didn't like a long
knife. If I had a knife like that, I'd cut the fish in two. I liked a small
knife."

For many years Walter worked in that plant. He developed a system,
a knack for doing his job as quickly as it could be done. His eyes shine
as he relives the days when he and five other men were able to split
one thousand pounds of fish in ten minutes. "Yep, I was fast. Fastest
probably than any of them. Except my brother. He was faster than I
was.

"We had different men to do different things to the fish. The thousand pounds in ten minutes we had six men splitting the fish. Six men
taking the heads off. Twelve men all together.

"We'd take care of a box. A box weighed a thousand pounds. We'd
be waiting before they hoist another box up. We was fast. Got them
taken care of real fast."

The fish were not dried at this plant. "No, we didn't dry 'em. We
salted them in a big box and then we used to pick 'em out. We used
salt every morning, a big box full. A big vessel used to come after 'em.
All salted. In the butt. Tall barrels, I guess they call them tall barrels,
now. We'd put them in the vessel that took them to Gloucester, I think.
But we didn't dry no fish."

Walter's secret is a simple one. "Mine was, always keep your knife
sharp. See, a dull knife will slow you up. We was fast. We used to be
out waiting for the boat to come in. We used to be out playing horse-
shoes. I enjoyed myself."

223. Walter's heading knife.

Walter worked at the plant in Minturn. There was another fish plant located on the other side of the island. At times it was necessary that Walter work at the other plant. "Well, they're both plants about the same size. I never worked over there much. They didn't have anything to work with.

"Everything there was done with pitchforks. I mean instead of hoisting the fish to you, they used to pitch the fish. Down at Harry Johnson's [in Minturn], he had a rig that the box went upside down and the fish went right to you. I think you didn't have to handle them more than three times and they was all taken care of.

"There [Swan's Island] somebody had to pitch them on a table. Then you split them. Then somebody pitch them in the water. Then we had to pitch them again to get salted and to be taken away. It was harder.

"That's why with this rig we was able to take care of sixty thousand pounds a day. That's what made it easier. He had a good rig.

"Well, at them times, you'll laugh at this, we call eight hours a day. We—at least I—got twelve dollars a week. Monday through Saturday. And that was straight pay. Twelve dollars a week. That don't seem like much now, but then it was big money.

"I know one time we was working on the fish, did about forty thousand that day. Anyway, we thought we wasn't getting enough money. And we all talked it over and said, 'Let's go on a strike! If he's got all those fish he can't get taken care of, he won't let them spoil.' We went out on the walk and stood there.

"The boss come out and saw us and said, 'By God, boys, ain't you workin'?' And we said, 'No, and we ain't working till we get fifty cents per hour.'

"He had to pay it. Couldn't let all them fish spoil. Then we went on pay per hour. We'd slow up. Then we'd get more hours, more pay. They kept paying by the hour. We'd usually get two more hours. We'd slow down, not go so fast."

Around the time of the second World War, the fish plant closed down for good. Most of the men who worked there, Walter included, began fishing for lobsters to earn their keep. "We all knocked off at the plant and went to catching lobsters. Of course I was lobstering while I was working at the plant, mind you. I started at the same age, fifteen, and I used to set them out by the harbor then.

"That was before I went to work. I didn't go lobstering all winter, though. All's I had was a little skiff and an outboard motor.

224. "It was a nice living just the same." (*Photo by Julien LeSieur*)

"I like lobstering. Long day, though. Five in the morning 'til five at night. I would haul one hundred traps one day and then let them set. Then I haul one hundred the next day. I stop when I get tired. I had two hundred traps in all.

"The last day I was out it was good fishing. I was haulin' this trap and I felt something was caught around it. I tugged and tugged 'cause I didn't want to lose that trap. Well, come to find out, my trap had hooked onto a big old anchor of a boat. I 'bout ruined it.

"Come to haulin' the second trap, nothing happened. I pulled again, and blood started coming from my nose and all over the skiff. I grabbed a buoy and it started again, so I said, 'It's about time you was getting home.'

"I got down to the wharf, down to the end. I don't think I tied my skiff, I don't remember. I made my way up to the house and fell on the grass. I hollered to my girl that I thought I was bleeding to death. She took me up to the nurse and she told me to go to the hospital. They told me to watch my stomach, I had ulcers or something. Told me not to haul any more traps. That ruined that. It was a nice living just the same. I miss it now."

225. The old stone quarry on Swan's Island in Maine.

Edwin Gott

By Deborah Garvin

Sitting in an old lawn chair under a small tree in uncut grass is a tall slender man with graying hair that is almost white. Edwin Gott, who lives in the village of Minturn on Swan's Island, is at eighty-three one of the three oldest men on the island.

On this particular afternoon, as the sun's rays dart through the leaves to dance on his shoulders, Edwin reflects back through his life. His vision is turned inward toward memories of the past more often than outward toward the small cluster of people gathered around him.

Like many men on the island, Edwin began working at an early age. He had his first job when he was eleven years old. "I used to work as a delivery boy for the local store near my home. I got twenty-five cents a day. That was big money back then. A whole lot of difference now than when I was a kid, I can tell ya that."

He pauses and his thoughts seem to burrow inward. "Oh, I used to love to go to school," he smiles, after a few moments. "But when I was fourteen, my mother got sick and I had to start working at the quarry. But I loved to go to school. Only went to the first two years of high school. My favorite subject was arithmetic. That's one thing I got goin' for me, I can figure in my head. We used to have contests in school. I was always up front. I never lost."

Edwin grins as he thinks about the time he helped his cousin with her homework. "My cousin had a problem that she couldn't do, so I told her to get me a piece of paper and a pencil and I'd have it for her. She said, 'No, Edwin, you can't do it. You didn't finish school.'

"In a few minutes I had the answer for her. She never said no more 'bout me not finishing high school." Although he left school after the tenth grade, Edwin doesn't feel he missed anything. "Oh the first two years are like the last two. It [school] never changed.

"Started when I was fourteen working in the quarry. I was tool boy.

A dollar a day, six dollars a week. That was in 1911. I would take those tools to the shop to be sharpened, and bring them back again. I'll tell ya this. I can still feel to this day lugging those drills. I can remember that."

After working in the quarry, Edwin went on to work at the Bath Iron Works for two and a half years. Then he went to Rockland, Maine, where he was the mate of a dragger [fishing boat].

"I lived in Rockland for seventeen years. I'd go fishin' in and out of Rockland."

Edwin wrinkles his face in distaste. "I worked in a fish plant, but not for very long."

After working in Rockland, Edwin returned to fish from his birthplace, Swan's Island. "This is my home and this is where I'm gonna stay," he reflects. "It really hasn't changed that much on the island, but there are more things to do now than there was when I was a youngster.

"Now everyone has a speed boat, a car. It's a lot easier to get back and forth from the island 'cause of the ferry.

"I guess I must have been fifteen before I saw a car. It was a Metz, nice car, the doctor owned it. Oh, and there was baseball. Had a good team when I was sixteen. We used to play all over the area. Never lost a game.

"We still have baseball. That's the big thing on the island." Edwin pauses for a few minutes, thinking about how it was then and how it is now. His eyes brighten as he remembers something special that he liked.

"Oh, I love dry fish, could eat them all the time. You don't see them anymore. I sure would like to have one now.

"I used to dry fish in the fall when the flies weren't so bad. Just keep them out overnight, then hang them up. They'd dry nice, just a little salt so you don't get them too salty, then you can eat 'em. You can do anything you want to them, cook 'em. Love dry fish, could eat one right now."

Once again Edwin stops talking, and for the longest time he has a look on his face as if he is searching for something else to say.

"I've had some narrow escapes, I'll tell ya that. One day I was out [in his boat] and there was a big storm. It was the gale winds. Took me four hours to get home. Big storm, big storm."

Edwin is quiet for a minute as he nods his head back and forth, remembering that day.

"I started out with nothing and I think I'm gonna end up with nothing," he finally says. "I oughten say that. I'm living all right."

"I'm eighty-three years old, going on eighty-four." He sits up in his chair, folds his arms across his chest and his eyes seem to glow.

In a soft voice, he continues, "I come out here on nice days and just sit. When you sum it all up, it's just a dream.

"You look back, it seems like you just dreamt it. Eighty-three years. Sometimes I wonder."

226. Basil Joyce and his home on Swan's Island, built by his father in 1891.

Basil Joyce

By Janice Coyne
Photography by Lynn Kippax, Jr.

Basil Joyce is a tall angular man whose startling blue eyes dart shyly into the safe corners of his well-kept white clapboard home as he greets a visitor. He moves with such rapid strides that his seventy-seven years suggest youth rather than age.

Basil was born on Swan's Island. The Joyces came to the island in 1806 and have been there ever since.

Basil still lives in the same house he was born in, which was built by his father in 1891. It is a large white Victorian house in Atlantic, a small village on Swan's Island. The house is the same as it was when it was built, with only a few minor changes. There is a sense of preservation about it. Basil never put in any running water or plumbing. "I couldn't really bear taking something apart to do it. That's my problem, I don't want to change anything. Course, I had to take the wood-stove out, which nearly killed me. I couldn't get the wood in anymore [as he got older]."

The kitchen has a warm dignity of its own. It has floor-to-ceiling cabinets made out of whitewood. "Mother said the woodwork was beautiful when it was new, don't ya know, because I mean it was whitewood, they called it. But they didn't have nice varnish like they have now. It was dark and sort of homely. And that molding around the top of the cupboards is hand ploughed. They had all different kinds of planes with different knives, and made the molding by hand. That was quite a performance."

The yard, like the house, is in very good order. "Well I always kept it up, my father always kept it up." It is a large area, with a few neatly spaced tall trees.

In his younger days, Basil used to wallpaper and paint houses on the island. Some people might call it "jobbing." "I waited on them. I did

anything I could do that they wanted done. Didn't pay too well, and there wasn't much in the wintertime, you see, so you didn't make any money.

"You used up all you made in the summer, eating in the winter. But I did have mostly summer people in the summer, I had three different ones that I worked for, and one charming person, Frances Wilson, but she's long gone. She was very nice, had a great sense of humor, which was wonderful."

There weren't too many people who made a living the way he did on Swan's Island. "We didn't have that kind of work, we didn't have that kind of summer people. I mean we never had very much with money, don't ya know, like they have in North Haven or anything like that. If they did, they were afraid to spend it.

"This Miss Wilson that I tell you about, if she had any, she'd have had more fun than a barrel of monkeys, 'cause she spent every nickel she had when she was here, that she could scrape together. And she loved it here, she just loved it here.

"I gave that up [being a handyman], most of it when I was about forty-five. Once in a while it kinda got to me, the last of it. I couldn't take it any longer." He says some of the people he worked for were hard to get along with "but mostly pretty good. They're all gone now and I don't know the new ones much. I don't care if I do or not, because they're all younger and they wouldn't be interested in me. I'm not working anyway."

The island has changed since Basil was a kid. "Because the three sections of the island didn't get together, don't ya know, like they do. Everybody was on foot then, they didn't get very far. Each village was sort of sufficient unto itself."

But today Swan's Island is more like one united town than three separate little villages. Basil says the reason for this is "because the schools consolidated, you see, and the children all grow up knowing each other. In my day, I mean, it was a strange place to go to the harbor. I think I was thirteen years old before I even went to the harbor [three miles away]. I wouldn't have gone then if I hadn't gone with my mother, I guess.

"We played amongst ourselves and, uh . . . we had bicycles and we rode up and down the gravel road. And then as we got a little older, well we gathered at the post office. So we all grew up going to the mail every night. There were about twenty-five of us then. A lot of young people. That was sort of a meeting place for everyone to get the mail, about seven-thirty in the evening. Then we'd pair off and the boys would walk home with the girls.

"But the fourth of July was a big time. All excitements on the other side of the island, and they had big doings at both Odd Fellows and Redmans. We'd walk over. We'd get all rigged up and walk over in the dust and by the time we got there, we'd have dust up to our knees. There'd be dances at night and all kinds of interesting things for the children and grown-ups.

"We used to have old silent movies, they had an old gasoline-driven motor that ran a generator for that. Sometimes it stopped in the middle of it, and the lights went out and everything was lovely. It was in the Redman's hall which is no longer there. They thought it was a fire hazard so they took it down."

Basil says that was quite a meeting place back then. "They showed movies once, sometimes twice a week, but not at all in the winter. But of course everyone had to walk up there, 'cause you couldn't get up in the car."

The halls aren't kept up now. He explains why. "Well probably the

older ones who started the lodges have lost interest or died, and the younger people didn't take hold. But they're trying to revive the Odd Fellows, The Rebeccas are trying to keep up the Odd Fellows. They've done the best they could. It's too big a thing anyway. I mean if they get one story off, they might be able to keep it up. [It is a three-story structure.]

"The town meetings," he says, "were different from what they are now. They seem different now anyway, but carry on somehow I guess. The older generation, my father's generation, would no more think of missing a town meeting than slitting their own throat. I don't think anyone takes it that seriously now. They used to have some heated arguments. Raising money for this, raising money for that, or not raising money, as the case may be. Somebody wanted to build a road, somebody else didn't want it . . . oh they'd have a great time. Now it's more or less they have a town meeting before the meeting."

People also used to go "neighboring" as they called it in those days. "I mean you didn't always have to call somebody up every time you wanted to see them. I mean, you wanted to see somebody, you went to see them. You didn't call them up to see if it was convenient for them or not. But . . . as a matter of fact, I don't know, I think I was nine years old before we had a telephone.

"They hadn't had it on the island too long. They had telephones, a few people, but my father didn't put one in until I was nine years old, I guess." Basil says that really didn't change the lives of the people on the island much, "other than the fact that you could speak to someone without going to see them, if you were lucky enough to get on the line.

"Well the last of most of the big changes have been made in the last twenty to twenty-five years, really. Course, everywhere you go, something's different. I mean, oh, I don't know how old I was . . . I was grown up before the radio came and then that was quite a long time before television.

"I was eleven years old I think before the first automobile came on, the first one I'd ever seen. It was an unusual thing. We had a few resident doctors here and they had the first cars, I think. Then people kept getting them, the old Model T first. But it wasn't any fun then, because it was all dirt roads then and nobody used their cars, only in the summertime a little while, because you were stuck in the snow or mud, one or the other. My brother and I had the first second-hand Model T Ford in 1942, I think."

The ferry brought changes to the island. It raised the price of land, it brought tourists in the summer, and it brought a source of communication with the mainland to the people on the island. Before the ferry, Swan's Island people went to the mainland on a steamship to Rockland. "That's a long jaunt, 'specially if you get seasick." The trip to Rockland took five hours, leaving the island at 5:30 A.M. "From this side we had to get up at three.

"Anyway, I had to walk up to the corner here, to get on what they call the mail team, horse and wagon, in the spring and ride to the other side of the island. The wagon was going this way in the mud, down to the wharf. [Basil demonstrates how the wagon tilted by tilting his hands.]

"You couldn't tell, I mean the weather may be calm at three o'clock, but by five-thirty it might be blowing us out to west, which it usually was.

"They took it off in, I don't know, forty-two I guess. The government decided they needed it worse than we did. They left us without anything. We had something because the mail had to be delivered, of course. It came for a while to Stonington. Then Fred Thomas had a little bigger boat that he took to Bass Harbor, around the island to what they call the quarry water. That kept going until the ferry came."

Basil feels that the same changes that are taking place on the mainland are also taking place on the island. "Although not as much probably, 'cause we've got fewer people."

Even if Swan's Island is changing with the times, Basil Joyce has chosen to stick with the old ways. He has chosen to keep his house as it was before the birth of the twentieth century, not wanting to take anything out to put something else in. He represents what the island was in the past. "I'm funny I guess, that way."

229. Boom of pulpwood waiting to be sluiced down Roach River. (*Photo by Steve Burbank, courtesy of Kennebec Log Driving Company*)

River Driving

Each spring for almost three hundred years as the deep snows of Maine, Vermont, and New Hampshire melted into tumultuous stream beds and the ice-locked rivers began to flow, the river drives of northern New England started.

Thousands of cords of wood were pushed from the northeast jungles southward over the waterways to the pulp mills and lumber mills of New England. Mountain men used the south-flowing currents, horses, pickpoles, peaveys, boats, chains, winches, and their own strength to bring to market the wood they had been cutting all winter.

Since the seventeenth century, river driving has been practiced in New England, and generations of men have called themselves river drivers. Rivers were used for transport instead of wagons or trains or trucks because, to quote Ted Quigley, an experienced driver and logger, "Why that's the cheapest transportation in the world!"

River drivers were the cowboys of northeastern America. They rode long logs instead of horses, hurled peaveys instead of lassoes, and ranged the mountain waterways instead of the Western plains. Still, they were the same breed of men as the cowboys, drawn to their work for the same reasons.

It was the romance of the trail that brought them together each year. The tough joy of the outdoors, the camaraderie on the drive, and the sense of being independent—"my own boss"—even while they worked together. No master driver could hold his men for very long until he understood that it was the drive itself which united, compelled, and disciplined these men—the drive to push the wood south. A good boss, like Ted Quigley or Bert Morris, had to be every inch the driver his men were, able to walk the logs with the best of them and worthy of respect.

In Maine the last river drive was held in 1976. After that the drives were outlawed by the Maine state legislature. Those who voted to outlaw river driving came to the conclusion that the logs were polluting the rivers. River drivers and their bosses don't agree (see chapter in this section on pollution).

Whether or not this is true, the drive was a dramatic example of man's ingenuity, guts, and daring. As Austin Kennedy of Jackman, Maine, pointed out to us in 1975, it is a story worth telling. "If somebody don't get after things like that [river driving], it's an art that will be lost forever. There will be no remaking of it."

With this warning in mind, we began to "get after things like that" in 1975. During 1975, 1976, and 1977 we interviewed twenty-two people from the northern portions of Maine whose lives revolved around the river drive. It was the biggest team effort we have ever made, with twenty-five students conducting interviews, transcribing, and writing. The large tasks of piecing the material together, story writing, and editing were assumed by Kelly Emery, Bill O'Donnell, Beth Mann, and Abby Dubay.

The goal of the group of writers was simple but demanding: "Through writing this story, we have tried to recapture the real adventure of river driving in a way that we can all visualize the unique experience these people had"—an experience no one in Maine will ever have again.—PW

230. River driver
Harley Fletcher.
(*Photo by
Whitney Draper*)

These are the people in northern Maine we interviewed about river driving in 1975, 1976, and 1977.

Bob Viles — North Anson
Gerald Bigelow — Bingham
Bill McLaughlin — Bingham
Wilfred Sanipas — Moscow
Austin Kennedy — Jackman
Yvonne Kennedy — Jackman
Russell Kennedy — West Forks
Stella Kennedy — West Forks
Carroll York — West Forks
Percy Burgess — Dayton
Martha York — West Forks
Barbara McLaughlin — Bingham

Ted Quigley — Bingham
Bert Morris — West Forks
Grover Morrison — Lincoln
 Center
Ida Allen — Moxie Falls
Ralph DeMusis — Caratunk
Walter York — Caratunk
Jed Calder — Bingham
Nellie Burgess — Dayton
Annie Farley — Jackman
Ted Quigley's granddaughter —
 Bingham

The following students have contributed to this section:

Kelly Emery
Bill O'Donnell
Beth Mann
Abby Dubay
Terry Merrill
Anne Gorham
Margaret Welch
Lorrie Kingsbury
Joe Iriana

Suellen Simpson
Robin Thurston
Caroline Ricketts
Sabrina Coyne
Meg Dempsey
John Wood
Fran Ober
Herbert Baum III

Sandy Frederick
Andy Dimock
David Bragdon
Libby Caldwell
Thom Truman
Mark Emerson
Anne Pierter
Dale Berube

231. Sluicing wood through the dam at the foot of Spencer Lake. (*Photo courtesy of Kennebec Log Driving Company*)

232. Raft of logs on Moosehead Lake. (*Photo by Steve Burbank, courtesy of Kennebec Log Driving Company*)

Herding Logs

River driving was somewhat like herding cattle. The drivers had to guide the lumber through streams, rivers, and lakes to the mills where the lumber was processed.

"That drive started way up by the Canadian border. They drive all spring and they drive all summer right on through the fall. They had sections, ya know. Every so many miles, the crewmen there to tend that section." That was the way Austin Kennedy explained the overall structure of the river drive.

After the wood had been cut, the drivers had to slide, or sluice, the wood into the streams. Austin said, "The brooks are high in the spring. There is the snow runoff. You have to take that wood out. Once that snow is gone, the water goes out. You see, they built a sluice. Built an A-frame and planted it up on the sides and the bottom, and they sluiced them logs down through there."

Deciding at the start of a drive up north if a small stream was high enough to float logs was a tough decision, but as Ted Quigley told us, "We'd take a chance." When the logs were on their way down the streams, the drive had started in full force.

"It's like walking on a bowlful of jelly!" is what Bill McLaughlin thought of balancing himself on the logs, breaking up log jams that popped up all along the drive. "Sometimes, you know, they'll spin quick, though most usually they been there so long they're slippery and slimy. And when you step in there, boy, away you go!"

There was very little special equipment that the drivers used to work with the logs. In the days of the long logs, the men wore caulk boots (caulks, or nails, on the soles) which helped them to keep their footing. The standard tools used to control the logs as they were floating down the river were cant dogs or peaveys (six-foot poles with a hook on the end) and spiked poles, which were even longer and were called pickpoles. The other major tool was the pickaroon, or "idiot stick" as

233. Sluicing at Spencer Lake Dam in 1955. (*Photo courtesy of Kennebec Log Driving Company*)

234. Sluice at Chase Stream. (*Photo courtesy of Kennebec Log Driving Company*)

235. Spencer Lake sluice in operation. (*Photo courtesy of Kennebec Log Driving Company*)

236. Workmen using pickpoles at sluice gate to keep the wood from jamming. (*Photo courtesy of Kennebec Log Driving Company*)

the drivers called it, used in cleaning away stray wood left in the river after the drive had passed through.

The job of cleaning up the wood washed ashore during the drive was called "picking rear." If the wood washed some distance from shore, that was called "high rear," as Gerry Bigelow explained.

"Well, in the spring of the year, the water and ice will force wood sometimes two or three hundred yards back into the woods from the water. And you go along the woods and drag it to the water. Either throw it in or leave it for the final rear to come through." The final rear was done after the last river drive of that particular year.

A log jam was a common nuisance on the drive, and the men had four ways of breaking it. First, they tried to break the jam by hand, and if that didn't work then they tried to chop up the key logs forming the jam. If chopping the key logs failed, the next step was to try to dynamite the jam. The last resort in breaking up a jam was to raise the water level, or heist. In heisting, the dam was opened and a new head of water was released. (Grover Morrison says a good head of water is about seven feet.)

Ted Quigley told us about some of his experiences with log jams. "We carried dynamite in our pocket and caps in shirt pockets. Lot of times if we had a log jam and some of the key logs were underwater, of course we couldn't cut 'em out with an ax so we just have to get the dynamite and tie it to a string and put it under and set it off, and of course it blew the whole thing up.

"Well, we'd work on it [the log jam] until it got pretty dangerous, and then, of course, the foreman was supposed to stay until the last thing. I remember one time we stayed and I stayed, of course, because I wasn't afraid to work and I could use a cant dog and they could tell I was one [river driver] before I raised my hand.

"But anyway, at this damn brook I started to choke her and the crew got ahead of me. There was a log come and hit the one I was running on and knocked me right off. I went under and when I came back up, I had my cant dog and glasses in one hand and my hat in the other. One guy said, 'You should know better than try and keep up with us.'"

Moving the lumber across lakes and ponds was a different process than floating wood down the fast-flowing streams and rivers. A giant lasso of big chained logs (boom logs) was used to surround the wood and pull it across still water.

Ted Quigley explained what was done. "They would have at the mouth of the river a lot of boom logs and make a big circle, fill them up and tie it together and then hook 'em onto a motor boat and start."

Bill McLaughlin described the boom logs. "They're about thirty feet long. And they're all bolted together and chained together to hold the

237. "Picking rear." Crews use "idiot sticks" to throw wood washed ashore back into the water. (*Photo by Whitney Draper*)

238. Jam of logs May 19, 1916, in Hollingsworth and Whitney Company's boom at Winslow, Maine. (*Photo courtesy of Kennebec Log Driving Company*)

logs back." There were about 120 of the logs on each side, and when both sides were joined, there were approximately 240 boom logs forming an enclosure, or "raft," that towed the wood across the lakes.

The use of the boom logs was not restricted to the lakes, however. Sometimes they had to be used on the river, as Bill McLaughlin pointed out.

"Like down on the river, you know, you come to a place that is just silent water, just barely moving. Or sometimes the wind will blow it back, so you take a boom, a single boom, you go around it, and you just kinda keep herding it right out till it gets into the quick water again, and then away she'll go."

240. "Rough, solid individuals." (*Photo by Joe Myerson*)

The Men

"The best logman is the man who wants to work on the river." So says Bob Viles, master driver for fourteen years with the Kennebec Log Driving Company (KLD).

"A man needs to be familiar with what he is doing. That's the first quality. That's what I look for. A man who wants to work and shows he wants to work. Those are the best qualities in a man, the man who wants the job.

"You know, as we've grown over the years we've employed many people. If it fits into their schedule, most of them want to work as much as they can. I think you gotta take a likin' to it. If you don't like what you're doin', you won't stay with it."

Ted Quigley, river driver and logger, says that men "came from everywhere" to work on the drive. "Oh my goodness; foreigners, Polacks, Swedes, Canadians, all nationalities. One time I could almost talk Swedish, there were so many of them."

Bob Viles agrees, "We've had quite an assortment of people: doctors, lawyers, ministers. You name it and we've probably had it. Eighty to ninety per cent of these people are all from here. They were rough, solid individuals. They were real tough as far as weather conditions. When they played, they played hard. They'd quit for a couple of weeks and then when their money ran out, they'd come back."

Wilfred Sanipas came to northern Maine from New Brunswick, Canada, when he was fifteen. He joined his brother, Leo, who worked as a river driver on the Dead River. Their family did a lot of boating in Canada, so when Wilfred came to Maine and began working on the river drive, he had had some experience with boats and he was already at home around the water. "I done a little bit of everything, I guess. From pullin' it to luggin' it, draggin' it . . ."

Austin Kennedy, of Jackman, Maine, recalls his first step toward becoming a logger and river driver. "Well, the first time I went into the woods I was eight years old. My brother was ten and we just went in to visit my father. He was a foreman in there, and we liked it so well that we stayed."

At the age of seventeen, Ted Quigley came to Maine from Quebec to "make my fortune," Ted told us jokingly.

Just as Wilfred Sanipas had had experience with boating before he joined the drive, Ted came to Maine with some knowledge of logging. "I knew it because I grew up on a farm, and in the wintertime, my father would log a little and I would help him.

"In 1912 I came over, but I only stayed two months. I was taken sick. The next year I came, I made it." Ted came here with family and friends and found it "a little tough getting started but not too bad." He adds, "I made it. Here I am."

241. River drivers form arch of pickeroons for the wedding of Donald Hovey and Karen George in Skowhegan. At head of line on each side are Wilfred Sanipas (*right*) and Bill McLaughlin (*left*).

We asked Gerry Bigelow, who "was born in Bingham, probably die in Bingham," how he first got involved with the drive.

"I didn't know what to do when I got out of school, so I told myself, 'I'll try the log drive.' It's a job gettin' started out, you know. Started sluicin' . . . just pushin' away. Then after that, as the years progressed, I got from pushin' pulp to these last few years when I've been a boat operator.

"The early bird catches the worm. If you go there first lookin' for the job, you'll get a halfway decent job. If you're a little late, well then they'll get you walkin' the tramp, back and forth."

Although Bob Viles has been master driver for the KLD, he tells us that he, too, started at the bottom and had to work his way up. "I used to drive logs just the way everyone else starts. One year I worked as a runner. I ran all the messages. It was on Indian Pond and I was seventeen.

"I was born and brought up in this county. My dad used to work the river drive and my grandfather was a director in the big river-driving run. It's been in my family all my life."

"Wild" Bill McLaughlin, a very experienced man on the drive, told us of his feelings about his work on the river. "I had a lot of chances to quit, you know, for more money, and go to work and have a real good job like I got now." Bill operates a backhoe now that the drive is over. "I coulda' took this job anytime—a lot easier, too, you know. You don't get dirty.

"I just couldn't leave it [the drive] until it was done with, that's all. If it had lasted another ten years, I'd still be there."

242. "Buster" Violette clears logs that have jammed up against the boom log on which he is standing. Buster was on the drive thirty years. (*Photo by Joe Myerson*)

Drivin' a Stick—
and Other Jobs

"Sluicing gets monotonous because all you do is walk and you pull your pickpole out and push." Gerry Bigelow explained, "You just walk back and forth, and after your first week you think you're going to go bananas. Then maybe they might give you a break and put you on as a deckhand on one of the tugboats.

"Then after that you go back to polling and then you may go for what they call high rear. In the spring of the year, some of the pulp gets pushed way back into the woods and you go in and pull it out to the edge of the water, and so forth. That's a little break from that boring, monotonous job."

"Yeah," Bob Viles added. "I done a lot of that [sluicing], too . . . a good many years. That's hard work. Standin' there all day, you know. Just drivin' a stick in and pull it back, drive it back in, you know. Work eight to nine hours—well, last part of the years it was only eight or nine hours, but when I first went to work it was seven days a week and they'd work anywhere from fourteen to eighteen hours a day."

How much does a river driver earn for all of his long, hard, wet hours of labor?

"When I came in, in June of sixty-nine, the pay was great," Gerry Bigelow said sarcastically. "At the time I was getting $1.69 an hour. I think it was about sixty hours a week."

"The average person was getting $2.65 an hour at the end of this last year," Ralph said. "It never got very high."

"It was peanuts," Gerry added. "Believe it or not, you have to put up with a lot of bull crap. One year one guy will tell you to do it this way, then you might have a different boss or something and he wants to do it another way than the way you're used to doing it.

243. (*Photo by
Anne Pierter*)

"When you get used to a job, you know what to do. Then this other fellow will tell you something else. You look at him, 'I been here a little longer than you have.' But I do it his way. Well, you start and somethin' goes wrong. Then he says, 'Well, if we would have done it this way [Gerry's way] then . . .'

" 'Why didn't I think of that?!!'

"But the last few years that we've been goin' out, they really didn't care, you know. They weren't down on ya' too much. But the crew there, the last of it, was the same people year after year, so they knew what was going on."

The Boats

Boats played an important role in 'the river drive. The types of boats used on the drive were not always the same, but they always had to fill the same function. Boats were needed for pushing, towing, and winching.

"When I first started I didn't know a boat from nothin'." That's how Bill McLaughlin described the beginning of his career in boating on the river drive. "I just told 'em I was a good boat driver. That's the only way you can get along, you know. If you wanted a good job, you told 'em, 'Oh yah, I've done that.' An' they'd try you. And if you done halfway decent, away you'd go. Just bluff your way, all the way."

Gerry Bigelow described the boats used in the drive. "They have regular wooden boats and horse-powered, and bateaus. You got pullman and horseman; then you've got your tugboats, and you've got small steel boats with inboards, and rowboats, and whatever.

"They have a kicker boat and they have what they call a washtub they use for a winch. And the pusher boat. That would be three. At Indian Pond at one time they had a winch boat and two pusher boats.

"A winch boat, you can use it for various things like when the main boat, the tugboat, brings your raft in. He'll let go of the raft and the fellow in the winch boat, well, they'll push your boat. They'll come in. They'll break it. One boat will pull way down towards the sluice gate and double back and hook in again while the other one will just be pullin' down on the other side.

"And all this time this wood is being forced right down. Then the guy that doubles back, he's hooked in again and he's tied down to a certain point down towards the sluice gate and the other fellow's still towing down. Then possibly if he's still got room and the wind's blowin' towards the other side, he can double back, then jump into the wood again and pull it down even more.

244. "Bill" McLaughlin, left, and "Buster" Violette with pickpoles. (*Photo by Whitney Draper*)

"So, all the time you're just forcin' the wood into this one little area. Then after that, the wood is usually so tight that your winch boat, you just sat right there and you have it tied up with your motor in gear, having it kick the wood towards the sluice."

Both Wilfred Sanipas and Gerry Bigelow have worked a winch boat. In Gerry's words, "We've been all the way around. On a winch boat you have an operator and a deckhand. Usually, once you start winchin', the boat operator becomes deckhand, then operator. The boat, all it is, well, you might say it's automatic."

Gerry explained how the winch boat and the pusher boat worked together. "It's [the pusher boat] a fairly good-sized boat. It has a little blade in front, maybe twelve, fifteen feet in length and maybe a foot and a half wide. And the blade just drops down and just pushes the wood towards the gate and turns. You pull back on your rudder to close up your basket underneath, just back up into the wood and turn around, come again.

"And then from there, after you get the wood all loosened up, usually your winch boat will go out to the middle of the raft, hook into the boom again and pull right to the middle of your sluice gate and all these pusher boats are pushin' at the same time and after you get almost all the way to the sluice gate, you let go of it, jump outside, and they'll untie. When the sides are already tied in, they'll snap that out, double it back out, and come around again to hook in and haul it back down again. You got to know what you're doin'.

"Sometimes when you jump boom logs, they'll crisscross, the chains will, and it's a son-of-a-gun job. The guy that's out there winchin' and hookin' on all this time, he's usually got to grab two rings and get two boom logs side by side, you know, so not to cross them and all that. Sometimes you think you're going to save on time or something and you're in a hurry and the wind's blowing against you and you're loosin' wood up the lake, you just got to grab one and you don't try to make a quick sweep. Sometimes you make it, sometimes you don't.

"Sometimes you can use a wooden boat with eighteen horse [for a winch boat]. It all depends on the wind and things like that. The pusher boats, I'd say you'd have to have a little more power. These pusher boats we had here, they had caterpillar engines in them like in a small bulldozer or something! They were, I would imagine, oh, twenty feet long, eight, ten feet wide, these pusher boats, so they're a good-sized boat.

"These motors in some of these boats are, well, the one I run has a fifty-seven Plymouth car engine. It's not the best of equipment, I tell ya. You want to be thankful you always had a screwdriver and an adjustable wrench or somethin' because you was always tinkerin'. So you're part mechanic, log driver, swimmer, knot tier, blacksmith, and nut!"

Another boat used on the drive was a flat-bottomed boat which Bill McLaughlin described. "Square at both ends, with an outboard on it. And that, they use that ta pick the rear with."

When asked which of all the boating jobs he liked best, Gerry said, "Tug. Go to sleep and let the deckhand run the boat." Wilfred Sanipas agreed. "Yeah, that's a pretty good job. The guy with the tug. You can just sit there and drink coffee. It's easy."

Working with the lumber on the lakes and ponds may seem easy at first, but as Gerry pointed out, working with the boats called for experience. "Well, it takes good judgment. You gotta be alert all the time. You got to know the depths of the water. Like there's places in the lakes and stuff that's real shallow, ledgy and all of this and you can't get bombin' around in a boat just goin' full buoy, looking for adventure or something. You have to be pretty alert, you know.

"You got to know your winds, you use them to your advantage 'cause you can work all day in a boat pulling the raft, and you can be bucking the wind the whole day when you could be usin' it, like rowin' your raft or something like that. You just have to—you got to think quite a bit. It's a lot like walkin' once you get used to it. You're on water. You got to make the boat operate for you."

Bill McLaughlin agreed. "You had to know right where to go. If you didn't, you'd go ground her. So it was quite a trick to go and take three thousand, five thousand cords up river. Take it in the cut-off and steer it all the way down the river. Then get it there so you didn't break the boom or hang up with it."

The work was hard on both the rivers and the lakes during the drive, and Gerry gave a good description of it. "There was a few times you might come into an eddy, they tell you to go under this little eddy, or backwater, where there's no current or anything and they'd tell you to get all the wood out of there.

"And when you get in there, about six inches underneath the water there's all these tree stumps, your boat's getting hung up, and you've got to pry this off every five minutes, and the woods in there, along with dead heads and blood suckers and black flies, and you're going bananas, you know? To heck with it, we'll leave that one right alone. And the guy comes by and says, 'How come you didn't clean that one out?' So we did. 'Must be the high water that took it back in.'

"You see, the lake is always goin' up and down and you can't really clean it. You can clean one place out one week and turn around two days later and you have to clean it again."

For a boatman, knowing the waters was all-important. "I know every shallow spot in it, every crook, every turn—everything. You have to know if you take that big boat out," said Bill.

"At Indian Pond there's [a place in it] where it comes right together. They call it the narrows. It's just a little narrow place and then it opens again into another lake, a great big lake. So you had to work your raft in and around there real careful to get it through so you don't break the boom.

"So they had this new fellow there. He wanted to be on the boat. They made him captain of the boat. They put him on the boat. So, he came down through the boom, he got around, and he got hung up. He was new at it though.

"Somethin' about boats that when new people get on them, they really get excited about it. I don't know why. They are always askin' me and I say, 'I don't care if you drive her all the way through the bottom. I ain't gonna have a heart attack about it.' Most everybody that's been

245. Pickpoling from a flat-bottomed boat. In center is Bill McLaughlin. (*Photo by Whitney Draper*)

in control of them have had a heart attack," Bill said, with a laugh. "The sweat rolls right off 'em! They get real scared!

"I remember once one year there, they had a fellow on there, Stanley Trepasy. I think he's dead now. He was a deckhand on the boat and he was goin' up the river. The captain, he got tired and he wanted Stanley to take it [the tiller]. So, he says, 'Okay.' So Willy, he went and laid down and went to sleep. They had a bunk right in the cabin.

"Well, they got goin' up the lake—goin' like heck and evidently he musta' gone to sleep or somethin'. There was a little island right in the middle and he came right up and 'vroom!' went right up on top of that island.

"And there he sat. Knocked old Willy out of the bunk there. He fell on the floor. He didn't know what happened! They got him [Stanley] off an' took him away, an' that's what they call it now—Stanley's Island. It's always had that name ever since he's been on it."

246. Hauling logs out of the woods in the 1930s.

Logging in the Winter

River drivers worked as loggers in the winter if they lived in the area. The same men who swung axes in the woods in the winter were hurling cant dogs in the spring and summer.

As soon as the spring thaw came and the streams and rivers began to run, the logging crews stopped cutting and stockpiling wood on the "landing" beside the water and began driving logs to the mills. The crews of local men were joined by Indians and Canadians who came just for the drive. Because Indians were known to be lithe walking the logs, as well as skilled boatmen, they were especially welcome when hiring time came.

For men like eighty-one-year-old Ted Quigley, eighty-eight-year-old Bert Morris, and the Kennedy brothers, Austin and Russell, both in their seventies, logging was as much a part of their lives as river driving.

"The first time I went in the woods, I was eight years old," said Austin Kennedy, who now lives in Jackman. "My brother was ten. We went in just to visit my father [Joe Kennedy]. He was a foreman in there, and we liked it so well that we stayed. School didn't keep them days in the [bad] weather, you know. There wasn't any school. The roads weren't plowed. If you wanted to go to town, you had to go on snowshoes.

"We was cookie. You had to wash dishes and carry lunch to the men in the woods. Cut wood, you know, a lot of wood. What did we get for doin' it? We didn't get anything. We just got bored, that's all."

Another beginning job for boys was "swamping." Ted Quigley started as a swamper at age sixteen when he walked over the border from Canada to work in the Maine woods.

"Swamping—that's clearing out the roads for the choppers," said Ted. "Cleaning out trees, scraping and cutting out roads so they could go right back to the back end.

247. Austin Kennedy at home in Jackman. (*Photo by Bill O'Donnell*)

248. Russell
Kennedy
describes logging
years ago.

"The men worked in crews. You had four or five men in a crew. You had a swamper, two choppers, someone to tend the sled and horses [called a teamster], and someone to help unload at the landing [called a yard man]," Ted explained. Each crew had a team of horses to pull the sled, which was a wagon on runners.

The highest paid men on the crew were the choppers and the teamster. "Way back then [1910–20] they got paid by the day, not by the hour. They got about two-fifty or three dollars a day.

"Two choppers could get six or seven thousand [feet] a day," said Ted, who rose to the position of superintendent during his fifty years of logging. The choppers used crosscut saws and bucksaws, two men to the saw, to fell the trees. They also used axes to notch the trees and to trim off the limbs.

The logs were peeled by stripping off the bark back in the days when Ted, Bert Morris, and the Kennedy brothers started logging. Austin Kennedy explained why the trees were peeled. "They was easier to handle, and the wood dried. It was lighter, too, lighter if you was gonna drive and if you was gonna truck it. Course, there wasn't any trucking back in them days, all driving [river driving].

"Not only that, but they didn't lose no wood, ya see. When they bark it in the mill they lose some wood, bound to. Peeling, you take just the bark. You don't take no wood at all. But course that's all gone now; they don't peel no more.

"They had what you'd call a spud. It's a peeling iron," Austin told us, "which was about a foot long. It would be about two and a half inches wide, made something like a spoon. First you'd break it [the bark] with an ax. Then you'd take the spud and you'd go in and roll the bark off.

"They'd peel that tree probably in three minutes, three to five minutes. When the bark's running good, the bark will fall right off.

"Some trees will peel easier than others. If trees don't have too many limbs, too many knots, you know, nice smooth tree, the bark will come right off easy. But if there's a lot of knots, working around them knots, it takes you a little longer to get the bark off. But they peel them, they peel all that wood.

"They used to pay them on topple ten cents a tree. To cut it and peel it, that was topple. For black oak they paid twenty cents a tree. A good man could cut a hundred topple a day and peel them, and they'd take it just as they come, big, little, and medium. They figured on making around twenty dollars a day them days.

"That weren't too far back. Let's see, I guess I was about twenty-five years old. That was fifty years ago! Fifty years ago, now that seems just like yesterday to me!"

Horses moved the logs from the place in the woods where they were cut to the landing or yard beside a brook, stream, or river where they could be driven in the spring and summer. Ted said the company he worked for kept sixteen horses for hauling.

The logs were loaded into sleds, which were rough wagons on runners that could be pulled through deep snow. Ted said the sleds were called drays. "Pop dray they called it." He pointed to an old photo taken in 1936 of two sleds hitched together pulled by a single pair of horses.

"Twenty-two cords there. That was a tremendous load. The record the year before was seventeen and we wanted to beat it, so we did," Ted said.

Percy Burgess of Dayton also hauled wood after it was cut. "I was what they called a scoot tender," he said. He made his own scoot sleds for hauling, which were horse drawn. "Skidders weren't invented in those days. I logged the hard way."

Percy also built brows, which were platforms of logs that made it easier to roll the logs onto the scoot sleds. Most of Percy's logging was done in southern Maine, but he also logged in the north. "I was up north in the big woods. I was logging up there for about three years. That's where they really log, up there."

The logs were scaled at the landing by a man that Ted Quigley referred to as the landing man or the yard man. Austin Kennedy scaled for a while, and he told us how it was done. "I used to scale up here for Jackman Lumber Company when they had this train going up through here. They had a railroad led right up into the woods. That was a big operation.

"Scaling, well that's measuring the lumber. On long logs you had to caliber rule. The rule had a wheel on it. You'd measure the length of the logs. And then you'd caliber it. Now that would give you what the log would saw out.

"Then on pulpwood, they had a left rule, you see. That was a hundred units through cords. You could measure your pile. If it was eight foot long and four foot high, that would give you a hundred points per cord.

"You have to learn from another scaler. When they start you off, they start with an experienced man teaching ya. When you learn the ropes, you go up and the head scaler checks your work to see how you're coming, keep an eye on ya. After you've scaled awhile, you're all right. You don't make mistakes."

In the yard or landing, the logs were marked with a letter to identify the owner. "Each company had their own mark," Ted said. "Mark 'em with an L or B or C or X or whatever. When they went to drive, when they went down river, each company got their own logs." At the end of the drive was a sorting station where logs were separated according to owner.

How were the sites for the logging operations selected? Two loggers described "cruising" for contracts with lumber companies, which took experience and a sure knowledge of the woods and logging operations.

Austin Kennedy was a contractor who "cruised" in search of lumber in northwest Maine. "Well, you cruise when the company owns a piece of land and wants you to see how much timber is on it. You estimate, you know. You have to have a pretty good knowledge of the woods. We expected it to come in pretty close. We didn't want it to be too far off."

His wife, Yvonne, agreed. "If he said there was a thousand cords in there, it was pretty close to it. Sometimes he'd go over. If he took a contract for a thousand cords of wood, he had to find it on that piece of land."

Grover Morrison of Lincoln Center described some of his cruising experiences during his fifty-two-year career in the logging business. "This operation was done for the Diamond Match Company. They wanted seven or eight million feet of pine. We heard about this, and I knew where there was a block of pine near Mattagammon. That was twenty-eight miles north of Patten. We went up there and cruised it, and the lumber was there. We put in six days of cruising, but there was no way to get there, only by water. The company didn't like this, as well as me.

"We didn't like the idea of being so far up in the woods with no road. So they said, 'Do you think you could get a road there?' I said, 'Well, I can try.' So I put in three more days cruising for the best spot to put the road through.

"Well, I looked it all over and I came back and reported to him. I said, 'Yes, it can be done, but it will cost a lot of money, because you have to put nine miles of road through the jungles of Maine—over them ridges, those ledges, black ledges. And they run in all directions.'

"I had wound around those ledges and over them and across them and almost under them to get there, but I made it. Then he says, 'What do you think it will cost?' I said to him, 'Well, I'm going to say it's gonna cost about forty-five thousand dollars.'

" 'Well,' he says, 'how much lumber do you feel there is?' I says, 'Six and a half to seven million feet. But here we have the expense of building the roads and the camps.' To get the men to go so far back into the jungles of Maine, you certainly have to throw out some inducements to do it. The inducements will be the accommodations on the other end such as decent food and decent beds along with wages.

"My experiences of life doing these jobs, building these roads, bridges, culverts and what-have-you—we carted so much gravel to build good gravel roads, all the cost of the roads and work you put in on them . . .

"When you are all done, you pick up and leave. Chances are you never see the same road again—after you cart the gravel, cut the trees out of your way, pay the men to work, pull out the stumps and the majority of the larger rocks. You build the camps and bridges with the material in the way. And then after you're done logging, you leave it all behind."

Life on the Drive and in the Woods

What was the life of the men on the river drive and the loggers in the woods? All agreed that the days were long. "You had to work from daylight to dark," Ted Quigley said. "The stream water didn't last too long, and we had to work while it was going."

Austin Kennedy agreed. "I *guess* it's a long day. You worked till nine or half past nine. Out in the woods all the time. We never did see that camp in daylight."

Ida Allen remembered her father's long work days. "Men used to work," the eighty-six-year-old pioneer of Moxie Falls said. "They didn't live [to be] old like they do now. They'd go out to work with lanterns, that's all there was, so as soon as it come daylight they'd be in the woods and working. Then they wouldn't come in until long after dark, you know."

In more recent days, the long working hours were shortened by such master drivers as Bob Viles. "I used to notice that when I went down and talked to the crew, by four-thirty in the afternoon they're all so ugly I can't even talk to them, can't communicate or get anywhere. After we initiated them to ten hours a day and one day off a week and it worked well, then we went to nine hours. We had more production and less accidents."

Even so, the days tended to be longer than for most jobs, the last drivers agreed. Bill McLaughlin said there was no set starting and stopping time. "Usually they'd start about seven o'clock. Some days a little bit early—five, six o'clock. An' they'd get done at five o'clock and come eat supper. Sometimes they'd go back and work after supper until nine, ten."

Gerry Bigelow and Ralph DeMusis said work weeks in the 1970s usually amounted to about sixty hours a week, considerably more than the forty hours most workers have grown accustomed to in these days.

249. Men warm their hands over a fire during a fall morning break. Left to right: Ralph DeMusis, unidentified lounger, Ed Calder smoking a pipe, Donald Hovey, and Bill McLaughlin. (*Photo by Whitney Draper*)

The camps for loggers and river drivers were built by the men themselves. When Ted Quigley started logging, the camps were "all built out of long logs—big timber. You built your own camps, big camps. Camps that would probably house seventy-five or eighty men or maybe more.

"And the cook's room on one end and the men's camp on the other end. Then they usually have a nice big office, you know, opposite the buildings. And hovels for some forty or fifty horses."

Grover Morrison described the construction of the camps. "Mostly long logs were used in building the camps, cut full length. There was log wells—all logs. The corners of the camps was notched slank together, and sometimes when boards wasn't too plentiful, we wed small poles on the roof and poles on the camp floors and then we had an adze that we adzed the top of the poles with and that made it more smooth.

250. Ida Allen. (*Photo by Anne Gorham*)

"I remember one camp we had cedar splits on the roof and the only boards there was in that camp was in the doors and the cook tables in the cook room.

"We used tarred paper on the roofs and you know about that now. If them knots wasn't all smooth, they would poke up through the paper. That left a rim right around that tarred paper. This stopped the rain from leaking in.

"On the logs inside, the men would drive nails in the logs to hang their coats and caps and what-have-you.

"The log heater stoves would take three- and four-foot wood. The big stovepipe was eight inches. It would go up to an elbow, along a long ways, then another elbow and up through the roof. And along beside the stovepipe, there would be poles so men could hang their stockings, coats, hats, and moccasins.

"Today, that heat instead of going up through the pipe and the length of the camp, it would go up through the pipe and outside it would go. When it goes the length of the camp, it heats the camp more."

Ted Quigley was asked if there were long lines hanging across the inside of the camp. "Always, always," he replied. "Always two big heaters, big woodpile in between. And they have poles or lines on both sides for them to hang their stockings and clothes and shoes."

Ted recalled days that were so long the clothes didn't have time to get dry. "On stream drives the water didn't last too long [there were no dams to raise the water level when it was low]. We had a great cook at that time and he'd holler, 'Time to get up, boys. Your stockings aren't quite dry, but it's time to get up.' They'd reach up and their shoes still swinging where they hung 'em."

Logging camps like the one Grover Morrison described were left behind after the logging operation was over. The river driving camps in the early 1900s were often temporary camps that were moved with the drive. Later permanent camps were built for the men who worked each section of the drive.

Russell Kennedy described the early river driving camps. "We had driving camps. You took all your beddin' and all your equipment, all your grub on the drive. After we got so far, three or four miles from camp, we'd move the camp. Next night we'd stay in a new spot.

"We must have had three big tents to hold eighty, eighty-five men. We used blankets and wood puffs. Sleeping bags you never heard tell of. They had a cook shack, oh, probably about fourteen foot square. Out on the end of that they got probably three or four logs on the back, and a log on the end and put on a roof made out of cedar splits. The front was all open. They made the cooks' bunks in the front.

"In front of where we slept there was a big open fire. You worked fourteen to sixteen hours. They called that a day.

"The pod auger days. Ever hear of that word? That's when you work so long they feed you four meals a day. They fed you at five in the morning, nine o'clock lunch, two o'clock lunch, and seven o'clock supper.

"You most generally wound up with beans—beans and biscuits. Lunch and supper we had potatoes and beef, too. There were about eighty, eighty-five men, and we never had a cook stove. Course, we had bean hole bean kettles for bean hole beans. Then we had a big open fire where they cooked all the boiled stuff.

"Then in the camp by those big open fires, course, they had those big open bakers. The two ends are closed and the top is rounded. There was a shelf—that's where you put the baker sheet. But, of course, ours was four or five feet long.

"They fill it all full of biscuits and you set it up to the fire and you bake the front side. Then you take it out and turn it around and bake the back side of the biscuits. Bake a cake the same way. They made cookies, cakes, and everything just the same way, but it was all open fire.

"Of course the cooks today couldn't do that because they wouldn't know how to go about it. But that's what they were brought up to do, them cooks. We lived good on the drive then. They fed us good."

When we asked the men what they did for entertainment, we got answers that varied according to the years and places we were talking about. Gerry said that when he lived in the camps (the 1970s) they played "anything from football to wiffle ball. Sometimes just pass, play with Frisbees, go swimming right there in the lake. Take a ride out and have a beer. Nine miles to a beer store, and then some evenings we just go down the road and look for deer and moose.

"A few fellows brought a guitar or somethin' and set there and sing and hoot and holler. They got better as the year progressed. I think we all did."

In Ted's day, thirty years earlier, the camps seemed a bit quieter than in Gerry's. There were very few things to do in the evenings except play cards, read a book, or tell stories.

"The Canadians would bring harmonicas and they'd step dance."

Ralph DeMusis described for us the parties they had at the end of the drive. "We had a few get-togethers over the years I'd say. Few times a year when we'd be playing. We had a fellow from Oklahoma one year who played the guitar very well. We used to get together quite a bit with him and there was always somebody. Always seemed to be two or three people a year that played, so we'd have get-togethers. Everybody had a few beers, of course, have a good time.

"Well, my wife and I sing together, and we've written songs and, ah, well the fellow from Oklahoma, he used to sing a lot of Irish songs. They were a lot of fun. We even had a party at the Marshall Hotel one night and we were having a good time. I'd learned a lot of them [Irish songs] and we started to play and had a good time. And there's Jed [Calder], of course; he wrote the 'Log Driving Song.'"

Austin Kennedy said, "Wherever they was, they had their spree. That's the nature of the river driver, lumberjack. That was part of his life."

Family men who lived in the area tended to be less rowdy than people who came in from other places just to work on the drive. Ted

Quigley's granddaughter said she had heard the loggers around Bangor
(Penobscot River) had a reputation for wild week-ends on the town.
"They say they tear up the town. I told that to Grandpa and he said the
loggers he worked with around here [the Kennebec River drive]
weren't rowdy like that."

Ted tried to explain. "I don't know whether they were different, but
we did have more disagreements on the Penobscot than we did over
here at the Kennebec. More natives on the Kennebec, I suppose, 'cause
the Penobscot drivers weren't all Bangor fellows, all from everywhere."

Ted told a story to illustrate his point. "I was down in Bar Harbor
one summer loading wood, and it was a hard place. The first ten days I
was there, it was foggy. The only thing we could see was fog horns. We
never saw the sun and I was so homesick, but anyway, they took me
down to run the place, and to run it I had to run it alone.

"Saturday nights the boys used to go over Bar Harbor and get something to drink and come back and get noisy. They got ahold of some
alcohol and along about four o'clock I could hear quite a racket, so I
looked out and they were having the darndest squabble, the darndest
fight that you'd ever see.

"Anyway some of them started it. One of them didn't want to go, so
they took a rope and tied him to a tree. I fired everybody the next
morning.

"So I called the office. I said, 'You told me I had to run it alone and
I'm alone this morning.' So they said, 'You come to Bangor and we'll
meet you there and we'll pick some up.' So I went to Bangor the next
morning. I picked up three or four of the same ones that I fired. Pretty
rough."

To get liquor in the camps, Ted said some of the men would "hire a
public boat there summers and they'd go get it. Bootlegging. Some of
the fellas there we used to call the methanol bunch. They used to take
that methanol alcohol and fix it all up with sugar and water, and
goodness sake, it put the bite right into them.

"Some poor fellas would work so hard and they'd never save a cent.
They'd work hard all winter, mend their own clothes, do their own
wash, and go to Bangor or some big city and blow it themselves; stay
there until they are broke and then come back."

Bill McLaughlin said he was saved from such a fate as a young man
by his boss, Bert Morris, who saw to it that Bill didn't have a chance to
squander his money. "That old codger. I don't know if he done that to
everybody, but to me he was more like—tried to be my father.

"I was single, you know, and I was kinda wild. On a Saturday night,
I'd wanta go out and I'd have me about a hundred dollars and he'd
say, 'Payday didn't come today.' He wouldn't give me my check.

251. Bill
McLaughlin.

"Come back Monday morning and he'd say, 'Here's your check. Now look how much money you saved!' One time I remember real, real good. Friday night and we had to go seven miles up the lake. It was right back of Indian Pond. The cutoff is around seven or eight miles above there, and there ain't nothin' up there. There ain't no road goin' in and there ain't no road comin' out. Just by boat.

"So he sent me up there. I got up in there, and I said, 'Oh well, I'll be back tonight. Then I'll go to town.' And he sent another boat up, a tugboat to tell me, 'Well, we got one boat broke down, and you're gonna have to stay there the week-end.' So I had to stay there Saturday and Sunday, and I coulda strangled him when I got back."

We asked Bill if Bert looked after the other young drivers the same way. "I don't know. I never asked about the other fellas. I just worried about myself. But he was a real nice fellow to work for. He fired me

252. Bert
Morris.

one day. We went to Greenville one time. They used to have mostly all Indians up there. We got raising hell one night and me and the Indians took off to Greenville.

"We all got drunk and came and we sassed the cook. We wanted breakfast about three o'clock in the morning and he didn't want to give it to us, so we decided we was gonna cook it ourselves. So we went in and cooked it anyways.

"The cook quit. He went back to Canada, I guess. Bert got up that mornin' and he said, 'You're all fired. Pack your clothes.' He fired all the Indians. That mornin' I was in packin' clothes—I was sick anyways, you know. He said, 'I want you to go down the road,' he said, 'and lay in the wood. And I'll pay ya for the day.' And he said, 'Get back here tonight and go back to work Monday mornin'.'

"So I came back that night. Four o'clock that mornin', he come over and he said, 'Well, the cook's gone. Now you gotta help me cook.' I had to get up at four o'clock and I had to help him cook till they found a cook. He was quite a character, that bird. He was a real good fella."

The Marshall Hotel in The Forks seemed to be a favorite spot for the men on the drives in recent years. Gerry Bigelow told us, "You're not supposed to drink on the job. After hours, your spare time is your own. As long as you're ready, able, and available the next day.

"Some fellas would stay there [at the camp] on the week-ends. They had to cook their own meals. Or they'd go to the Marshall Hotel. Get all hogged up on the week-ends and hit her hard Monday morning. A lot of good log drivers died there."

Every man who knows his job also knows some tricks of the trade that make the job easier. For instance, caulk boots were a must when the men walked the long logs in earlier days.

"You'd break your neck if you didn't have on caulk boots," said Austin Kennedy. "The logs are slippery. And them rocks are slippery. There's a kind of slime on them. Gotta have caulk boots. When you travel on the river, there's a lot of sharp rocks and ledges and things. If you had on rubber or moccasins, your feet wouldn't take it. You gotta have big thick soles.

"That was some boots we had. They was loaded with sharp caulks. They had to be good leather to hold the caulks. There's two rows of nails [caulks] in the bottom of the boots right around them. There's a few more in the heel.

"You don't step on nothing. You jump in a boat and you gotta be careful of the boat crew, careful of the soles. They'd go right through, but they had to have 'em going on that slippery logs and rocks. You couldn't drive without them."

Dealing with black flies in the spring was as much a part of the job as pushing the logs down the river. We wondered if the river drivers had any special ointments to keep the black flies away. "You'd need some iodine and baby oil," Gerry Bigelow said. Then he laughed. "Some guys would use this old woodsman tar. I don't know what was in it. They'd set right there and they was just as brown with it. They'd start sweating and it would just roll right off. Once you get it on your clothes, it takes three or four washings to get it out.

"You don't wear too much blue because the black flies get attracted to blue for some reason. Anything—light blue or dark blue—it doesn't matter. It was just instant. 'What have I got here?' But usually if you

253. Ralph DeMusis, second from left, tells about moose flies.

was out in the middle of the water or something, there was always a breeze of some sort, so you wouldn't have any flies. But you get along shore, you feel like you're going to get picked up and carried away."

Ralph DeMusis of Caratunk told us how he had been caught by the horse flies. "I'd forgotten that after you get wet those big moose flies or whatever you call them, they love you after that. I jumped right in the water it felt so good. It was the summer and I hadn't been swimming yet and, oh, it felt nice.

"And when I got out, I had about thirteen or fourteen of them on my back while I was trying to get my shirt back on and my shoes on and everything. And everybody else, they was hiking away because they couldn't stand it. And they were laughing at me. Jesus, they just about carried me off."

Black flies weren't the only pest that bothered the drivers. Blood suckers were also a problem. "A lot of guys, when you're picking rear in a lake or something, they'll tie their pants right up tight to keep the blood suckers and stuff away from them," Gerry said. "Either tuck your pants in your boots or get a rope and tie it right around."

Sometimes the men had a good time competing with each other in tests of strength and endurance. It was especially fun when one of the out-of-state men tried to show off for the native Mainers, who knew just exactly what the results would be. Gerry told us a couple of stories that illustrate this.

"There was this one fellow from California, he came for two consecutive years. He was only eighteen or nineteen. This fellow was telling how he was writing home to his mother, you know, telling how he was getting big and strong in the Maine air. He says he could pick up this piece of wood over his head.

"And Jed [Calder], he was in charge of us, he said, 'Go right ahead. Pick it up.' So the guy comes and picks it up and gets it about to his chest. He [Jed] said, 'I thought you could pick that up?!'

"About this time, Jed picks it up and holds it right over his head. 'That's the way you're supposed to do it, you know.' And the guy just looks at him.

"We had some people from Connecticut and different places like that and we went down to Skowhegan and these two fellows, they couldn't move this piece of wood. There was this one guy—he was from Connecticut. I forget his name—we just called him 'Connecticut' anyways. This Connecticut guy says, 'What's the matter with you guys, you weak? I can move more wood than you!'

" 'Well, go right ahead!'

"Now, he picked a log that two guys would have all they could do to drag to the water. I couldn't move it. Then he says, 'Well, I can drag it to the water.' This guy was maybe six foot, hundred and eighty pounds. 'Why don't you put it right on my shoulders. I'll carry her.'

" 'Well, come right over here!' We picked it right up and put it on his shoulders—drove him right into mud over his knees!

" 'Stay right there, sucker!' "

The risks that the men took each day along the river became a part of their lives. They came with the job. "I got stabbed with an idiot stick a couple of times," Gerry Bigelow said. "We formed these lines, what they call a chain. You got a lot of wood in the woods. You all line right up in a straight line, stand there throwing it back to the next guy.

"I was throwing it back and a guy reached up and caught me right in the hand, right here with that hook. It snaps you right around, wakes you right up," he chuckled.

"And another time I stabbed myself. It was just one of those mornings when nothing goes right. I was going to go stick this piece of wood and we were working on these ledges, Indian Pond. And it just

254. "I got stabbed with an idiot stick a couple of times."

bounced right off and struck me right in the foot. So the captain and I stood right there and looked at it and I said, 'Jesus, I hope this don't hurt!' Pulled it right out and the suction sound . . . took a little trip to Greenville [to the hospital]."

"There wasn't too many men that drowned. Not for all the chances we took and all of the work that we've done. We was pretty lucky," said Ted Quigley.

Bill McLaughlin told about two near misses when men almost lost their lives on the drive. "We was goin' down Solon Dam there. They had the gates open. It was kinda rough water. A fella was sitting on the edge of one of them flat-bottomed boats. And I don't know what happened. Next thing he was gone. He was down in the water. He couldn't swim. He went right down out of sight.

"I reached right down in the water and I caught him right by the corner of the shirt and I pulled him right up out of the water. And a young fellow—they called him 'Buggymaster'—got ahold of him on the other side, and we pulled him up into the boat. When he came up out of the water, he was white as a ghost.

"Another time. The water is real fast right there in front of the sluice gate. So this fellow was standing on the back of a kicker boat. The sluice gate was right behind him, he was standing on the back of the boat, and they was towing all the boom. The boom had gone down around the back of the boat.

"When they took off in a big tugboat, they got goin'. Sometimes they take off a little too fast. And that log caught the bottom of that boat, and when it did, it flipped him right over backwards.

"And he went down right over in front of that sluice gate. There's a pan that sticks up there and he went right down below the pan. And I just happened to be standing right up on the top [of the sluice gate], and I reached right down quick and got ahold of him by the hair on the head when he started to comin' up. And I picked him up, boy, and just the minute I got him up out of the water, they drove her into that tramway!"

From all accounts, not many men were lost on the drive, and when a man was lost, the tale of his death was recounted again and again. Austin Kennedy told us about the only death he had seen in his years of driving—and we heard about the same death from Bert Morris.

"We lost just one man that I can remember of when I was driving," Austin said. "He wasn't on my shore. That was coming down from Indian Pond, way up above The Forks. This was right before the building of the Indian Dam.

"Bert Morris was in that boat and another fellow, I forget his name, and a fellow from Bingham and a guy from Skowhegan. They hit a rock and it busted the boat and threw them all out. They all got ashore but this fellow from Bingham. He got drowned. That's the only man that I ever remember seein'. But they did lose a man on Cole Stream. It was Martin Donahue's brother. Martin Donahue, he used to be the master driver for quite a few years."

When a man died in the woods, it was the custom to carry him out without ever laying him down, Ted Quigley told us.

"We had heard that there was a log jam and I went down there and worked with the crew in the jam," Ted remembered. "By lunch we hadn't broken it, so I had to bring the word up and have them heist again to bring another head down. Something came over me that I better go over myself.

"When I got up there, there was no sight of the superintendent, nobody knew where he was. We looked around everywhere and couldn't find him. Then some of the boys found his hat. Of course I shut everything down and everyone went out looking for him. Two fellows poking around shore on a raft made out of logs could see the soles of his rubbers showing. So then I had to call and say that there was an accident. I had to walk quite a ways to find a phone. And then I had to go back again and tell them that we had found him and to get permission to lug him out.

"So we lugged him out that night and the old custom then was you were never to lay a dead person down even when they shifted hands. You can't lay it down, and that night we didn't lay it down. We got him out that night at two o'clock. We carried him about six miles through the snow. Snow clear to the road. And they never laid him down."

Bean Hole Beans

On a windy day in late August we traveled, once again, to The Forks, Maine, to meet with Russell Kennedy, logger, bear trapper, river driver, and *bean hole bean* baker.

Bean hole bean baking is a tradition in Russell's family. "Years ago, there were times when everyone baked 'em in the ground," says Russell. And when you were river driving, "You most generally wound up with beans. Beans and biscuits."

The first step in the preparation of bean hole beans is to dig a hole. The size of the hole depends on the size of your bean pot. The hole Russell dug for us was about three feet deep, and his pot was about a foot in depth. This hole will serve as the "oven" to cook your beans in.

After the hole is dug, line it with pieces of granite or slate. This is where the fire will be built, with bark and kindling.

We asked Russell what was the best kind of wood to use for the fire. "Well, course up here we use hard wood. But I talked with a man the other day, he and his boy come up from down 'round the coast. He asked me about bean hole beans. His father, or somebody, used to sell bean hole beans. He dug a great big trench on the beach, you know, all sand, lined it with brick and burnt ash and alders. But up here we usually use hard wood."

After he lit the fire, Russell threw small stones in and around the fire. "Just throw them anywhere," Russell said. The small stones get hot and hold the heat many hours.

By now, it was just about three in the afternoon. We wondered how long the fire should burn before the beans would be put in.

"How be if we let that burn till six? We'll let it go for three hours. Then you put your beans in. Some let it go for six hours. By that time, it should be warmed up enough to cook 'em."

A few hours later, after visiting around the area with some old *Salt* friends, we returned to the Kennedy house to find Mrs. Kennedy pre-

255. This hole will serve as the "oven" in which to cook your beans.

paring the beans for baking. We asked her to share her recipe with us. She was more than pleased to do so.

"Well, I put them to soak for overnight. And then in the morning I parboil 'em. When the skin breaks, you put them in a pot. And then, I put a layer of salt pork, then a layer of beans, and then salt pork and then beans. I've got about a pound and a half of salt pork for two pounds of beans. Then I put a half cup of molasses. I put that and mix two teaspoons of salt, a teaspoon of dry mustard. Then I have an onion of medium size that I put in. I put that in whole, then I put water on my beans to cover them up.

"When we cook 'em in the oven, we don't put as much salt pork. Without as much, it's more apt to burn. Russell doesn't like pork mixed in with the beans. Some Irishmen, you know, and Frenchmen like the pork mixed in with their beans."

We went back outside for the next step. Russell was putting the coals around and over the pot, which he had placed in the hole. We asked him if he filled the spaces in all around the pot.

"All the way. Right over the top. I put pretty near a foot of dirt on

256. "Then I leave it down there for a good eight hours."

top. Can't let none of the heat out. Pack it all down tight. They cook right down in there. Then I leave it down there for a good eight hours. I'd be afraid they'd burn if I left 'em under any longer."

"Couldn't you leave it down there longer after the heat has lost its strength?" we asked.

"No, there's a hot spot. It's hot down there, and it takes a long time for it to cool off."

"Course, the big kettle would stand more time 'cause they got more in 'em, see. But the little kettle can't. You might burn 'em. When we go logging, we leave 'em in overnight, for twenty-four hours."

Russell was up bright and early the next day to take the beans out of the hole and on to the breakfast table. We ate our bean hole beans heartily, along with lots of other things Stella Kennedy prepared for us.

"Is this the first time you have ever had bean hole beans?" Russell asked. The truth was that we, and most of the Maine born staff members, had never even heard of them before. This basic staple of the river driving days was new to us.

257. Nellie Burgess. (*Photo by Bill O'Donnell*)

Women in the Camps

River running and logging in the Maine woods was a saga of strong men, but behind these men were some strong women who worked equally hard, and who loved living in the woods.

We talked with Nellie Burgess and Yvonne Kennedy who were cooks in logging camps for the same reason; they wanted to keep their families together. Each had husbands working for logging companies, and they went along as cooks for the camps. Their children lived in the woods with them.

Yvonne said she was twenty-six when she started cooking in camps. Her first year she didn't quite know what she was getting into.

"I started with about eight to cook for up to Bigelow Mountain. That was my first job. He [Austin Kennedy, her husband] and I went up there and I cooked that winter. I had my little girl, three years old, with me. We'd go in the fall in November, come out, oh, about the end of March.

"I got up at half past four and started breakfast for the men. A typical breakfast for them was beans, fried potatoes, bacon and eggs, doughnuts, and even pies they liked. Course, they worked hard so they needed a lot of food."

Nellie told us that they had a special book they used for cooking in the camps. "When you had to cook for so many you couldn't take a regular recipe and double or triple it. It wouldn't come out right. Like when I made a pan of biscuits for 'em I had to use eight cups of flour. Just for a small batch for breakfast. A lot of 'em would eat toast. Toasted bread around the stove. You had big old bread toasters, put it on the bread stove.

"Then we had a dish on the back of the stove with butter in it, and a little brush with butter on it and stack it on a big dish and put it on the table. Lots of 'em had biscuits and a lot of 'em had toast. And there was something else, too; for milk we had Carnation that came in cases, not cans, and we'd dilute that and have that on our cereal. Course, in the mornin' they'd have oatmeal. Oh they had all kinds of stuff for breakfast. They lived good."

"The men were all gone by half past six. They had breakfast and were gone. Each one would take his own lunch if they were too far to come back. Lunch pails, you know," Yvonne told us.

Both women cooked for between twenty and thirty men. In Nellie's camp she had two huge stoves. "We used to have a big cook camp, you know.

"Two stoves, two ranges back to back. One of them would be baking bread, the other would be baking pies or meat or something in 'em, you know. Probably make a dozen loaves of bread at a time and twelve dozen doughnuts and a dozen pies."

We figured that they must have had quite a shopping list, and Yvonne told us this, "I would order the bacon for a week because we had no Frigidaire, nothing but cellars.

"My husband dug vegetable cellars in the ground near the stream for the meat and vegetables, and he'd have another cellar right in the ground so we kept our fresh meat for a week. We'd have a lot of hams and bacon. If I had fresh pork I had to feed it for, you know, for the first part of the week so I'd keep my smoked meat for the end of the week. We had beans all the time, it was a good standby." She said she baked her beans every night. "Before I went to bed, I'd put a five-gallon pot on, a great big iron one. I'd fill it with beans every night. They'd bake all night long. I baked 'em at night 'cause I was busy during the day with breads and pies and stuff. So I had to plan to bake the beans at night. While we slept, the beans baked."

They got their supplies by horse and sleigh mostly. "My husband had a man that toted or carried the food from the horse and sleigh or whatever they had in the summer. We had tote roads, just tote roads. They'd send out the horse and sleigh for them. It was more or less like a sled."

We asked about all the other things that they did besides cooking, like carrying wood and washing.

Yvonne had a man called a cookie who used to help her. "When you have so many, I couldn't do it all, so he cleaned the camp, and then he'd do the dishes for me. Oh yes, I couldn't have done it all alone 'cause it took a lot of food."

Nellie said that her cookie was as busy as she was. "He'd bring in all the wood and water, keep the fire going.

"I remember long towards spring I sent to Montgomery Ward's for a wash machine. The one you had to crank it and it was all corrugated inside. Everybody fought to use that washer and I used to do my wash on Sunday morning.

258. Yvonne Kennedy. (*Photo by Kelly Emery*)

"I'd wash my clothes on Sunday. I had water in a big boiler on the wood stove and then I'd pour it in the washin' machine. Well everyone wanted to crank that machine. I had all kinds of help that morning."

Yvonne had it tougher. "I had to do all the washing with a scrubboard and big tub full of water. I would go down by the stream and fill the tub full of water, build a little fire, heat the water—that's what I call a rough life.

"The men did their own washing just like I did. With a tub and scrubboard."

When we asked her what she did in her spare time she replied, "I didn't have any! I used to wash, scrub—I had to keep my family clean and the camp. So when I wasn't cooking, I was cleaning. We stayed there over the week-ends most of the time. Stayed right there. That was my spare time."

Ted Quigley's granddaughter told us about her grandmother who was a cook in one of the camps. She said her grandmother's arms were like a man's. "She would have these great big bowls and big spoons with long arms so you can put the middle up against your arm for leverage and turn. She was a strong woman. She had to be."

We wondered if it was unusual for women to be cooks, and Ted Quigley told us, "They had a lot of women. A lot of the men and their wives worked together."

When we asked Yvonne the same question she said, "Yes, there weren't that many. Unless I was working with my husband, if it hadn't been for that, I would have never gone in the woods to work."

It was, Nellie remembers, "hard, but everyone was so good. In that camp I was the only woman, and they used to treat me like a princess. They'd go down river and bring me back candy and magazines and the children candy.

"There was one man who lived up there in Bar Mills. He was some kind of inspector. He used to walk in the main road. In the winter you couldn't get in and out of there unless you had a horse. Every time he came down he'd bring me magazines. Lots of 'em."

We asked Yvonne if everybody liked her cooking and she said, "Oh, most everybody. There's a lot of people that are picky, but that doesn't matter. Some liked the food, some didn't."

Of course out in the woods there were plenty of dangers, especially animals and most especially bears. Yvonne told us a good story about an experience she had with bears.

"We had these cellars, these meat cellars. If we had ham and bacon, you can smell this, and the bears love that stuff. One morning at four o'clock my husband was coming in and a bear was up at the cellar window tearing it down. He saved my bacon and ham then.

"We had little pigs in a pen, and that great big bear came into the pen and grabbed a little pig and walked away with it. Standing up on his hind legs he carried it away in his arms. And the little pig was crying like a baby.

"I was nervous; he scared me. So I had my husband put wires all around the windows because I was all alone. I didn't want the bears in there; they never bothered me again."

Nellie had a good bear story for us, too. "They had to leave one fellow in camp to watch it for the bears in spring. They were so plentiful. They came in and hit their paws in a barrel of molasses and got into it or sugar or anything.

"They said one little red-headed fellow was scared to death. He got on the top bunk and had his gun right there. The bear came in and helped himself. That man just sat on the top bunk and shivered."

Both women worked as hard as any man in those camps. Yvonne said of those years, "I just made it my life and I enjoyed it. Sometimes I think about it and really I've had a good life. I liked it and the children loved it."

The Lure of the Drive

Each year, with the first stirrings of spring, the men of northern Maine joined the drive to move the logs over the water, pulled by an almost elemental instinct. Why did they go, and once there, why did they stay, putting in long hours, straining muscles, and enduring black flies?

The reasons the men themselves most often give are the joy of working outdoors; freedom from many of the constraints of society ("Didn't have to worry about washin' your feet every night."); and the friendships formed on the drive ("The drive is like a big family. You all got to work together, you all got to travel together.").

"There were a lot of reasons for going on the drive," says Bob Viles, master driver. "The traditional part of it, the strong part of it, and the work is different. There's a lot of teamwork involved. It's a natural thing. All the men are skilled people.

"Many years ago you worked and the driving was fun. Back then we made a living. Drive in the spring, summer, and fall. Then we'd go back to the woods and stay all winter. Of course, everything was all seasoned back then."

"The river drive is a very good experience for anyone," Gerry Bigelow told us. "It's outdoors . . . fresh air. I keep referring to Indian Pond, but I've worked there for the last two years. You stay right there, you have three meals a day, and it's just beautiful up there."

Almost all agreed that they liked being outdoors and that they had a sense of freedom on the drive. After meeting these men, we don't think they would have stuck with the drive so long if there hadn't been some amount of freedom.

"I was my own boss all of the time," was the way Wild Bill McLaughlin put it. "Like if you wanted to work—like oh . . . oh say you wanted to work tonight. You just ask a couple of fellows if they wanted to work.

259. (*Photo by Anne Gorham*)

"If they said 'Sure,' just go tell the boss when you were goin' to work and he would say, 'Go ahead.' You work as late as you wanted to and then you come back."

Nobody was ever a complete boss over the drivers, we learned from Ted Quigley. "They come, borrowed me to bring the rear down that river for the Kennebec Log Driving Company, and they landed me up the river dam. They landed me in the evening and of course the next morning I had to take over and it was very difficult.

"We were sleeping in them darn old shacks, you know, along the river, and the blankets were all there for years. Mice have nests in 'em and have a good time. We'd go to bed and get all set, all content, and you'd feel them things moving. So anyway we kept coming to that time and it was very, very hard. We got pretty near into the fogs and I got quite the—I worked for a master driver then his name was Melvin Ross.

"I threw the cant dog on the boat and told him to take that and do what he wanted to do with it, that I was done. The very next afternoon the fella I worked for so long come up. He and the walking boss then, the superintendent, asked me, 'What the devil you doing here? You're supposed to be on the drive!'

"I says, 'I was, but I quit last night.' He says 'What's wrong?' I says, 'I've had enough of that.' 'Well,' he says, 'you showed your spirit anyway,' and he hired me right then, right that day."

The man who holds the record for quitting, however, is Bill McLaughlin. "I quit seven times in a week. I used t' take the blame, you know. If somethin' happened, I'd take the blame for the fellows. I'd say to hell with ya I'm gonna quit—so I quit.

"Anything [that] would happen—if someone would sink a boat, they'd say what happened, and I'd say I done it. I knew he [Bob Viles] couldn't bother me anyway. Let him fire me. I didn't care."

Then there were times you couldn't fire Wild Bill no matter how hard you tried. "My uncle fired me two times in one day. Fired me and he says, 'You're all done.' So I left and I said, 'Ah, the hell with him, he can't fire me.' So I went back, he said, 'What are you doing back here?' he said.

"So I worked for about an hour and he got mad at me again. He wanted everybody to work right in one bunch, you know, right around each other. And I didn't like that, I wanted to kinda stretch out and work, you know. Instead of stumbling over each other's feet and drivin' a pickeroon in your foot or somethin'.

"So he got mad, he said, 'You fellows either get together or quit or get fired . . .' He said, 'You're fired!' He got mad right off quick. And I got mad, too. I said, 'You old son of a whore, you can't fire me!' I kept right on workin'. I worked all that day until about, oh, about four

260. Bill working with pike pole. (*Photo by Joe Myerson*)

o'clock. And the fellows said, 'Well, you must be workin' for nothin', you're fired.' I said, 'I don't care what he says, he can't fire me anyways.'

"I was mad. And about four, four-thirty he said, 'Go get that truck and go pick up the men.' I said, 'O.K.' And away I went. Didn't have no driver's license or nothin'."

The bosses needed the men in their race to get the wood into the streams while the water was high. Ted Quigley told us how he handled matters one time when some of his crew became a bit wild. "I fired everybody. Next day, I had to hire most of them back."

Gerry Bigelow remembers an easy-going boss. "One boss we had, he was only twenty-one, twenty-two years old, and about three o'clock each day, 'O.K., everyone in the boat!' We'd get into the boat, go out to the middle of the lake . . . 'O.K., let's go swimmin'. It's just—that's a break for ya. Gettin' paid while you have fun. In not many jobs you do.' "

Choosing the right men to hire usually wasn't a hard decision. But one time Ted Quigley discovered he had made a mistake. "We'd been in, I don't know, a long ways from anywhere. Twenty-two miles from The Forks and twenty-two miles from another town. This guy came in one night and he had a long, thin coat. Of course, that's something to remember seeing in the woods.

"Well, anyway we kept him for two or three days and anyway I had to let him go because he wasn't desirable. I told the clerk, I says, 'My God, never hire a man with a long thin coat.' You know they kept that up for a long time. That was the clerk I had then.

"This fella came in with a long thin coat and when I came in that evening he said, 'There's another guy in there with a long thin coat who's looking for a job.' I says, 'Go tell him we don't want him.' I says, 'There's no luck with men with long thin coats.' "

There weren't many requirements to be a good river driver from the bosses except two, which Ted Quigley told us about. Good river drivers had to "get along with each other and do their work."

When compared with a factory job, Gerry says that "river driving is ten times better."

Ralph DeMusis, one of Gerry's fellow workers, agrees. "It was good to be outdoors and have a nice river to work on. Something to relax you if you were uptight or . . . I don't know. I just liked it."

"Well," says Gerry, "didn't have to worry about washin' your feet every night.

"Working conditions weren't really that bad," Gerry told us. "It all depended on the weather." Ralph added, "We even had fun in the rain if it wasn't too cold."

Then Gerry recalled, "Those rainy days . . . oh, you just sit there. Like if you're runnin' a winch boat, you just gotta set there and just idle in forcin' wood. You know, you're hooked into the raft. The boom logs itself just forcin' the wood toward the sluice gate and you're just settin' there, just idlin'—goin' forward, and it's just pourin'.

"And you're just standin' there. 'What am I doin' here?' You say, 'Well, I'd like to be inside havin' a nice cup of hot coffee now!' That's when everyone buys a big quart thermos and just sits there in the pourin' rain and drinks it!

"But myself, and I think I speak for quite a few, they really enjoyed the river. They didn't like being cooped up.

"The drive," Gerry Bigelow tells us, "is like a big family, you know what I mean? You all got to work together. You all got to travel together. Usually you have everything in common. Like, everyone around here likes to hunt and fish, drink beer, you know. It's all closely knit."

Learning to be a river driver took place in a family context, with an older driver training a greenhorn, as Austin Kennedy pointed out.

"Oh, you have to learn with some of the old fellows," he said. "Young fellow goes on the drive, who's never been on the drive before, the boss or some of the older drivers will kind of look out for him till he learns how.

"They don't put him out there tracking a jam in that white water or

261, 262. (*Photos by Joe Myerson*)

fooling around with dynamite right off quick. He has to learn, he has to be on there a few years. Somebody who's handled a boat and stuff like that, you know. You gradually learn, you pick it up."

The camps were a mixture of Canadians, Indians, and Americans, with a sprinkling of other nationalities. Bosses and men alike agreed that there were no nationality clashes, and that the camps were usually peaceful. As Bill McLaughlin explained, "It's like a family, they all get right together and tell everybody everything. Things you wouldn't imagine.

"You know every year you was all gonna meet and you was all gonna be there. You know about their wives. You know when they're gonna have a kid. You know when they ain't. You know if they ain't got no money or if they have got money. It's right in there. Everbody's business."

Work and play were closely related on the drive. Gerry Bigelow explained the situation. "Well, we was supposed to pick rear, high rear, down by Austin's Stream down there. We got there and no one wanted to go near the poison ivy, poison ivy everywhere. So we said the heck with it and we'll all chip in and go up and buy some hot dogs, loaf of bread, mustard, relish, and have a cookout.

"I think there were nine of us, chipped right up and got, I think, about five pounds of hot dogs, couple loaves of bread, and a jar of mustard and relish. Sat down and cooked hot dogs all day. Threw rocks in the river, you know, in the stream, goofing off. Turned around that night, waded across the stream, got in the van.

"He [the foreman] says, 'You pick that shore?'

" 'Oh yeah, picked her clean.' "

A rather unfair question was asked of Gerry Bigelow. He was asked if any specific men he worked with stuck out in his mind as being special or extremely interesting. His answer summed up what all the river drivers seemed to feel about the crews they worked with.

"Just about everyone that I worked with on the drive. They all stand right out to me."

Changes

Machines have severely altered the way the woods are harvested. Gerry Bigelow expressed his feelings about them. "Trees, cutting trees with a harvester, I didn't like it. You're only supposed to cut soft wood, but you've got to knock down all the hard wood and all these little trees and everything, and when you get done, it looks like a football field."

Jed Calder added, "Well, now that's the trouble with this goddamn machinery, far as in the woods goes. It destroys watersheds and it changes watersheds and there's a lot of erosion. And, like you say, in a lot of places, stuff won't grow. Oh, it's just washed right out. Everything is subordinated to the dollar. That's the whole point."

263. (*Photo by Joe Myerson*)

Austin Kennedy recalled the changes he has seen. "I seen a change from long logs to pulpwood. There weren't many pulpwood at all when I first started driving. All long logs. There isn't no more big timber. It's all small stuff.

"But they're still lumbering and getting a lot of wood. You notice it on the trucks. It's all small wood. Years ago they wouldn't take wood that small. They wouldn't consider taking it. The biggest, the best. Selective cut, ya know? They wouldn't think about going in there and cutting all that little stuff.

"They improved the bucksaws and came out with the power saw. They're still with the power saw now. But they have those big machines now, they're a tremendous big piece of equipment. I don't know if you've ever seen one or not, but they run 'em night and day. They take a tree, that equipment goes right up and limbs it out and tops it. Then it comes down and cuts it right off at the bottom and picks it up and lays it right on a pile, just like that."

The End of an Era

Men will no longer be seen pushing logs down the Kennebec or any other river in the state of Maine. Many men, such as Austin, Ted, Gerry, and Bill, made river driving their lives. During the fall and winter they worked as loggers, and during the spring and summer they worked as river drivers. They enjoyed the work. River driving was the foundation of their lives.

The drives are over, and the logs will now be moved by truck to the mills. The river drivers do not accept the reasons for ending river driving and had much to say about it. Bob Viles said, "If you have five rivers in the state of Maine, you should use them for transportation. That's pure common sense!"

"I don't think that you'll find many old-timers who think it polluted the waters," said Yvonne Kennedy. Austin Kennedy told us how he felt about the pollution issue. "I can't see that the water in the river is that much different now than it was fifty years ago. I could never see where the pulp would mess up the river any, or the logs. Because with the big runoff in the spring, the high water just washes that river, flushes it right out.

"Course, there wasn't any dams in them days. And there was no pollution in the river of pulpwood or logs. I didn't see no pollution. But since they built the dam, of course, that's different. They pulled that back, some of that wood, they had that there for a long time.

"Some of that wood sinks. I had been told that anyways. I saw a diver once on the lake, I was on the drive and he was out there diving. He was down in sixty-foot water and he said there was a lot of pulpwood on the bottom of the lake. But before they had the dams to make them lakes we never had no trouble with bark or pollution."

Austin continued. "They talk about pollution. What's going to happen here now, between here and that new plant when all those big trucks are there in the summertime going up them hills shifting gears and blowing smoke."

264. Towing 7,000 cords of wood on Indian Pond. That's 35 acres of wood according to Arthur Stedman, director of the Kennebec Log Driving Company. (*Photo by Black Star, courtesy of Kennebec Log Driving Company*)

Jed Calder had a strong overall view of the atmosphere in which the drive was ended. "The whole thing about the drive is it typifies the way this society has gone. And the way that it's going, it's dehumanizing, that's the whole thing. With machines taking over everything.

"Years ago, like in the woods and on the river, men worked in fairly small crews. They got to know each other and it was a pretty decent thing. But now it ain't no good. It's machines. Them old-timers will tell you that, too."

Nobody can listen to the river drivers and their wives without feeling that something important has passed from our way of life. We think again of what Austin Kennedy said:

"If somebody don't get after things like that, it's an art that will be lost forever. There will be no remaking of it. These things . . . should have been recorded."

265. (*Photo by Jason Wheeler*)

River Driving Ballad

By Jed Calder

(The "River Driving Ballad" was composed by Jed Calder during
the last year of the river drives in Maine in 1976. Copyright © 1976
by David "Jed" Calder, reprinted by permission of the author.)

My name is Jed Calder and I work on the River Drive.
My foreman's name is Buster and he also does reside
Near the banks of the Kennebec River in Skowhegan, Maine,
But when the rear gets in this year,
We'll never drive again.

We been driving this old river, boys, for a century and a half
Just to get that wood down to the mills, and it almost makes me laugh;
Some educated fools from out of state, they figured it should end
So the idiots down in Augusta say
That we can never drive again.

Well, the mighty Kennebec River, boys, is something to be seen,
From Moosehead Lake down to the sea, she's prettier than a dream
With islands and back channels, white water and dead;
Great eddies and great remedies
For a river driver's head.

We're hangin' the booms in the springtime, and we sluice in the
    summertime,
They're raftin' wood across the lake, 5,000 cord to a time,
But now the fall's a-comin' on, and it's time to take the rear—
Better head up to the cutoff
And get Joe McLaughlin's tail in gear.

Well, there's Buster and Gerry Bigelow, and the Sanipas boys and me,
Glenn Turner and my father, and Ralph and Bob and Bunny.
The Messer boys are hung over and they're prayin' for a headwind
So we can hitch her up at noontime
And they can start right in again.
Well, I will tell ye' something, boys, that's gotta be quite a crew,
Buster's been here 30 years and he knows just what to do.

From the Forks down to Caratunk, and over the Wyman Dam,
By the first week in September, we're headed for the Solon Dam.
And from Solon down through the Libby Country, and into North
    Anson,
That oxbow, she don't slow us up,
And we're into Madison.

Well, we take those three days there, always on the run,
And it's flyin' rear through Norridgewock, and down into Skowhegan.
Well, we spend a day at the Great Eddy and head for Shawmut
    Shores—
It's two weeks of hard pickin' there,
Then there'll only be one week more.

But by then it is November, and the water's gettin' mighty cold.
And we're slidin' on them ledges so, and there ain't no place to take
    hold.
Yeah, from Shawmut down to the Winslow mill ain't more than about
    three miles,
But the wood's jammed up on the ledges good
And it takes us quite a while.
For two straight days we don't move more than two hundred yards,
Just a-slippin' and a-slidin' and a-fallin' on our tails.

But finally we do get her in, and it feels a-mighty good,
So we have us a little party, then, just to forget all of that wood.
A little liquor, a little smokin', a little b.s.in' all around,
But everybody's thinkin' this
Is the last year we'll take her down.

My name is Jed Calder and I work on the River Drive
My foreman's name is Buster and he also does reside
Near the banks of the Kennebec River in Skowhegan, Maine.
But when the rear gets in this year
We'll never drive again.

"We Never Bought Anything We Could Make"

The title of this section was taken from a remark made by Monty Washburn as he showed us how to make sumac sap spiles. A man with a rich supply of stories about all the things he loves—the woods, fishing, hunting, and the old-timers from his childhood such as "old uncle Ell" —Monty has shown us how to do more things and make more things than any other person we've interviewed in *Salt*'s eight-year lifetime.

"When I was a kid, we used to make all our own sap spiles," said Monty. "I guess the store-boughten ones only cost a nickel at that time, but we never bought anything we could make."

All the articles in this section are collective proof of Monty's words, documenting as they do the making of products at home by people who have expected from early childhood to craft, improvise, or manufacture many of the goods of their daily lives.

The section begins with a chapter about a horse-power farm in southern Maine where the harrowing is done by tree branches dragged over the ground. It continues with the making of sumac spiles; cider making with longtime friend Reid Chapman; and buttermaking and molasses cookies with another old friend, Mary Turner.

Other articles included are a demonstration of paddle making and whistle making by Monty Washburn; a collection of old home remedies; and interviews with a score of Maine people who tell of the simple Christmases of their childhood when nobody expected "more than one store-boughten present," and the sleds and skates and doll's clothes were made by those who loved them.

266. Clifford Jackson at his Snug Harbor Farm in Kennebunk, Maine.

Settin' on His Independence

By Kim Lovejoy
Photography by Mark Emerson
Interviewing by Kim Lovejoy, Mark Emerson, J. York, and, on one afternoon, visiting students from Whitefield Junior High School in New Hampshire.

A lingering afternoon of Indian summer, with its clear blue sky and warming rays of sunlight, can let one drift backward in time. For a moment, thoughts turn to the days when the last of the earth's bounty was harvested for winter, and fields were spotted with golden haystacks. Scenes from those days come alive in today's time at Clifford and Belle Jackson's Snug Harbor Farm in lower Kennebunk. There the seasonal activities are carried on just as they were before the mechanization of farming. A tractor or a wobbly baler can't be found in their barn—only a sturdy horse, two generations of cattle, and plenty of hay.

We first met Clifford Jackson in the spring when he was readying the ground for planting. Most farmers pull a harrower behind a tractor to loosen the soil. Clifford was kneeling by four freshly cut birches and a beam.

"I'm just buildin' a thing to smooth the ground with, a brush," he explained quietly. The wooden beam had holes drilled in its side, each about the circumference of a young birch tree. Step by step, he wedged the four tree trunks tightly into these openings, and the stiff, bushy tree tops together formed a brush that his horse dragged along the ground.

One of the tools that Clifford used is an antique drawknife, a cutting tool with a handle at each end of the blade that is drawn toward the user. He held the drawknife with both hands and began whittling the tree trunks to fit in the holes of the beam.

The first one just squeezed into the opening. He raised a sledgehammer and banged the trunk to tighten it in the hole. For the second birch, he broke off a sliver of thin wood.

267. Clifford
uses a drawknife
to whittle the
trunk.

268. A corner of the brush is finished as Clifford pounds the trunk with the blunt side of an ax.

"I'll wedge it in there so it won't come out." He hammered the sliver into the ax-cut birch trunk until the white bark was wedged tightly against the beam's surface. The other two were pounded in with the sledgehammer. "They can't pull out," he said. To complete the construction, he sawed a few stray branches off the brush. The rest of the job is delegated to Molly, the horse, when she pulls the brush over the soil.

We asked Clifford what the brush does to the ground. "It makes it smooth where ya plant, see, fills all the holes." The branches sweep up the bunches of grass and disintegrate dirt clods that might smother little seeds. The wooden beam "holds it together so you can stand on it if you want to. If you've got a big bunch you want to pull into a hole, you can stand on it, and it'll dig in hard."

Clifford led Molly from her enclosure, hitched her up to the brush, and looked at us with a turn of his head. "Heh! I'd say this is the way our grandfather done it. People [today] don't do it that way."

269. Clifford tightens a birch trunk in its holder by pounding in a wedge.

270. Clifford slides another birch into position.

We wanted to know why he farms the old-fashioned way. He told us, "What farmin' I do is too small. If I went an' bought ten thousand dollars' worth of machinery, it'd be more than a farm would be worth. Heh! That's the trouble with a lot of these people, these men that had farms around here. They went and spent ten thousand dollars for tools, and then they didn't have farms big enough to pay for 'em.

"I don't think anybody that was tryin' to make any more money would try to do it the way I do it. We don't depend on it to live on. If we did, we'd go short."

Yet I sensed that there were deeper motives for Clifford Jackson's simple, independent way of farming. As time went on, I could feel his reverence for the old style of doing things. He speaks modestly and earns respect. On this day he talked about the Amish people of Pennsylvania, whom he had once visited.

"They do more farming there with four or five hosses than they do here with ten thousand dollars' worth o' big tractors. Hosses 'n' mules, that's all they use. They don't have no automobiles, they ride buggies, make their own harnesses, guns . . . I was just talkin' to a man who was out there a couple weeks ago. Said he went in a harness shop

271. Hitching up to Molly with "a gimcrack!"

where there was as much as a dozen of 'em, makin' harnesses, sewin' 'em all by hand. Just their way of life."

Molly was getting restless, so Clifford went back to business, attaching the chain to the horse's harness. He showed us the hitch, and with a twinkle in his eye that we didn't quite understand said, "That's a gimcrack. A gimcrack! I suppose you think it ain't no good, huh?" Then he saw the puzzled look on our faces and chuckled.

"Didn't you ever hear o' that? Well, these ole country musicians, they used to make up three or four different kinds o' amusements or things to play on, lug 'em on their back, an' they called 'em gimcrack."

"But," I asked, "what connection does it have with the thing you were hitching?"

272. "These was all farms here when I was a boy."

"Anything you make that doesn't really amount to anything, they call it a gimcrack. Anything's gonna fall to pieces, or is a failure, it's a gimcrack." We all understood and laughed. "A foolish thing is a gimcrack."

Clifford stepped up to stand on the beam of the brush and shook the reins, and Molly walked through a gate that opens to a portion of the twenty acres of field. Some of the soil that had been plowed in the fall was dry enough to go over with the brush. Potatoes would be planted in this plot, so he didn't need to be too particular about clumps. Clifford walked beside Molly and held the reins as she pulled the brush over the garden.

"This sweeps all that grass up on top so you can rake it off." Clumps of grass and dirt pebbled the trail of the brush. After Molly had passed back and forth over the field many times, he stopped to tell us about farms in lower Kennebunk when he was a youngster.

"Just a dirt road 'n' very few houses. These was all farms here when I was a boy. Big farms. Two big farms over on the corner when I was a boy—Littlefield's and Peabody's. Both sides of the roads was big farms . . . All of 'em bought all down to the beach and made lawns out of 'em, housin' developments."

"Why do you think people decided not to farm?"

"Well I don't know. I suppose they figured they'd make a livin' easier some other way. I suppose they've got to do what they like to do best.

"My grandfather's name was Jackson. He came from England to work in the shipyard, and he used to build wooden ships over here. He just done a little farmin' for himself. Everybody grows up in the country knows how to do it. I worked around on a farm when I was a boy." Clifford lived near the Mousam River, not far from the farmhouse where he lives now.

"Durin' the Depression I lived out in Ohio. It was much tougher than it was here, I'll tell ya that."

"Did you farm during the Depression?"

"No, I worked on the railroad out there. Hundreds of people livin' on the dumps of Cleveland durin' the Depression."

"What are some other things you remember about it?"

"I just remember that people had a job and was makin' money, they was better off than they ever was in their life. Anybody that had a job you could buy so much with your money. Lived two weeks on eighteen dollars for a grocery bill. Buy a suit o' clothes for eighteen dollars. If you was makin' sixty-seventy dollars a week, then you had hard work findin' some way to spend it.

"But them that didn't have nothin' was starvin' to death, in the land o' plenty. It was terrible out there around Cleveland, Detroit, all the big steel cities. They used to have them soup kettles. Sometimes they'd stand in line all afternoon before one o' them soup kettles, an' by the time they'd get up there, it'd be empty. All around Pittsburgh 'n' Cleveland they had them. Soup kettles.

"But now you have this Social Security 'n' relief 'n' everything. They didn't have none o' that stuff then."

The Jacksons returned to Maine in 1947 because Clifford's health wasn't faring well in Ohio. He worked in the Portsmouth Naval Shipyard for a long time, and produced what he could from the garden.

"I had a man who used to live here with me. He used t' farm, used t' keep a lot o' hens. He done everything by signs. They say you're supposed to plant corn when the oak leaves on the trees are as big as a squirrel's ears. He wouldn't do nothin' until it went by the signs."

Clifford Jackson's farming doesn't involve signs. It's an accumulation of years of experience that enables him to grow vegetables and strawberries successfully. His simple methods only require the assistance of two school-age neighbors, Peter and Mark DeTeso.

Planting begins about the same time every year, around the first of May. When the ground dries out enough, he plants peas and potatoes,

273. Like a shot of growth hormones, the sun captured in these mini-greenhouses gives plants a boost.

and soon after he plants corn, beets, beans, and cabbages. Not until the end of May, when "we ain't apt to have a frost here down near the ocean," are less hardy seeds like squash and cucumber planted.

The growing season in Maine is short, so Clifford does his best to give tomatoes a boost. In late May he told us, "It's cold, it's too cold for 'em. That time of year it's cold. Now the rest of May 'n' part o' the next you get that cold wind off o' the ocean every day."

He starts tomatoes from seed in cans of soil. When the plants are about to outgrow their coffee-can pots, he transfers them into the field. Years ago he made dozens of open wooden boxes. Clifford puts a small box around the plants and lets the heat of the sun bathe them. Just as the temperature drops daily, he covers each hot box with a sheet of glass, and the tomato plants inside stay cozy. This continues until the weather is warm. He never leaves the glass on when it's hot enough to burn them.

"I do it to some others. I can do it to anything, cucumbers 'n' melons, or anything." He says that it makes a few weeks' difference in their production.

Strawberries are a good cash crop in Maine. This year the Jacksons planted ten new rows of strawberries which will bear next year. Clifford and his young helpers picked the fruit from about the same number of old rows. They used to wholesale strawberries in Boston, but now "we have more customers than we have stuff."

Pests aren't a great problem. "We don't get so many bugs down around here as they do some places. There's some of 'em sometimes, y' know, makes a difference. Some years the aphids 'n' stuff on the strawberries are real bad. Sometimes we put codeine around the strawberries to keep the grubworms from gettin' 'em. Grubworms sometimes eat a few potatoes.

"I suppose these corn borers are about the worst pest there is. To spray for them, you have to do it at the right time, just before pickin' time when the silk's out. Sometimes people that've got a small garden just for the house take 'n' put mineral oil right on the silk of the corn and the ear worms won't do anything. But you couldn't do it with acres.

"The different kind o' ground it grows on makes a difference in the taste o' corn 'n' stuff. There's some kind o' soil corn grows on 'n' it's dry. And it don't have as good a taste to it as some that's growed on soil that has plenty of moisture. Lots o' people think it's a special kind o' corn that tastes good, but it's the kind o' soil it grows on that makes a lot o' difference about how it tastes.

"Any soil that has plenty o' lime in it, has plenty o' moisture in it, will grow good corn. To grow good crops you have to have plenty o' lime. You can tell whether it needs lime or not if they test it.

"They've had lime for a long time. But before they had chemical phosphate, they got the chemicals out o' seaweed to put on their land. I can remember when farmers were so anxious to get seaweed they'd come from way up to Alewive in the middle of the night, stay up all night, and come here to try to get seaweed before somebody got it ahead of 'em. That's the way they got their lime 'n' their potash, 'n' stuff you get in commercial phosphates now. They got it out o' seaweed. And then when they started gettin' commercial phosphate 'n' stuff, why it was cheaper for 'em to buy it than it was to wait for the tide to go out and try to get it before somebody got it ahead of 'em. But that's the way most of 'em around here got their chemicals to go in the ground."

The Jacksons have an endless supply of fertilizer from the animals they keep. Clifford enjoys having cattle and breeds some to raise or sell. On our first interview, two of the cows were pregnant. When we returned to the barn a few weeks later, he showed us two bright-eyed calves. With a pitchfork he tossed them some hay. The older ones got a share of grain. "They never feed the young ones grain till they get a year or so old." He shoveled the fresh manure through a sliding "trap door" into a pile in back of the barn. "I don't give them no grain, don't give no milk yet." They start giving milk when they're about two and a half years old, Clifford said.

"These beef cows don't give much milk anyways, just enough for the calves. Sometimes in the summertime I get enough for my coffee. Let the calves have the rest. They milk 'em."

Molly's stall is nearby. Clifford gives her plenty of water and grain. The harness that she wears when pulling heavy loads hangs from the wall. "This is the collar 'n' hames," Clifford told us. "They go together like a hoss 'n' buggy. They have all different sizes for different size hosses." Until recently the Jacksons had a fine pair of oxen that worked in the field. The farmer sold them because "I didn't use 'em any, they was gettin' so large."

There's a proud rooster named Jake who struts around the barnyard, crowing over his domain. Sometimes he fights his reflection in the bumper of the car. But the animal that Clifford calls a "feisty bugger" is a gander who stands guard over his mate. When she's sitting on eggs, sometimes eleven at a time, he flaps his wings and hisses menacingly at anyone who wanders too close. "They don't like to have ya steal their eggs," Clifford warned. "There's a window back there. He can see his reflection in it, an' I don't know whether he thinks it's her or not, but he'll go stand at that window for hours." Generally, he said, only half of the geese eggs will survive.

The Jacksons have raised turkeys, chickens, sheep, and even pigs at one time or another. People who purchase young pigs to fatten now find the cost high, about twenty-five dollars per pig. Clifford added, "I sold plenty of 'em for three dollars."

A workshop in the back is filled with fascinating old tools. Most of them were there when Clifford bought the farm. There are venerable objects like a grindstone that was once propelled by a foot pedal, an iron tool that was used by old-timers to graft apple trees, and two hay mowers. Outside in a shed is a "scoot sled," a platform on double runners used for hauling wood and other loads. Although he values these remnants of days gone by, age is the only thing we ever heard him complain about.

"When you get old, you ain't good for nothin', you know it? You can't see nothin', you can't hear nothin'; everything you got starts shrinkin' up. Your head, and your eyes, 'n' everything you got starts shrinkin' up, 'n' gettin' smaller."

Rarely does he speak of his age so fiercely. It's more evident that Clifford Jackson believes in the maxim "make hay while the sun shines." That's exactly what we watched him do on a beautiful September afternoon. He had hired a man to bale hay from the large field. For the smaller field, he hitched Molly to the old hay mower and cut it himself.

According to Clifford, the time to cut hay is "when the hay is ripe 'n' it starts to head out, before the seed starts droppin' off it." He plucked a head from some hay in the barn and scraped it upward against the grain with his jackknife, exposing the seeds. "It's the seeds in what they call the head, see? Hay is ready to cut when the seed will still hold on it. If you wait until it gets bigger, older, 'n' starts to dry up, the seed will all fall off of it. And there's a lot of grain value in the seed.

"Some kind o' hay goes to seed quicker than others. There's different kinds, orchard grass 'n' redtop. We just pick out when the weather's good. It has to be dry when it comes in. If the hay's put in wet or damp enough, 'n' green enough, it'll catch afire in the barn."

Enough hay is gathered from Snug Harbor Farm to feed the cattle nearly all winter.

The last cuttings were coming in on that Indian summer afternoon. One of the DeTeso boys stood in the front of the hay wagon and urged Molly to pull it near another haystack. Clifford has constructed the

wagon bed and sides to complete the function of four wooden wheels that he found. He and the other boy filled their pitchforks to heap it high.

Occasionally, some hay drifted away from the wagon, but they didn't mind pitching it up again. They worked silently and harmoniously. We stood at the top of the hill and watched the trio in the golden sunlight, bringing in the hay as the colorful leaves on the trees signaled a changing season.

Later, as we departed, a student from New Hampshire asked Clifford if he keeps himself busy in the winter by making maple sugar, as many New Englanders do.

"There ain't the right kind o' maples around here. These are swamp maples. The sap is no good. You have to have what they call rock maple or sugar maple. There isn't many around here unless there's some that somebody set out. I don't know why it is, but they don't seed themselves."

Since maple sugaring isn't his winter occupation, what does Clifford Jackson do to pass the months of dormancy?

"Oh, not much. Just set on my independence."

Sumac Sap Spiles

By Suellen Simpson
Photography by Sandy Frederick and Mark Serreze

"You want to go down and cut a piece of sumac? We'll make a sap spile. Everybody got their boots on?"

So began another interview with an old *Salt* favorite, Monty Washburn, who lives in Kittery Point, Maine. A man with all sorts of knowledge, stories, crafts, and humor to share (Monty has shown us how to make flintlock guns, and how to find fiddleheads and wild honeybees, *The Salt Book,* pp. 379–98), he had agreed to show us how to make a sap spile, used in the collecting of maple syrup. The spile funnels the sap from the maple tree when it is tapped.

The first step of the process is to find a staghorn sumac tree. Staghorn sumac is a shrub or small tree that grows on dry hillsides or around the foundations of old buildings. This type of sumac tree should not be confused with white sumac, or "poison sumac," which grows in swampy areas and has a sparse white blossom.

The staghorn sumac can be identified easily by the conical-shaped cluster of red seeds that appear at the top of the tree, usually in late July. These seeds serve many purposes. Honeybees use them for making honey; deer find them a good source of food; and people have discovered they make a refreshing drink when crushed and mixed with sugar and water.

Monty explained why this particular tree was used. "You know the reason that this makes good sap spiles? It's got such a large center of pith, and it's soft. You can push it right out, so the first thing to do is chop off a little piece here and take the center out of it. See, it's very soft wood. It's also real pretty inside.

"So, we'll cut a piece about three and a half, four inches long, something like that, and then even off each end, and with a piece of wire,

276. Monty Washburn cutting a branch of staghorn sumac to make a sap spile.

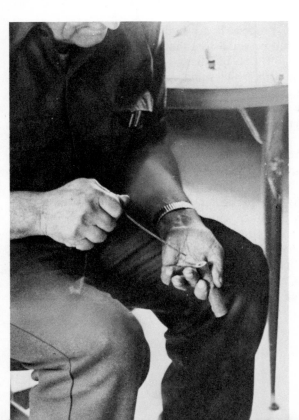

277. Pushing out the soft pith of the sumac.

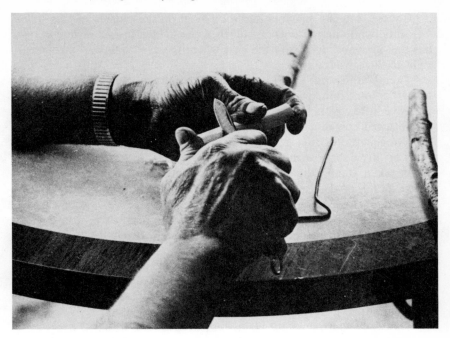

278. Removing the bark.

you push the center of it right out. See? You can push this stuff right out. Now we'll take the bark off."

The bark came off very easily. In fact, we compared removing the bark to peeling a banana.

"Then you have to put a little taper on one end of it. This is the end that goes in the hole in the tree. Now, this is something that isn't necessary, but I like to do it 'cause I think it looks a little better. I like to make a little spout so I can watch the sap run out.

"Now, that's your sap spile."

The next step in the process was to tap the tree.

"You just bore a hole in the tree and tap it [the spile] in with a hammer. This taper will seal the hole so you won't get any leakage around it here.

"And, of course, a lot of people will bore a hole clear into the center of the tree, and there's no need of it. You just get into the sapwood, and that's all you need. Probably in most average-sized trees, if you bored a hole an inch and a half deep, you'd get just as much sap as you would if you bored one six or eight inches deep because all the wood comes up on the outside of the sapwood.

"Course, you can see your sapwood right on the outside of this spile. The little white on the outside and then the golden inside. A maple tree has this sapwood, too. And the part where the sap comes up through is right in the outside layer.

"Then you just put a nail underneath and attach your bucket on that, and if it don't rain, you'll get some sap [undiluted sap]. A lot of people have little covers for those things, so the rain won't get into it."

We asked how much sap you could get from an average-sized tree.

"Oh, gee. You could get a lot of it. If it were a good year, probably forty or fifty quarts or more.

"It takes about forty gallons of sap usually to make a gallon of syrup. Some of the trees will produce a little more sugar than others, and it don't take quite as much. But syrup weighs, or is supposed to weigh, eleven pounds to a gallon. Some people make it a little thicker and it weighs twelve, but I think the accepted weight of a gallon of maple syrup is eleven pounds.

"I've made a couple sap spiles this year to keep in practice. I haven't tapped any trees in years, but when I was a kid, my mother and I used to tap some maples up in back of the house every year, and we used to make all our own sap spiles.

"We'd tap approximately eight, ten, or a dozen trees. There was a line of 'em by the stone wall in back of the house. I used to tease my mother in the spring, 'Hurry up and get those trees tapped!'

"Oh, we might boil down a gallon of syrup if we were lucky. I said that we didn't have to bother with a humidifier 'cause the house was always full of steam.

279. "You just bore a hole in the tree and tap it [the spile] in with a hammer."

280. Monty tapping a maple tree with the sap spile he has just made.

"I would guess we'd probably boil sap for a week to get a gallon of syrup. We'd boil it during the day. We had just plain kettles, and we'd set it on the back of the stove and start boiling it again in the morning. When it got half boiled down, and started to get sweet, I used to get into it—I just couldn't wait. And, of course, on cold nights what sap was in the buckets would freeze, except the sugar wouldn't freeze, and I used to like to drink that in the morning, too.

"An awful lot of families made syrup when I was growing up. Anyone that had maple trees almost always tapped their trees and made their own syrup.

"Right up in back of my house [his childhood home was in West Peru], well, up the stone wall a little ways from where we tapped the trees, was a big sap orchard, and they had a big saphouse up there. They used to tap trees and sell maple syrup.

"We used to slog around on our snowshoes sometimes to gather up the buckets and lug them by hand to the house. It wasn't any commercial operation. I don't know if it was worth it or not, but I guess it was. We used to put it up in quart jars. I said commercial maple syrup was about eleven pounds a gallon, but I guess ours was closer to fifteen, because ours was real thick.

"After you let the syrup set in those jars for six months, you'd take 'em up and there'd be great big crystals in the bottom of 'em. Just colorless sugar crystals. And hard? Oh, man! Talk about the big rock candy mountain! Those things were harder than flint. And you'd get in there with a knife and pry them things loose, and they were an all-day sucker. You had candy all day long!

"When I was a kid, we used to make all our own sap spiles. I guess the store-boughten ones only cost a nickel at that time, but we never bought anything we could make!"

Cider Making

Story by Ann Bath, Sharon Crisman, and Joe Iriana
Photography by Ann Bath and Sharon Crisman

"Everybody made cider back when I was a young fella. I made a lot of it, drank a lot of it, and gave a lot of it away." It was a crisp fall Sunday morning in southern Maine when Reid Chapman spoke these words, as he stood before the apple trees on his farm.

"Most of the farmers liked a glass. When the preacher would come around, anytime anyone came to visit, some farmer came over, he'd say, 'Hey, you got any good cider?' I'd go down cellar and draw a pitcher," grinned eighty-four-year-old Reid as he remembered the barrels of cider he had made.

"Cider was real cheap stuff, and it had a kick. You couldn't afford them days to pay all kinds of money for whiskey or gin. Couldn't get it here anyway, unless it was bootleg stuff."

281. Reid Chapman.

282. "We got this cider press from Sprockett and Shaw in Somersworth, New Hampshire."

283. The hopper.

About twelve of us from *Salt* had come to help Reid make cider. At an earlier visit we had discovered an old cider press tucked away in his barn. Reid had agreed that we could come back and pick some apples and get the old press going again.

When we got there, we found lots to do. Everyone was very busy picking apples and cleaning the dusty press. Finally, after several hours of preparation, we got under way making apple cider.

As we were looking over the old Hocking Valley Press, Reid began to talk about it.

"Got it from Sprockett and Shaw in Somersworth, New Hampshire. Oh, probably thirty years ago, but I'll tell ya . . . My brother and I bought it together and I forget what we paid for it, forty-seven, fifty dollars, or something like that, years ago.

"We got a little gasoline engine, a peppy little motor, about two-and-a-half horsepower. The engine came with a cement mixer that I still have out back. You'd hook up the press to the engine with belts; we'd have it set up somewhere and he'd make cider and sell it and I'd make some.

"When the motor's on she pulls, so you have to have her braced. The job is going to be startin' the motor and setting her up."

Later when we tried to get the motor going, it wouldn't start, so we rigged up a handle, and ran the press by hand.

Reid told us more about the press.

"Oh, that's the hopper."

This is the upper portion of the press into which the apples are fed before they are ground up. In the bottom portion of the hopper is the sluiceway. This is where the apples are ground up by a rotating drum. You can adjust the opening of the sluiceway by tightening or loosening the adjustable metal plate. How it's adjusted depends on what type of apples you have, whether they are hard or soft, large or small.

Directly below the sluiceway is the pummy cylinder, which collects the pummy. "Pummy's the ground-up apples," Reid explained. The pummy cylinder is an open-ended cylinder of wooden slats that sits upon a skid.

The skid sits in the cider trough, which rests upon the wooden frame. The pummy cylinder can slide to the forward section of the press where the pressing is done. A solid wooden disk fits into the open end of the cylinder. It is used for pressing the pummy. The disk is connected to a threaded shaft that, when tightened, forces it down into the pummy cylinder. This action compresses the pummy and forces the juices out. From an opening in the trough the juice runs out into a container.

We asked Reid what type of apple he uses to make cider.

284. The cider
cylinders and
skid.

285. The trough
and disk.

"Well, you can make cider out of any kind of apples—wild apples, even ungrafted apples, makes good cider. Oh, they'd pick up all the apples in the woods and make cider out of them."

Years ago, Reid said they didn't have to spray the trees.

"When I was a kid, the apples was all right, most of them. Now and then one wasn't. And you know what I doped out, what makes apples wormy . . . is so many cats. They catch all the birds. I ain't heard no- body else say it. But the woods is full of cats down here. Oh, big tomcats."

Reid says that Rhode Island Greenings, Northern Spies, and Bald- wins make the best cider. "I never heard of Rhode Island Greenings here in Maine. We used to have a lot of them in Connecticut. Damn good apple.

"McIntosh, oh, they don't make such good cider, although they're the highest priced apple there is."

The apples that we used to make cider were Ben Davis apples.

"It's an old Maine apple. It's one they used to ship to England years ago. Used to haul them way up country some thirty miles from there, I heard the old fellas say. They used to drive down with a load of apples in the wintertime. When the boat would come in, they'd been hauling apples on sleds down to go to England. Over at England they didn't know what a good apple was. And they were glad to get anything.

"They're a cheap apple, poor apple, but they keep a long time. Bugs don't like 'em. Them's Yankee apples."

Reid says he used to let his apples sit in the barn until they were soft. "If ya let the apples set till they're soft, ya'd get more juice.

286. "Old Yankee apples." (*Photo by Dale Berube*)

"You take these apples, they should've been picked a month ago. Ah, maybe two or three weeks ago, and then if you want to get all the juice out of them, you put 'em where it is warm, in the cow stable. It used to be warm.

"They'd be softened up and you'd get twice as much juice when they were softened up. Then I'd keep 'em there till November, oh, about the middle of November. Then I'd squeeze them out and have it for Thanksgiving trade, everybody'd buy a gallon or two.

"We made cider from the first of October until Thanksgiving. Too cold after that."

To clean the press Reid used to press a couple of gallons of cider. "Takes the taste of the wood away from a press that's been setting awhile.

"Let it set for a while, then run apples through, a gallon or two. Throw it away. Oh, you could use it for vinegar maybe."

Once you've picked your apples you are ready to begin. It's hard to say how many apples you will need. We picked about five bushels of apples just to be sure.

"A good bushel of old-fashioned apples, like Northern Spies, would make two gallons . . . twelve to fifteen bushels to a barrel of cider. Well, that's fifty gallons to a barrel."

287. First step is to feed the apples into the hopper. Then they are forced with a stick into the sluiceway.

The first step is to feed the apples into the hopper. They are then forced with a stick into the sluiceway where they are ground up into pummy. In order for this to happen, somebody has to be turning the crank constantly.

As the apples are ground up, the pummy collects in the pummy cylinder. You can throw in anything that you want with the apples since the apple pummy will hold it, according to Reid.

"I've ground up beets for color and beets got sugar in it . . . makes alcohol . . . makes it peppier.

"I used to throw in a couple handfuls of hay as I was making it." This stops the pummy from coming out the slats once you start pressing. This is especially true if your apples are soft.

When the cylinder is filled, slide it and the skid forward so that it rests underneath the pressing disk. Next, force the disk into the cylinder by tightening down on the threaded shaft. This compresses the pummy and forces the juice out the sides and bottom of the cylinder. The juice then collects in the trough and runs out of the hole into the crock or container. Reid suggested, "It should set, then be pressed again. The juice will keep running out of it.

"The best cider is the last of the pressing."

This procedure should be done a couple more times, then Reid

288. Turning the crank while apples are fed into the hopper.

289. The cylinder and skid rests under the pressing disk.

290. Next you force the disk into the cylinder by tightening the threaded shaft.

throws the pummy out. "It ain't good for nothing. It's sour, there ain't no fertilizer in it. I used to pile it down in back. There was some pheasants around here and they used to come and eat the seeds, then I'd shoot them."

The cider will be muddy after it is made, but it will clear.

"Let it set and it will clear in two days or so.

"You put the cider in barrels. [First] ya wash your barrels out, clean and soak 'em in sody [soda]. Then after, you put them in the pond and let them soak up. Well, that's so cracks, you know . . . [The wood will swell and fill the cracks.] Then so they don't leak."

Once the cider is pressed, the next step is to decide whether to have sweet cider or let it go hard. In either case, it has to be stored. Reid used to make large quantities and store the cider in fifty-gallon barrels in his cellar.

"Sweet cider don't stay long. It starts to work. It works and it ferments. To keep it sweet, you have to bung [cork] it up, put a plug in it. If you want hard cider, you keep the bung out of it.

"Them little bubbles, when it's working, that makes it taste so good."

We asked Reid how long you should let the cider work. He said, "About a month to six weeks. Well, a lot of people like cider that's been made two or three weeks, though. When it's bubbly, just started to work. Them little bubbles.

"Well, you can never tell. You have to watch it and keep the stopper loose on it, when it starts workin' 'cause it'll work up and foam over. If you keep it plugged up, she'll blow up and spoil your whole room.

"Once that cider starts workin' you have to keep the bung out of it or otherwise you'll be in for a surprise.

"Well, I'll tell ya, you're going to get in trouble if ya ain't careful. If you're going to keep the thing plugged up, the damn thing's going to blow up all over."

Reid recalled that when he used to sell cider, occasionally people left it in the front parlor and forgot about it. Then it started working and blew up all over the room.

"I knew of several women who blew it up and had to repaint their whole room."

Reid said it is difficult to tell when to bung it up the last time for storage. "Yah, you leave the bung out, then bung it up, when it's through working. Then it's pretty good for a while, but then it might start working again. You have to watch it all the time, especially if you put beets or sugar in the cider."

Reid was one of the first people around here to experiment with adding sugar or beets. Over the years he's built up some good advice.

"If you just want color, you just need three or four beets [to a barrel]. It makes a nice wine color. And they'll turn to sugar and make your cider speedier. But if you want more speed, put in a quart or two [to the barrel] of sugar.

"Sugar don't make it go hard, but it keeps it sweeter, it makes it worth more, so there's more alcohol in it."

We asked Reid how much sugar you should put in the cider.

"Well, it all depends on what you want. Oh, some of them used to put twenty-five pounds in a barrel. But you put ten or a dozen pounds in and you got something. I used to have a mustard cup with a handle on it. One glass of that cider was enough, all you could handle."

But sugar isn't always needed in much quantity to spice it up. "Sometimes with good apples, you don't have to put much sugar in to get a hell of a kick. It all depends on the apples. It was the apples.

"Oh, yes, we tried all kinds, and the barrel that had the most kick to it would be the one we put the sugar in. They were nice and foamy. When you'd draw it out, there'd be foam on it, and it'd taste just like ginger ale, but it was warm when you swallowed it.

"Some of the best cider had the most kick in it. We'd get an old molasses barrel and stand it up on end, bring your cider home and siphon it down cellar, let it run through a hose and then the molasses barrel would hold twenty gallons, and then you'd pour your cider into that. Oh, about four to five inches of old molasses would be in the bottom of it and that all goes into the cider, and oh, God, what powerful stuff you got! You don't want more than one glass of that.

"Oh, I've had all kinds of cider. I've put sugar, I've put corn . . . cracked corn. The more corn you put in the more speed you get."

Down in his cellar, Reid used to have some barrels of cider that had a kick to it and others that didn't have a kick to it.

We asked him how many barrels he had in his cellar at a time. Reid remembers that he usually had two to four barrels, and once he had as many as seven or eight barrels.

Reid wouldn't let much of his cider go to vinegar, but sometimes he let a ten-gallon keg go.

"Oh, sometimes a barrel would be kind of shallow cider, and I'd keep the bung open and let it go to vinegar. If you let it get all the air it wants, it'll turn to vinegar. If you keep it bunged up, put a little plug in it, it'll keep.

"Some of the farmers would have a warm cellar and let the acid heat up the alcohol.

"You see the acid in the apples, in the cider, will eat up the alcohol if it gets to the air and is warm, too warm. A cool cellar is a good place to make old-fashioned cider because the acid don't eat up the alcohol in the cider, and if you let it eat up the alcohol, it'll go to vinegar, that's apple vinegar.

"Cider's a damn good drink. We always kept a jug of cider during haying time. Christ, a good barrel! You lap up a gallon in a day by going easy, you know. When you're pitching hay up in that hot hay wagon, you're sweating your life out. That's the way we used to get it in. You put a load on and then come in and unload, pitch it off, or take a hay fork and take it off. I used to raise some good hay.

"I learned this from my grandfather and my mother. You take a jug out into the field and you pour out for each man. If it's good stuff, just one glass and pitching hay he works it off pretty quick. Then you give him another. You want him to feel good and work.

"My old grandfather was a shrewd old Yankee, and that's what he used to do.

"I didn't drink much cider when I was a kid, I never drank much of any. When I got up to Maine, well I was a young fella then, probably in my twenties. I used to go down with an old man, name was Jim Mead. He's an old lumberman, comes from Massachusetts. He bought a place down here and loves cider. Yah, he was a real cider hound! And I'd play cribbage, cards, with him at Saturday night. And he'd send his wife down to the cellar and draw a pitcher of cider. Well I was drinking cider and didn't know if it had much of a kick to it. Well I got up and went outdoors, and I couldn't walk in a straight line!

"I was coming up, and it was snowing, about a foot of snow then. And when I turned around and looked back, there's this crooked line of tracks! And I didn't realize I was getting hot. We were sitting there in a warm room, drinkin' cider and eatin' doughnuts and playin' cribbage.

"Oh, Jim was a fella that liked to get feelin' good, so he made it [cider]. One time he had a keg down cellar, he'd say, 'I'm going to dump it,' he was a wise old guy. And I had a fella workin' for me, and I brought him along. Jim says, 'Come down and help yourself, I'm going to dump it, it's getting sour!'

"So I draw half a glass and I was wise to him. Damn good cider, and he wanted us to drink a lot of it and get feelin' good, see. So I said to John Neadeau, he was workin' for me, I said, 'Be careful of that. Take a glass, but that's all you want.' Jim wanted us to drink more and get us feelin' good, see. Oh yes, cider.

"Oh I could tell you stories about cider. Given 'em two glasses and gettin' home and get hell from their wife.

"It didn't happen too much. I wouldn't do it. Two or three times and you get sick of it. Sometimes you'd get 'em hot, you'd have to help 'em in and they'd stagger around, they can't walk. One glass would be all they wanted. One big glass."

Before we left, Reid warned of something, and gave us a sure-fire remedy for it.

"If you ever get drunk on cider, you're sick for four or five days. The best thing to sober up after drinking cider is clam water and lemon juice."

291. "Oh, I've had all kinds of cider."

Buttermaking and Molasses Cookies

Story and photography by Kelly Emery
Interviewing by Wade Zahares, Abby Dubay, Jeff Bonney, and Kelly Emery

It is always worth the trip to West Peru to see what Mary Turner has been up to lately. The last time we had gone to her weathered, isolated farmhouse, knit into the side of a wooded hill, she told us everything from how she raises veal cattle to how she shot a moose one day (see *The Salt Book*, pp. 413–30). This time she showed us how to make butter.

The damp cold air and the last of autumn's clinging leaves were signs that winter would soon be upon us. Mary welcomed us warmly from the door of her woodshed, and soon we were basking by her wood stove and eating molasses cookies fresh from the oven.

If there's anything Mary enjoys, it's a kitchen full of friends eager to hear some of her stories, have a bite to eat, or sit around and chat. Just about anybody is welcome in Mary's house at just about any time. She's bound to be busy doing something that she is willing to share with you.

We had no idea what Mary was going to be up to when we arrived. It could have been anything from milking cows to digging potatoes.

"After you called last night, I got to thinkin'. I got to kill some of my chickens, but I got churnin' to do, too, so why not do that. That's better than killing, 'cause I got to thinkin'—they might think I'm damn cruel seeing me cut them ol' roosters' heads off, then throwin' 'em, and lettin' them flop.

"You see, I had the milk, 'cause I sold the veal cow and I had to milk my cow out. So I thought of churnin'. I said, 'There, by gosh, I could do this right in the house and it would be better than going outdoors.'

292. Mary
Turner making
butter.

"You don't see too many people makin' butter today. There's more money in veal cows.

"You only get a small amount of cream from a gallon of milk." Mary told us, "Sometimes I'll have a whole pail full of milk before I churn. Then I get those tall cooler cans and pour it in 'em and then I hang them down cellar. The cream comes to the top and I draw the milk out through a spickit [spigot] in the bottom. I can tell when my cream gets down there, 'cause I hold my finger in under the milk that's drawin' off. When the cream starts, your finger will be yellow. The yellow cream will come out on it.

"You got to be careful when you're keepin' your cream. You got to stir that cream every day and leave it in the ice chest. If you don't, the top will skim over and it don't taste so good, you know, it 'tain't so good. You stir it every day.

"Usually I have two jars full. I can set one jar in my ice chest and the other I have to put into pails or something 'cause I can't get two of them critters in there."

When we arrived, Mary had already washed out her churn and put in the cream. She'd been churning that crank for almost twenty minutes and it was already butter. Mary explained to us the process of preparing the churn and the butter press.

It was evident to us, by looking at Mary's old hardwood churn, that many pounds of butter had been made in it over the years. "I think it must'uv come over on Noah's Ark," Mary said, laughing.

"I was eight years old and my folks bought a farm over here, and this churn come with the farm. Let's see, I'm seventy-three and I've used it ever since. My mother used it. It has been used and used and used. I'm pretty sure this is hardwood. Softwood never would 'uv lasted."

As old as it is, Mary's churn is still turning out the best-tasting butter you could ever hope to have on your table. We know because Mary gave us a pound. "I don't sell it, I give it away," she said, with a smile. "The outside [of the churn] looks pretty grubby, but the inside is clean enough, so why worry about the outside.

"This old churn leaks like the devil, so I keep pans underneath here," Mary told us. "There's a plug on the side of the churn, and you can draw the buttermilk out that plug."

Mary told us that she keeps her churn out in the back hall when she's not using it. "I don't like to leave it out in the shed. It gets all covered with frost and like that, you know, it's cold!" We've got an idea that old churn spends as much time right in Mary's kitchen full of butter as it does in the hall.

"I can make up to fifteen pounds of butter in this churn," Mary tells us. "It's pretty full though.

"Oh, I've used it and used it. I'd like to see the pounds of butter I've made from that churn.

"When I first start in, I pour the hot water in my churn, boiling water, and I run the crank around, around, and around. That washes the churn out and fixes it so the butter won't stick to the churn. And I also take my butter stamp and I put that in and cover boiling hot water on that, and I let it set.

"So then, when I get ready, I take out the hot water and I put in cold water and I let that set. I slosh that all around, and then I run all that out. And then I put in my cream. The butter has already come now and I've drawed off the buttermilk.

"You can hear the sound and you know when she breaks and comes to butter.

"I draw the buttermilk off into a pail, and I use that to cook with. It's awful good. I make doughnuts and molasses cookies, biscuits, and what-have-you.

"Then I fix my hands. I take my hands and I wash them all good with soap and warm water; then I rinse 'em off in cold water. That's so the butter won't stick to your hands. You get that butter stickin' to your hands and you're in trouble. You got a mess.

"Sometimes I might have to put ice cubes in with my butter." The butter has got to be fairly cold or it will stick to the churn, your hands and the butter press. "It's too damn soft. I'm gonna get some ice cubes 'cause I want to make it harder than that."

After Mary put in the ice and the butter had cooled off a little more, she scooped the butter out, squeezed some of the moisture from it, and began to knead it and pat it firmly on the counter top.

"My grandchildren used to stand up around this counter, here. They'd come right up and I'd spat that butter and ya get a spatter from it, and how they'd holler!"

Mary has an old butter press that is used to form the butter into one-pound squares after it has been churned.

"The churn was my mother's, but this old stamp was bought from a lady down here [in West Peru], and she's been dead and gone for a long time. She was old, old, old."

When Mary presses the butter, it has to be pushed down into the press firmly and then leveled off on the top. When the sides of the press are removed and the bottom is taken off, she lays it on wet butter paper and wraps it up.

"I got my butter paper here. You got to wet it. If you don't, it ain't no good to ya."

The butter doesn't always come out of the butter press smoothly. "You see, that shouldn't do that. It sticks to the stamp and there's not a damn thing you can do about it. Son-of-a-gun. Don't that make me mad. It sticks terrible. The butter's not cold enough. Well, there it is. It don't look too pretty, but by gosh, it won't hurt the taste a damn bit."

Steps in Making Butter

1. Pour boiling water in the churn and run the crank around. "That washes the churn out and fixes it so the butter won't stick to it."
2. Drain out the hot water and put in cold water. "I slosh it all around, then I run that out."
3. Put in the cream (at room temperature), add about two handfuls of salt and churn for about 20 minutes. Mary put in a little better than a gallon and got just over four pounds of butter.
4. "You know when she breaks and comes to butter." When it does, draw off the buttermilk through the plug on the side of the churn.
5. Cool off the butter by pouring in cold water and churn a little more. If it still isn't cooled off enough for you to be able to work without it sticking to your hands, then add a tray of ice cubes and churn.
6. When butter is cold enough to work, drain off all liquids, and wring out the butter with your hands.

293. Pour the cream into the churn.

294. Mary and her granddaughter, Tracy Turner, take turns churning the butter for about twenty minutes.

295. Cool the butter and churn a little more.

Steps in Pressing Butter

1. Soak the butter press in cold water before using it so that the butter won't stick. Attach the sides.
2. Wet the butter paper. "You got to wet it. If you don't, it ain't no good to ya."
3. Take the butter out of the churn and knead the butter, pressing out all the air bubbles. Pat the butter firmly.
4. Pull off a little better than a pound (a little more than enough to fill the press).
5. Push it down firmly into the press. "That's got to be pressed right down in there or you ain't gonna get a pretty design. There's a print of a flower right there on the press."
6. Make it level by scraping off the top.
7. Take off the sides of the press and put the butter out onto the butter paper. The butter may stick to the press a little if it is still not firm enough. "You get that every once in a while, but," Mary reassures us, "it won't hurt the taste a damn bit."
8. Wrap up the butter in wet paper and store in the icebox.

296. Soak the butter press.

297. Wet butter paper.

298. Take off sides of the press and put butter out onto the butter paper.

Mary's Molasses Cookies

After the butter was made, Mary offered us molasses cookies freshly baked in her wood stove. The buttermilk she gets when churning was one of the cookie ingredients.

These are the directions for making the cookies:

Take some sugar, about a cup, and a cup of molasses.

A cup of buttermilk. "If you got any kind of milk that ain't sour, put in some vinegar and it will sour."

Then put about a cup of lard on the stove and let it melt.

Then put in flour, a quart,

A teaspoon of soda,

A teaspoon of salt,

Ginger, "I guess at that."

Then put in the lard and stir that all in.

"I spread them out a little with a knife when I put them in the pan. If you don't, they pop right up like a biscuit.

"I always put a little bit of sugar on each one."

We really can't say how many cookies that makes. "Well, I ain't exactly sure, but last night when I was done, my whole table was covered with 'em."

300. Monty Washburn.

Paddle Making

By Douglas Lamont, Steve Keating, Chris Adelhardt, and Chris Bates
Photography by Chris Adelhardt, Chris Bates, and Steve Keating

"When I start a paddle, I first look at the material I have selected and think . . . 'Somewhere, inside this piece of wood, is a paddle.'

"Then I start working.

"I saw, hew, chip, and sand away everything on that piece of wood that ain't a paddle, and finally I find one just where I knew it would be all the time. It was only waiting for someone to discover it!"

Monty Washburn of Kittery Point was showing us how to make canoe paddles the way he makes them. Monty's paddles are hand hewn and so lightweight that you can balance them on one finger.

As a woodsman and fisherman, Monty likes his gear lightweight. Not only paddles, but canoes as well. "I've had every kind of canoe, from wooden to aluminum, the whole works. This one's my favorite. I've had it for twenty years," he said, pointing to an aluminum canoe perched in the rafters of his shed.

"It's short, fifteen feet long, and only weighs fifty pounds. I can put it on my back and lug it anywhere in the woods and to the ponds. Hang it up on trees. Two people can fish in it quite comfortably. You can get up in it and walk around like you can in a boat."

If you plan on tackling a rough river such as the Alagash, which Monty has been down twice, you want a good hardwood paddle. Because he doesn't do much rough-water canoeing anymore, Monty uses light paddles made of spruce for fishing in small ponds and quiet rivers.

Once he finishes a spruce paddle, it weighs just about a pound and a half. "My old uncle used to make paddles years ago, and that's what got me interested in making paddles. My uncle made beautiful paddles."

Normally Monty makes his paddles in the wintertime inside his small, well-equipped workshop. Since it would have been hard to crowd all of us inside the six-foot by eight-foot shop, he made a paddle for us outdoors in good weather.

"Paddles like this will sell for close to twenty dollars," Monty told us. "Now you can buy cheap ones, and are they cheap! They look like something somebody hacked out of an inch board. But a good paddle will sell for around twenty dollars."

Monty has never sold any of his paddles. "I just don't want to get into business, that's all. Well, I gave away quite a few of them. I'd rather give them away. It ain't fun unless you can give things away."

The type of wood Monty uses to make his paddles is native Maine spruce. He told us that good Maine spruce is hard to come by. "Oh, I guess you could use any kind of spruce, but I like Maine spruce. It's hard to find nowadays.

"I look upon the selection of wood much the same as choosing a wife. I've only had one wife, and I'm still proud of my choice.

"First find a tree that is straight and free of blemishes. You'll know it when you find it because it seems to stand out from the other trees.

"After taking it home, store it where it will be warm and dry, so it won't warp. It has to be dry, and it should be a couple of years old in order to get it dry enough to work it in good shape and to make it light."

Monty arranged to have a friend cut the wood for him near his camp in Andover, Maine. Another friend milled it into stock one and one eighth inches thick, six feet long, and eight inches wide. He then aged it for four years before he started working the paddle.

Monty uses very few tools to make his paddles. The tools and materials he uses are listed below.

1. Spruce stock six feet long, eight inches wide, and one and one eighth inches thick, aged at least two years.
2. Marker to outline the pattern.
3. Saber or band saw to cut out the paddle.
4. Ax or hatchet to shape the blade and shaft of the paddle.
5. Draw shave or block plane for fine shaping.
6. Orbital sander and sandpaper.
7. Colorless plastic spray.
8. Ten hours of spare time.

As Monty told us, he studies the wood he has selected and lets the grain and shape of it determine where he will cut out the paddle. He tells himself, "Somewhere, inside this piece of wood, is a paddle."

After he decides where the paddle should be, he outlines it on the wood with a template. "I use a paddle already made for a pattern. I just put it on here and take a marking pen and draw it out.

301. Using the pattern, Monty traces the paddle.

"The best thing to cut the paddle out with is a bandsaw. But seeing I don't have one, I use a saber saw. It's slower, but I've got plenty of time."

Monty starts to cut the paddle in from the sides and goes down around the blade and then back up around the handle. Usually he makes this basic shape with one cut.

After the paddle is cut out, Monty draws a line down the center of the blade. He uses this as a guide when cutting so that the blade won't be lopsided or weighted unevenly.

He cuts most of the excess wood off with an ax, which leaves the basic shape of the paddle.

302. Cutting the paddle out with a saber saw.

303. Marking the paddle center.

This shaping with the ax is the key to making a good paddle. You're working with a pretty sharp tool and it's easy to cut too deeply into the wood. But, on the other hand, if you don't take enough wood off, you'll end up having to do too much sanding.

How do you know when you have the right shape? "By looking at it. When it looks good to me, I stop. I take about all I can off with an ax. Then later on, I use a draw shave."

Balance and lightness are what you should look for in your paddle, according to Monty. "Balance, lightness, well, that's about all, and, actually, thickness in here [the handle]. The blade should be thin.

304. "I take off all I can with an ax."

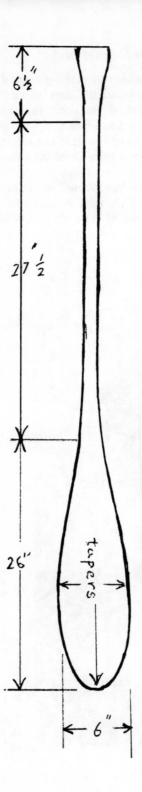

305. (*Diagram by Chris Adelhardt*)

6½"

27½"

26"

tapers

6"

"A lot of times you're still lifting your paddle out of the water and you make a paddle stroke and bring it back in the water. You paddle this way without bringing your paddle up out of the water.

"Also, it's much quieter if you're sneaking up on a moose," Monty said, grinning.

"So you want a good thin paddle and a good wide blade on it. You have to get it fairly thin through here [edge of the blade]. It has to taper from the middle out towards the edges." The tapering should move out from the center guideline toward the edges of the paddle (see Plate 305).

"It's pretty near a knife's edge, but it still has a lot of strength to it."

When Monty cuts out the paddle, the shaft is not round yet. To round the edges out, he starts with the ax. The shaft doesn't require as much shaping with the ax as the blade did because most of it can be done more easily with a block plane.

The balance point on the paddle is midway on the shaft, at about the spot where the left hand normally holds the shaft, Monty told us.

"Well, it's hard to say where the balance point is, but if you got a paddle with too heavy a blade on it, when you grab it, it's always sagging down and has too heavy a blade. So I would say just about where you grip it when you're paddling, which is normally about midway on the handle [shaft]."

306. Monty shaped the shaft of the paddle with a block plane.

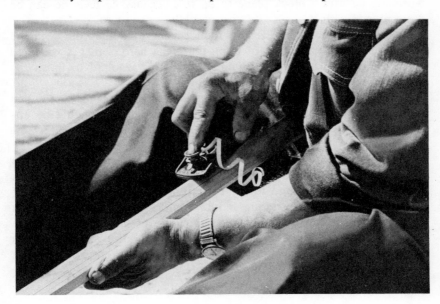

307. Sanding the blade with a sander.

After shaping the blade and shaft of the paddle, Monty uses the draw shave on the blade to smooth out any roughness before sanding. Normally he uses a block plane to do this because he feels he can be more precise with it.

The shaft of the paddle is also rounded and smoothed out with the block plane. The advantage of using the plane here is that it will help make the shaft straighter. After this, all that is required to finish the shaft section is hand sanding.

In sanding the blade, Monty first uses an orbital sander and then hand sands it with sandpaper. The blade, after sanding, should be approximately one half inch thick in the center where Monty drew his guideline.

From the base of the handle, the thickness gently slopes down from one inch thick to approximately five-eighths inch thick. It then widens and curves up and around to form the rounded handle. The width of the tip and the gentle tapering should conform to your hand so that your fingertips and palm rest in the depression of the handle.

After sanding, Monty usually engraves his paddles and then coats each one with a colorless plastic spray to keep them from waterlogging. He does this to all his paddles every winter.

308. "Giving 'em the plastic."

"This winter I'll get all my paddles out and sand 'em down and give 'em the plastic. Lots of times—here's something you shouldn't do and I still do it myself—you'll be paddling and find yoursef pushing off the bottom of the river or pond.

"This is bad for the paddle. What you should have is a spotting pole or setting pole that you'd use going up and down the stream. Sometimes I use the paddle instead. I still have a few bad habits."

Then Monty offered us some advice about paddling a canoe. "There are not very many people who know how to paddle a canoe from one side. Most people paddle on one side and when the boat starts to shift they paddle on the other side and so on."

To paddle on one side only, Monty told us you bring the paddle toward you and then, at the end of the stroke, you turn it and push out a little. The canoe has a tendency to veer to the right, and when you push out it brings the stern back to place, which straightens the canoe. "You do it mostly by feel, after you practice awhile."

Another piece of advice Monty offered was this: "I aways keep two paddles in the canoe, 'cause you never know when you're gonna be up a creek and need a paddle!"

Monty had a tale to tell about canoeing. "I remember the first time I ever went over in a canoe. It was about six or seven years ago. My wife and I were floating down the swift-flowing river down at the camp, fishing and just floating.

"All of a sudden the canoe got up on a little stub, so I stuck the paddle in the water and gave it a push one way, and I see her grab a branch and she gave a pull the other way and over we went.

"And I came up giving her hell. She said, 'It wasn't my fault.' And I said, 'It wasn't your fault, but you have violated all the prime navigation rules.' I says, 'The captain is supposed to let the women and children out first and go out last themselves, and I went out first and I'm the captain!'"

Later, as we looked at the tools Monty had collected in his small workshop, he picked up a bolo knife (shaped like a machete) and told us a story about it. This one involved his good friend Doc Taylor (Dr. Paul Taylor of Kittery).

"He gave me a squash, a big, hard, hard hubbard squash. The next day I took this bolo knife out and I laid the squash on the ground and I aimed to hit and went right into my leg, right to the bone.

"So my wife came to the door and said, 'You be careful you don't hurt yourself.' I said, 'Jesus, I already did.' I said, 'Don't get excited now. Get me a needle and thread.'

" 'What are you gonna do?' she asked.

" 'Sew that cut up.'

" 'No, you're not,' she said.

" 'Yes, I am, and if you don't get me a needle, I'll come get it and bleed all over your floor.'

" 'What color thread?' she asked.

" 'Plain white thread and a good big needle.'

"I had this little pair of pliers and I sat on the doorstep and I got my needle and thread and you don't realize how tough a person's hide is. It's just like old shoe leather.

"Finally I got four stitches in and tied it up and stopped the bleeding. Put some sulfur powder on it.

"Next Saturday, I went up to see Doc to shoot the breeze with him and I said, 'Goddamn squash, Doc.' He said, 'Why, wasn't it any good?'

" 'Yeah, it was good squash, but look at that cut.' He said, 'How did you do that? With an ax?'

"I said, 'Next thing to it. A big bolo knife.' I said, 'What do you think of that stitchin' job, Doc?'

"And Doc said, 'That's a pretty good job. Who did it for you?'

"I said, 'I did it myself.'

"Doc said, 'Guess you saved twenty dollars, didn't you!'

"Old Doc, he never could keep his mouth shut, though. The next year I went in the hospital for an operation and you know every nurse came in there said, 'Show us where you sewed your leg up.' Doc had spread the word.

"Oh, I've had my share in just about everything. I've pulled four or five teeth of my own. I just wanted to do it. I've always wanted to pull someone else's tooth, but no one would let me, so I had to pull my own."

309. Thilomena Sullivan.

Soapmaking

By Lorraine Kingsbury and Erin Campbell
Photography by Anne Gorham and Jeff Bonney

"You know, we're coming back to a time when we don't have so much and it's nice. I told my girls, the more things you're able to do for yourself, the better off you'll be later on."

One of the things Thilomena Sullivan knows how to do, and has been doing since she was a small child, is make soap. A tiny, vivacious woman whose beauty is undimmed by sixty-some-odd years of living, she emigrated to Boston as a young child.

"I was seven and a half years old. I was told that I would find gold on the streets, and I always thought that the little glitter things like you see in the linoleum here, the little glitter things [in the pavement], I thought that was gold or something.

"I was born in a mountainous place called Abruzzi in Italy. I haven't been back to Italy in thirty-nine years. I remember when I was young, we killed our own pigs and made hams and cheeses.

"Oh, I'll tell you about the cheeses! My mother would hang them up somewhere, and when I was kind of hungry, I climbed up and ate some of the cheeses. My mother thought a mouse had been there. I finally admitted I was the mouse.

"Instead of cows, we had goats. The goats would come to the front door and would be milked, and I would drink the milk and it was always nice and warm. When we had relatives go back and see the old country, they would bring us back cheeses as presents from our home town or from our goats. We like to grate the cheese and use it in our homemade spaghetti."

As she began making preparations for soapmaking in her home in York, Maine, Thilomena laughed as she remembered a family story about her soap. "My daughter and son-in-law went to the Appalachian country and they tented, and they left a piece of my homemade soap out.

310. While the grease is cooling, the lye is added to the ammonia and water to make a lye solution. It is then stirred constantly.

311. Skimming off the fat.

"A pig ate the piece of soap. I don't know what it did to the pig, but it was a riot. That must have been a hungry pig!

"The soap, it's terrific. I use it for my face, my hair, and I even grate it and use it in my wash. I would recommend making it outside because it does have a strong smell, and you wouldn't want that in your house.

"The first step in making soap is to collect the fat. I certainly wouldn't go out and buy fat. That you wouldn't do because it's too expensive.

"Now in the batch that we're making today, I have a little bit of oil.

312. Straining
the fat.

Being Italian, I buy oil in gallons, not in little bottles. When I render a
leg of lamb, I have lamb fat. Now bacon fat you could use for cooking,
like if I make gravies, which I don't usually do. But any other fat, you
save it. You take off the fat, and I keep it in the garage. I wouldn't
keep it in the house in the refrigerator.

"We're making a double batch, so we need six pounds of grease, and
the grease we've brought to a boil. That's important. Some people put a
raw potato in because that's supposed to be a clarifier or something. I
don't do it that way, though. I pass it through a strainer.

"After the grease is brought to a boil, it is frosted on the top. You
can just skim that off. It wouldn't harm the soap if you didn't skim it
off, though.

"Now that the fat is ready, it is set aside to cool while we make the
lye solution. You don't use an aluminum bucket to mix in. I'm using an
enamel one. You first add two and a half pints of cold water and you
add a thirteen-ounce can of lye.

"Now when you mix this, it is going to look like it's boiling. It has to
be mixed until it is completely dissolved, and you should keep stirring
constantly.

"I'm going to put the ammonia in and this is one cup of clear ammonia. It must be clear ammonia . . . otherwise it doesn't come out right.
Now I put in one cup of Borax and one cup of sugar and keep stirring

constantly. I remember when we didn't have that [Twenty Mule Team Borax], so we would use some kind of soap powder that we had.

"Our next step is to strain the grease. You place the strainer on the side of the pan and pour the grease slowly into it and let it drain.

"You can't make the soap without grease. Neither can you make the soap without lye.

"This soap, you could leave in water overnight [after it's made], and it doesn't end up as nothing. Some soaps you buy are so expensive, and when you leave it in water for even five minutes it's all gone.

"It looks like yellow soap when you're making it, but when it ages, it usually looks white. It all depends on the grease.

"Now keep stirring, and it should be getting thicker. The smell of the lye solution is very strong, but after a couple of weeks, you don't smell it anymore.

"After it has thickened and there are no more lumps, you let it set for a while, and we can go in for a cup of tea and come back and stir some more."

While we were around her kitchen table having tea, Thilomena told us more about her childhood. "We used to have a coal stove, and you know that smell of grease that was on the stove kinda smelled awful, but I remember Dad would have lemon peels or orange peels on the stove to take the smell off."

Then she outlined the final steps in soapmaking for us. "When it cools, you pour it into a mold of some kind. When it hardens, you cut it in the desired pieces. You could pour it in a box. In fact, I've seen people put it in bread boxes.

"After you've poured it, you leave it out all night. Now, if you want, you can add perfume. I have a little bit of Emeraud oil, so I'm going to make it perfumed. I think it's a waste of perfume myself, because the soap is so clean smelling. But you add your perfume before you pour the mixture into the molds.

"After I've poured the mixture into the molds, I don't bother to smooth it out.

"Now don't forget," Thilomena said as we began to depart, "the most important thing is you never dissolve the lye in a pot that is aluminum. It should be enamel. Also, you shouldn't make the soap outside if the temperature is below freezing," she said, glancing at a gray sky that threatened snow.

"Some of my friends have given me some fat, because you can't collect it all yourself," she said, her active hands spread out to include the world.

"So you get some friends together and you make a batch and you share the soap!"

315. "I've made dozens of these things. I can play tunes now. My mother showed me how to do it."

Whistle Making

By Mark DeTeso
Photography by Jay York and Mark DeTeso

In the middle of May we were with Monty Washburn at his camp in the mountains to gather fiddleheads—and a story for *Salt* about fiddleheads. As it turned out, Monty had more than one story for us.

Monty's camp sits far back from the main road and the main room and porch have a good view overlooking the mountains that stretch into the distance. When we came back to the camp after picking fiddleheads, Monty pulled out a jackknife and cut off a stick about eighteen inches long from a young tree.

We asked him what he was doing. "Makin' a whistle," he said. "I've made dozens of these things. My mother showed me how to do it. I can play tunes on 'em.

"I think maple makes the best ones. You can use anything you can peel the bark from . . . maple, alder, poplar. This is the best time of year to make 'em 'cause the sap is starting to rise.

"You can vary the tone with the depth of this cut here. The longer the cut, the deeper the tone."

Here are the steps Monty went through in making the whistle:

First, cut a stick eighteen inches to two feet long, give or take a few inches.

Next, notch it half an inch from the end.

Cut the bark all the way around about three inches from the same end. Tap the stick all the way around where the cut was made.

"Do this to the bark [tap it] so it'll come off. Not too hard or it will split the bark," said Monty. Then slip the bark off.

Make a cut at about the center of the section where the bark has been removed. "Just chip out a little piece right there," he said. The tone of the whistle can be changed by the depth and length of the cut that is whittled.

Then slip the bark back on and the whistle is ready.

316. Cut a stick 18″ to 2′ long. After notching it, make a cut and remove the bark.

317. Cut the bark all the way around about 3″ from the same end. Slip the bark on, and you've made your whistle.

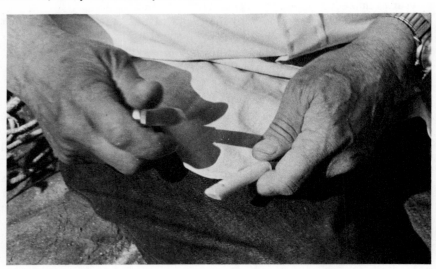

319. Looking in the woods for remedies, Eleanor Wormwood explains the use of fir.

Home Remedies

By Laurie Smith
Photography by Anne Gorham

Old home remedies played a big part in the lives of people in earlier years. Even when there were doctors in the community who were known as good healers, many people couldn't afford their services and relied on simple home remedies for most of their needs.

Some people still believe in these remedies and use them often. These are some remedies that were used in years past and are still used today, as told by Eleanor Wormwood, Christine Adams, and my father, Ralph Smith.

Eleanor Wormwood began telling about the remedies her mother and grandmother used when she was a child.

"Well, what I can think of first is when I was growin' up I had a lot of colds and my mother tried every remedy there was for a cold. The first thing she always did was take chicken fat, pour it in the oven and get all the fat out of it, so it was just like melted butter, and put it on my chest, front and back.

"Yep, she put it on your back and on your chest. Just rubbed us with that chicken fat. We were very susceptible to colds. I guess we always had croup, my sister and I, and she tried everything there was, and that's what I can remember most.

"She gave us loads of boiled onions to eat, which were supposed to be good for a cold, and stewed tomatoes, even for breakfast with toast in the mornin'.

"Another big remedy was a nutmeg. I think this was my grandmother's remedy. When it came fall, we had to have a nutmeg and tie it around our neck.

"Now I remember there was two ways we wore it. Both had to do with black. I don't remember the reason for it being black, but either they put a whole nutmeg in a little black bag and wore it around the

320. Picking rose hips for a cold.

neck or my grandfather used to drill a hole through the nutmeg. He'd
put a black cord through the hole and we'd wear it around our neck.

"Then I know she tried such things as heated vinegar and putting
salt and pepper in it and put that on our chest. Other times it was
kerosene on a woolen cloth worn around our neck. These are things I
can remember and, of course, there was other things that we was supposed to eat.

"We always went an' gathered wintergreen leaves, the checkerberry
leaves for tea for a stomachache. I remember havin' jars of those on
the shelves. They used to dry them and put 'em in apothecary jars and
my grandmother had 'em all lined up on the shelf.

"And then catnip tea. She used to give us a lot of that. I guess she
thought we should have something hot to drink all the time. Catnip tea
was just plain hot water—add milk and sugar in it and she called it
catnip tea. Course, there was no catnip in it. That's what she called it.

"Now sage tea was supposed to cure a lot of things . . . besides
colds it was good for stomach trouble and, goodness, I can't remember
all the things the older people believed sage tea was good for.

321. For mosquito bites, Eleanor takes the tips from a fir tree, pounds them, and makes "a horrible sticky, gooey mess."

"My father always raised his own sage. Besides using it for stuffing for Thanksgiving turkey, they used it for medicine as well. I think they put sage tea with some kind of grease, too. I think that used to break up congestion.

"And then, of course, there's red-clover tea. Course, that's supposed to be good for all kinds of stomach trouble and especially cancer. It used to be recommended that it would cure cancer but, course, it never did, but my sister always dries red-clover blossoms now.

"I asked her what we gathered Indian tobacco for. I can remember gathering Indian tobacco to use as some kind of herb, but I can't remember what for.

"Let me see, celery was always good for almost everything. Used to be good for nerves so they always wanted you to eat a lot of celery.

322. Eleanor picks wintergreen or checkerberry leaves used in making a tea for stomach trouble.

And of course the very simple one about a burnt finger, putting butter on it or wet the finger and putting baking soda on it. Both of 'em were not very good remedies 'cause they kept the heat in and made it burn worse. Cold water is much better, but I remember doin' both.

"That's what they believed in doin'. I think that was to take your attention away from the burn, and ya know you thought if you was doin' something, it was helping ya.

"They used spruce gum for a lot of things and pine pitch right off from a tree.

"One of my children kept getting bit by mosquitoes and poison 'em. I took the tips off from the fir tree—the three little sticky things on the end of the pine branch—and pound them all up and it makes a horrible sticky, gooey mess.

"It's just like pitch pine, and when you do it and make salve out of this it really works. That's an Indian remedy and that really works.

"We always had to gather rose hips. You know, those are the little rose buds that are seeds after the rose petals drop off. Dry those and make rose-hip tea. I guess there's some virtue in this 'cause it contains more Vitamin C than anything else.

"So they'd have that in the winter for colds, and thought it kept the cold away. I thought it was horrid-tasting stuff. It was kinda bitter.

"What I really use the very most is gold thread. It's a little plant that grows under fir trees or evergreens, and it has a kind of heart-shaped, clover-leafed, very glossy leaf. When it blossoms you have a little white flower.

"And you dig the plant growing there under the leaves and pine needles, and there's the root. It's very gold, certainly looks like sparkling gold, and you take that out and it's good right then and there for use.

"Or if you want to keep it for winter just dry it and save it. It's good for canker sores in the mouth or for people with sore mouths of any kind, or if you wear dentures if it hurts. I really believe in that, 'cause I use it.

"Well, that's all I can say."

We have extracted from Christine Adams, Ralph Smith, and Eleanor remedies for the illnesses that follow.

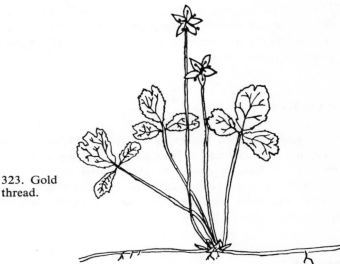

323. Gold thread.

Appendicitis

"When you thought you had appendicitis you would put kerosene on a cloth and put it over your side and this would draw the poison right out of the appendix."

Cuts in the Woods

"If you were cut in the woods, you'd take the pitch right off the white pine, put it in the cut, and tie a handkerchief or something around it."

Chapped Hands

"If you were a fisherman your hands got very chapped at sea, so they'd urinate on their hands so they wouldn't get chapped."

Mumps

"If you have mumps, tie a tarred rope next to your skin around your waist and allow it to stay there until you're sure they're gone. This was for a boy and the mumps wouldn't cross over the tarred rope."

Sore Feet from Shoes

"If you have a pair of shoes that are real leather, it gets pretty stiff. Take some salt pork from the pork barrel, cut off the fat and bind the rind around the sore place or blister as it happens on your feet. This will soften the leather, too."

White Teeth

"If you wanted to whiten your teeth they always claimed you went down under these bridges. They used to seal 'em with tar that was drippin'. It was hard of course by then, put it in your mouth and let it soften. Then you chew it till your teeth you figured was white. Of course, you never swallowed the tar, but there wasn't anything in it to hurt you."

Stomach Trouble and Cancer

"Red-clover tea was supposed to be good for stomach trouble and especially cancer, but if I recall it never cured cancer."

Boils and Sores

"Grated carrots were good for boils or sores. You put them on a sore which hadn't healed yet and it would cure it."

Removing Splinters

"Take a bottle, fill the bottle about three-fourths full of boiling water, rinse the finger and press it down into the bottle until the splinter is removed. If you can stand the pain, this will cure it."

Cankers

"For cankers or a sore mouth, gold thread can be used. This is a little plant that grows under fir trees and the leaves are clover leafed. You dig the root up and it's a sparkling gold and this can be used right then or you can store it."

Asthma

"They used to drink tea for asthma, plain tea. They drank it when they caught their breath after an attack. I don't know whether it cured the asthma or took your mind away, like some of these remedies did."

Bites

"For bee bites you could do one of two things. You could grate together carrots and raw potatoes, and put it on the bee sting, or put clay or mud on it. Some used the leaves from planter's plant which contained a liquid that helped the sting.

"For mosquito bites you'd take the three tips from the end of a fir bough. Then you pounded them all up and it made a sticky mess, which you used as a salve to cure the bites."

Uses of Strawberry and Sage Tea

"There were many uses for sage tea. It could cure many, many things. It was good for colds, stomach trouble, and then you'd mix it with some kind of grease to break up congestion.

"Strawberry tea was also good for stomach trouble. In the fall you'd gather the leaves, dry them, and then steam them to make your tea."

Diarrhea

"For this you would drink strawberry tea; this remedy was also good to increase your appetite.

"Another remedy for this was to take one teaspoonful of paragoric, one teaspoonful niter, a little sugar, and warm water. Drink it and this will cure it within an hour or less."

Headache

"Some people thought soaking your feet cured a headache. Others gathered plantain leaves and bound them around their heads with pieces of cloth."

324. Plantain.

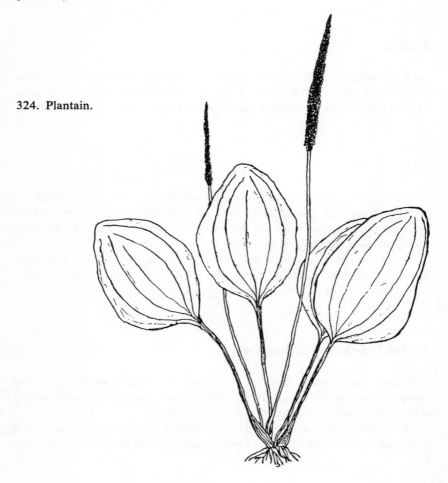

Whooping Cough

"For whooping cough they took a tea kettle full of hot water and put a wet towel over your head, and you'd breathe the vapor in. This would break up the phlegm in your throat so you could breathe. This really worked."

Toothaches

"Then they had a remedy for toothaches was to put a chaw of tobacco right on your tooth, don't chew it, just put it there and let it set. The codeine in the tobacco would fix a toothache.

"Another way was if you had a cavity, take a drop of iodine and in the cavity paint around the tooth with iodine. Leave your mouth open till it dries. This might kill the nerve in your mouth but it will cure it."

325. Indian tobacco or lobelia.

Earache

"This is a remedy for an earache. Find someone who smokes strong tobacco in a pipe, allow them to blow in your ear and it would go away in about ten minutes. Cigarettes don't work."

Warts

"You put cod liver oil on the wart for three nights, skip three nights and repeat it for nine times and the wart should go away."

Nerves

"For nerves you would eat a lot of celery."

Burns

"Of course the very simple one about a burnt finger was putting butter on it, or wetting the finger and putting baking soda on it. These two ways would keep the heat in, so the best was just plain cold water."

Hiccups

"For this you would cut an orange in half and eat the half of orange and if that didn't cure it you would squeeze one teaspoonful of onion juice out of an onion and that would cure them."

Charcoal Uses

"I remember charcoal used for many, many things. I know they mixed it with water and took it for gas and heartburn. They mixed it with a hot tea for bruises, and they mixed charcoal and olive oil for indigestion."

Liver and Kidney Trouble

"For liver and kidney trouble you would make strong sage tea and this was supposed to cure it."

Chills

"If you have chills on the bottom of your feet, rub kerosene into it and this will cure it."

Sore Eyes

"For sore eyes you would steam your eyes with black tea in hot water and this would make them feel better."

Gall Bladder

"To cure gall bladder trouble, you ate watercress and this was supposed to cure it."

326. Watercress.

Arthritis and Rheumatism

"If you had arthritis or rheumatism, you could wear a copper brace-let or put a copper penny in your shoe. This was supposed to make it go away."

Blood Pressure (high or low)

"If you have high blood pressure you should eat a lot of garlic, and if you have low blood pressure you should eat a lot of potatoes."

Dandruff or Losing Your Hair

"You would make tea out of the bark and leaves from a willow tree, then wash your hair with it. If you were losing your hair or had dandruff, this would cure it."

Colds

For colds there were many, many cures and these are just a few of the remedies that were used.

"You could soak your feet in hot water to cure a cold and draw it out of your chest, and you could take sage tea to cure pneumonia or a fever."

"Another way was to take the rose hips and make rose-hip tea that was said to have a lot of Vitamin C in it. This would cure a cold."

"For a cold we used to use skunk's grease, rubbing it on your chest up and around your neck and well under the ears. Then you took an old piece of flannel and tied it up around the neck and left it for three or four days."

"Then there was a chest protector you could buy out of Sears, and this would be tied around your neck next to your skin and this would cure it."

"Then you took ginger tea and drank a lot of this. Another way was to put mustard oil on a hot woolen blanket, put this on your chest and this would break up the phlegm in your throat."

"Another remedy for a cold was to cook chicken fat and put it on a piece of cloth on your chest and this would break up the congestion."

"What a lot of people used was honey and lemon to cure a cold."

327. Rose.

328. Mustard.

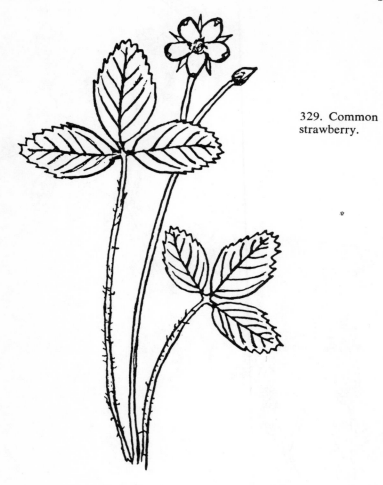

329. Common
strawberry.

"Take a nutmeg and there were two ways you could do this. First
you could wrap it in a black cloth and wear it around your neck. The
other way was to drill a hole through the nutmeg and put a black cord
through it and wear it around your neck, and this was supposed to cure
a cold."

Cure-all

"Stick your head in a bucket of sea water three times. Pull it out
twice. That'll cure everything."

Homemade Christmases

Interviews and transcriptions by Renee Sylvain, Douglas Lamont, Denise Merrill, Ann Bath, Kelly Emery, Bill O'Donnell, Andy Dimock, Sharon Crisman, Chip Zeiner, Joe Iriana, Nancy Lomax, Libby Caldwell, Beth Mann, Audrey Zahares, Wendy Gibson, Steve Keating, Abby Dubay, Dale Berube, Kathy Leach, Kevin Adams, and Chris Adelhardt

It came as a surprise to find that talk of Christmases of long ago failed to bring a rush and tumble of words, laughter, and excitement from those who remembered them. Instead, the responses were quiet and thoughtful, the words were slow and sparse.

None of us had expected it. The challenge of writing a story about old-time Christmases seemed an easy one, and it would be fun. Teams of students spread into our community and other Maine communities to ask a score of *Salt* friends about Christmases in the 1900s, 1910s, and 1920s.

Day after day for almost a month we sat in kitchens and living rooms listening to people who had shared their lives with us before; people who had showed us how to knit bait bags, make molasses cookies, and build boats; people who had told us tales about hunting and fishing, about lighthouse keeping and rum running.

At first their words left us disappointed, almost sad. "We didn't make much of Christmas years ago, not like now," many of them said, and a few even added, "Christmas was pretty much like every other day, in some ways."

Why had it been easier for them to tell us about bait bags and light-houses than about their childhood Christmases? The longer we sat, the harder we listened, the closer we came to understanding. We began to realize that the fault lay in us—the children of abundance. How could they reach us through the miles of tinsel, the elaborate twinkling lights and ornaments that festoon our trees, the piles of expensive gifts in

330. Pearl Street, Kennebunkport, in the early 1900s. (*Photo courtesy of Kennebunkport Historical Society*)

decorator paper, the parties, the frantic round of activities that characterize modern day Christmases?

And then we knew. The words they spoke were slow and sparse because they reflected times that were slow and sparse in the villages of Maine. Many homes did not have a Christmas tree. An orange in the stockings hung by the fireplace was a prize that came only at Christmastime. So was ribbon candy. Children got one or two presents handmade by their parents or relatives. Presents from stores were rare: "We never got more than one boughten present. We knew not to expect it."

There was not an abundance to recall from those Christmases of long ago. Instead, what was remembered was single and intense, a single gift or a single experience crystallized over the years like a tiny gem.

Sometimes the memory was a happy one, like the little red wheelbarrow Reid Chapman was given by his mother seventy-five years ago, or a China doll for each of the Furbish twins.

Sometimes the memory was of trying times, like a Christmas Eve in Cape Porpoise when the people prayed for the return of two fishermen lost at sea, or Ada Foss's sixth Christmas, when the little girl was called to the bedside of her gravely ill mother for a doll and a pair of shoes.

We have chosen to offer all these memories, the sad along with the glad ones. To sort the rough times from the good would do an injustice to the real people and real Christmases we have come to value in the course of our interviews.—PW

Reid Chapman has been farming in West Kennebunk for almost seventy years. He still chops his own wood and drives a forty-year-old tractor. It was Reid who helped us understand how a family could have a good Christmas without having a Christmas tree.

"We never had a Christmas tree. We were just ordinary poor people. We owned the place and us kids worked. We had a good father and mother and a lot of good neighbors.

"We had it [Christmas celebration] around one of the fireplaces . . . there's six fireplaces in that old house; it was an old, long house. We had feather beds that we could sink way down in them and they were very comfortable. I slept with my brother. Upstairs was cold . . . the bedrooms were all upstairs.

"And we'd have our presents in the morning. Sometimes we wouldn't get dressed; sometimes we had pajamas and sometimes we had nightshirts. The nightshirts would come way down to here," Reid said, touching his ankles. "You could roll up in 'em—keep ya warm.

"On Christmas morning we'd go down those old winding stairs and into the living room on the east side of the house. We'd all come down and our presents were out there by the fireplace. I got a little bucksaw and hacksaw one Christmas."

331. "We had a good father and mother and a lot of good neighbors," says Reid Chapman. (*Photo by Herbert C. Baum III*)

332. (*Sketch by Sharon Crisman*)

Reid spent his early childhood on a farm in Connecticut. "I was sickly. I had what they call consumption. The doctor said, 'If you don't get that boy out where there's pine trees, he'll die.'" So the family moved to Maine.

"I don't think we had any Christmas trees until we got to Maine, but we had them in the schoolhouse, Rocky Hill Schoolhouse. We used to have a time in the schoolhouse at Christmas.

"On the farm we didn't have a Christmas tree, but big stores like Brown Thompson had a big Christmas tree right up through the fourth story, right in the middle of the store. And they had it all decorated. One Christmas I went up in Brown Thompson's with my mother. Oh I wasn't too old. She'd always take us around to see all the goings on.

"I yanked on her dress," Reid grinned, as he showed us how he had tugged on his mother's skirt. "Women wore their dresses so they almost touched the ground. Big thick dresses in the wintertime. I can remember yanking on it.

"Way up on the Christmas tree was a little red wheelbarrow, and I says, 'I want that, Mama.' The wheelbarrow was way up top of the tree. It cost about seventy-five cents. And on Christmas day I got the wheelbarrow—it'd hold pret'near a bushel of wood.

"I just gave it to my grandson here about three or four years ago."

"The Christmas I can remember best is when I was six years old," Ada Foss told us. Ada, who is the daughter of a sea captain, was born on Beal's Island and later became the wife of a lighthouse keeper.

"That was when my mother was real sick. She planned Christmas for us three children. I was the oldest. I had two sisters. One was four years younger than me. The baby was nine months old.

"When I was six years old, that was my first tree, and I remember her being so sick. She called, 'cause we used to have a little bell and she rang the bell. My grandmother sent me in and I said, 'What you want?' My mother said, 'Merry Christmas, dear.'

"And I remember getting up on the bed. She had a pair of shoes and a doll for me, and I can remember that being my first doll. It was all dressed up, and it had a pretty little bonnet. I'll never forget that. She

333. Ada Foss of Cape Porpoise.

got a lady to bring it to her. It cost a dollar in those days. Today I suppose that doll would cost twenty-five dollars.

"And she tried on the shoes to see if they would fit, felt my toes to see if they were too tight. She said, 'If they are, your father will have to go and exchange them, 'cause you can't have tight shoes.'

"And then that next June she passed away. My grandmother said to us children, 'Well, we're going to try to have Christmas anyhow.' And my father got a little tree, and we'd trim it with popcorn and cookies. My grandmother would cut the cookies out herself in different designs.

"I can remember our grandmother talking to us and telling us that Christ had been borned. Oh, she had a way of telling it like a Christmas story. And it was good. We always remembered it. She was so good anyway, our grandmother. Whatever she done we thought was marvelous."

During the twenty-seven years Ada lived on lighthouses, she and her husband had to bring Christmas trees by boat from the mainland. "And there used to be quite an old man. He was fussy and he'd go in the woods, and he would get our Christmas tree for us. If it didn't suit him, he'd put it to one side and go back and get another one. We had apples and popcorn and cranberries and that was what we trimmed our tree with. Oh yes, and the children used to gather shells and used them for decorations.

"One time I said to my husband, 'I don't know what we're going to do for the children this year.' We didn't have too much money! His salary was very small, but he made each of the girls a cradle and I made all of the beddin', and we sent to Charles Williams' Stores from the catalogue and got them each a doll. And I dressed them and we put them away, and they didn't know anything about it at all.

"And the two boys, he made them each a sled . . . and they were so thrilled with their sleds. They weren't boughten, but they said they thought more of them because their daddy made them. And then he always made them snow shovels and the things we knew they would have to have, but it wasn't spending too much money. So that's the way we got along when it comes to Christmas."

Ada told us that the long winter months on lighthouses brought only one outside visitor. He was the flying Santa Claus, who flew over during the Christmas season, dropping gifts. "It was Snow [Edward Rowe Snow]," she said.

"We used to watch for that. We wouldn't miss that for the world. He'd fly over and drop the package. There would be something in it for all of the children and for Justin and I. We could hear him coming and we'd always rush out and be there. And of course we'd all wave to him and he'd wave back."

In Maine homes where there was very little at Christmastime, the children often got their images of Christmas from the tree and celebration in the schoolhouse or church.

This is how it was for Mary Turner. Mary grew up on an isolated farm outside West Peru. In her seventies now, she is quite a hunter and has told us some strong and funny tales about killing a moose (illegally) and hiding the meat from game wardens who came to search her place. She has told us that times were hard when she was young, but we didn't realize quite how hard until we asked her about Christmas.

"At home we didn't have very much," she told us. "We had enough to eat and enough cloth to wear, but as for money for Christmas, well, weren't much.

" 'Tain't like the Christmases now. We very seldom got any toys or anything like that. It was damn lucky to get enough to eat, say nothin' about spendin' money for Christmas. We'd have our stockin'. and we'd get an apple maybe, or something like that. We didn't ever get much. We'd hang a stocking back on the stove.

"We always lived back here out on the farm, and we'd go to the village and see those lights and just about like to go crazy. Yeah, I remember. But we had a Christmas tree in the school, and we had one evening that there'd be the Christmas tree and the kids would sing songs and things like that."

Mary sent us down the road to talk about Christmas with her seventy-four-year-old friend, Roger Farnum, and his wife of Bryant Pond. Roger remembered Christmases celebrated in the schoolhouse.

"We went to school in a little country schoolhouse, and the school teacher taught somewhere from thirty to thirty-four kids right in one room. We used to have Christmas trees, you know, and we had these entertainments. All the kids would have a program; we'd have to learn Christmas songs and dialogues.

"And people who didn't have a Christmas tree, they'd come from miles around to the schoolhouse right in the wintertime. They'd come in teams and keep the horses in my father's barn, and then go up to the schoolhouse. My father ran a little country store.

"We never had the toys back in them days that the kids do now, but we was tickled to death if we got a sled to slide on, you know, a factory-made sled. Most generally we'd get a sled that our folks had made for us and it had runners on it.

"And we'd get on some hill and we'd tread the snow down, the older people would, sometimes tread it down with snowshoes, pack it down hard, and after a while we'd get it down so we could slide on it. There'd come a time when there'd be a crust—there'd be a rain, you know. Then we could slide on a crust and that's what we had to play with back in them days.

"We'd be tickled to death to get somethin' like that. Of course, we had a great big bag of popcorn and a couple pieces of candy—ribbon candy. The kids would get it, and they thought they had a prize back in them days."

Christmases in the small fishing village of Cape Porpoise were community affairs fifty years ago, according to two of the women who remember them vividly. Wendy Gibson, a *Salt* student, talked about Christmas with both her great-grandmother, ninety-two-year-old Alberta Redmond, and her grandmother, Beryl Bilderback.

"The school children had their own Christmas concert and it was a big thing . . . the Cape children always had their concerts down here at the Fire Hall. It was always held in the evening. Everybody in the Cape went. It was just full of people. It was the big time at Christmas at that time.

"We'd start right after Thanksgiving getting ready for the Christmas concert. Every day, you know, we'd have our recitations and our songs, and we had a music teacher came in once a week. One year it would be a concert, like a musical program, and another year it would be all recitations. The little tots were always awfully cute. They'd get up there and they'd be frightened. They'd say a few words and then they'd run.

"Everybody in the Cape went when they had a community tree here at the Fire Hall. They all exchanged gifts and some were funny and some weren't. It was really a strong community feeling and everybody was close then.

"Of course Christmases then weren't like they are today because people didn't have the money, for one thing. The type of gifts you got were a nice book or a box of candy. I can remember getting a scarf. Oh, that was gorgeous, a beautiful scarf!"

The Cape people had their own special way of earning money for Christmas presents, Beryl remembers. "The Mill Pond used to be cut for ice, you know. And this was where most of the local men made their Christmas money. They always looked forward to the icing—to the Mill Pond freezing over. J. Frank Seavey had a big ice house up there on the left-hand side going towards Goose Rocks.

"And the boys in school would get dismissed from school so they could go up and help if they were related to the family or if they were the age where they could work on the ice. And this was the big thing then. Fishing was not as lucrative as it is today.

"This was their Christmas money and also their tax money. Taxes always came due at the most miserable time of the year—at Christmastime.

334. W. J. C. Millken Ice Company in 1911. Ice was a source of Christmas money.

"And if they had a good freeze-up and they could ice at that time, then everybody had a nice Christmas. If not, it was pretty meager."

The women in the Cape earned their Christmas money during the summer. "At the pier they had lunches and shore dinners. In fact, I got a menu where they had a lobster sandwich for fifteen cents. They sold homemade pies and cakes and cookies, and of course the women would save their money to spend at Christmas, or they'd buy their Christmas presents in the summer. This was how the Christmas at the Cape was about fifty years ago.

"Many of the families were related in the Cape. There were a great many Cluffs and Huffs around here, and many, many Nunans. And so they all had sorts of family jokes and things, which they had on the tree [at the Fire Hall]. That made it nice, a really fun time for the whole community.

"I think all of the old grieves that they had, if they had any, were forgotten at that time."

Santa Claus was very much a part of Christmases years ago, although he was more often heard than seen. He most certainly did not stand around in toy stores, and when he made visits to children in the flesh, he was usually a kindly relative.

The Furbish twins told us how they heard Santa's sleigh bells at Christmastime. In Kennebunk, the tiny ninety-year-old ladies welcomed us into the home where they were born, laughing about their height. "We didn't have time to grow any more," joked Ethel, glancing at Edie. "We had too many other things to do." And other things they did do. Ethel worked in the local shoe factory until she was well into her eighties and Edie cleaned houses "for everybody up and down Summer Street."

"We did hear Santy Claus come," said Ethel. "We heard the sleigh bells ring. We slept upstairs. We weren't supposed to look because he wouldn't come if we saw him, you know. It was my Uncle Harris, and he came in the sleigh and we heard the bells.

"They couldn't make us believe there wasn't a Santy Claus because we heard him! We heard his footsteps and everything. We had a little Christmas tree in that corner there, and when we come down in the morning we had each a doll. We thought that was wonderful.

"We had a little pug dog. And I made a cart so he could haul our doll. He would go just as good as could be. One day when he was harnessed up, Mother happened to get out her bicycle and go down the street. He followed after her and the doll fell out and got a cracked head. We had that doll for a long time, with a crack in the side of her head."

Children wrote letters to Santa Claus in those days, but the letters weren't taken to the post office. Eleanor Berdeen told us, "When I was little, we used to put our letters in the kitchen stove and they were supposed to go up in smoke. When we had oil burners, we used to put the letter down the furnace."

When she was a little girl, Eleanor Eldridge used to ring a bell on Christmas Eve to let Santa Claus know where she was. She told her grandson, Chip Zeiner, who is a *Salt* student, "They used to have me go to the back door and ring a bell to let Santa Claus know where I was.

"My parents would tell me when it was time to ring the bell just like their parents used to tell them when they were children. It was a family tradition, ringing the bell."

Ken Berdeen remembers an uncle who played the part of Santa Claus when he was a boy in Stonington. "My aunt's husband, Paul Small, used to like Christmas. He was a man you would think would never like kids, never fuss over them, but he did.

"He would come over on Christmas day and say, 'I saw Santa Claus! He's going to be over to my house, and I want you to be over there.

335. Ken
Berdeen. (*Photo
by Gerald
Dickson*)

You may not see him, but I want you over there. You look on the
roof.'

"And he had great big popcorn balls all made up. And he would get
on the back side of the house and he'd throw them over the chimney.
He would holler, 'Ho, ho, ho!' and us kids out there were excited
catching those corn balls!"

The Santa Claus that visited children on Swan's Island where Kay
Baum grew up "was sort of a hermit. He lived all by himself in a little
house that was on the edge of the woods. He was a poor man. I don't
know how he lived. Bread and jams and stuff people gave him, I guess.

"He would start out from his house ringing his bells all the way up
to the house and he'd come in your house and say, 'Yo, ho, ho!' and
ring his bells. We seen him. We'd actually get down where we could
see him going out through the door. Then he rang all the way going
out. It was fun, and it was so real.

"Probably the maddest I ever was in my life was when a kid about a year older than me told me there was no Santa Claus. At that time . . . I can't remember if I was twelve or thirteen . . . Osca, my sister, was with me. We was in the woods after a tree. We took him and put him in the snow 'cause we thought he was lying to us. We rubbed his face in the snow. I think the both of us jumped on him.

"You ask me about disappointments, that was the biggest disappointment I ever had. Find out there was no Santa Claus!"

Ice skating and sledding always were part of the memories of Christmases long ago. "The night before Christmas, we'd go sledding," said Roger Farnum. "They had what they call double runners in them days and it would be two sleds, one in front and one in back, and they'd have a long board [in between], hardwood most generally, and sometimes it would be a plank. We'd get on the hills and six of us would get on to that and slide down. We'd haul it back up. If there was too many, some would stay up and take turns."

In Cape Porpoise, Beryl Bilderback remembered, "We always went skating Christmas day. That was the big thing. You had skates, whether they fit you or not," she said, laughing. "And they didn't always fit. They weren't nice skates like you'd have today. We were lucky if our shoes fit, let alone the skates, but it was fun and we had good times.

"We always skated on the Mill Pond, and that was beautiful skating, way up by the Hutchins school and back. Everybody skated. The older people skated a lot then. You didn't have all these other things; you didn't have TV, movies.

"Somebody always used to fall in, to make it more exciting—if they got near the stream, you know. We always had big bonfires. Some of us would take marshmallows or hamburger or whatever, and it was a big thing for us."

One of the *Salt* students remembers his grandfather taking him for a sleigh ride at Christmastime when he was a small boy. "My grandfather would wrap us up in a buffalo blanket in the back of the sleigh," Kevin Adams told us.

"The horses had their wool coats, thick woolly fur. They wore a fancy harness with bells that jingled. We'd go up the field and through the woods on a trail. We saw winter white rabbits and pheasants that scampered or flew away as the sleigh passed by.

"My grandfather had a jolly voice, and looking back to us in the sleigh, he'd give a smile and start singing a carol, and we'd all join in. We circled through the woods and back to the house. As we neared the kitchen, we smelled my grandmother's cooking. Then we became aware

336. School bus disappearing out of sight at Dock Square, Kennebunkport. (*Photo courtesy of Kennebunkport Historical Society*)

that we were cold and wanted to go in to the warm fireplace. Soon we were all drinking hot chocolate by the fire."

Christmas was a day of good food long ago, as it is now, but rarely was turkey the main dish on the Christmas table. More often chicken or roast pork was served, and the women cooked for days in preparation.

"I'd cook all week for those big feasts because the family all come together. We'd start off in courses. We had soup or fish and then your main course. We had homemade bread, pies, and cookies," Betty Hutchins told us.

"My mother used to make candy out of carrots and beets," she said, explaining how the carrot candy is made. "Well, you grind up the carrots. It's a cup of carrots pressed down in the cup to a cup of sugar. You put a little bit of water in, not much. Then you put ginger in it. You cook it until it hardens."

Ada Foss told us that Christmas dinner for her family on the lighthouse was always chicken. "Chicken and everything that went with it. I did all my cooking for Christmas, apple pie, mincemeat pie, pumpkin pie. We had that every Christmas.

"Once in a while we would have a duck, but we never had turkey. My husband never cared for turkey. He did love chicken and so did the children, so we just had our chicken. We used to raise it ourselves. We made peanut brittle our own self. And then we had our own ice cream. That's one thing we had plenty of. The kids used to say, 'Well, Mama, can you make some ice cream?' Homemade ice cream is so much better than the boughten, I think."

What Roger Farnum remembers about Christmas food was the unaccustomed treat of walnuts. "If we had any walnuts, we thought we was getting something, you know."

Edith and Ethel Furbish liked nuts, too, and they remembered getting walnuts at Christmastime. "We'd get a bag of candy, and you'd have popcorn, nuts, and walnuts. Course, my brother Bert was here, too, and he had his bag, too. We weren't allowed to check one another's bag, 'cause they had our names on them."

For Ken Berdeen, Christmas meant roast pig. "In those days food was awful hard to get, and at that time some people would raise pigs. For your traditional Christmas dinner, we would have roast pork. Couldn't have no turkey, nothing like that because we didn't have any. We always had fruit Jell-O with whipped topping for dessert."

"We'd have somethin' a little bit different for Christmas, a chicken or somethin' like that to eat for dinner," Mary Turner said. "In some homes they used to all go for a turkey dinner. We kids never did, though. We were never invited to go anywheres.

"My father, well we had goose, sometimes. We was never lucky enough to get a moose. I don't never remember my father ever shootin' a moose. I guess I must hold the record for shootin' the moose of the family!"

Eleanor Eldridge had chicken for Christmas, too. "We had our own chickens, and we used to roast chickens and we had cranberry sauce, dressing, boiled onions, mashed potatoes, and sweet potatoes. Mother made a lot of pickles, too."

Reid Chapman especially remembers all the good food at Christmastime. "There'd be five or six kinds of pies and cakes and all kinds of vegetables. My mother was a wonderful cook. There'd be two long tables, as long as this room, and there'd be a dozen and a half people. A big feed with everybody singing afterward.

"My mother had an organ. She loved to play Christmas songs and hymns, and we'd all sing. So your neighbors got together and some of your close friends, and I think that they cared for one another a little bit more than they do today. As I look back on it, a friend was a real friend.

"Mr. Cook would ask the blessing [at Christmas dinner] and this is what he'd say: 'God bless the hands that prepared this food,' and I've never forgot it since I was a little kid. It's something you don't hear very often, and it always made me feel a little more thankful of what we got. You see what I mean."

The memories stirred by Christmas were not always of a treasured toy or an afternoon on the ice. While Ken Hutchins laughed and remembered the lump of coal in his stocking—"probably the biggest piece they could find in the coal bin," a sort of joke in those days—as well as the best present he ever got, a fire engine with three horses, the memories of his wife, Betty, are more sober.

"When I was eight years old in 1908, we were burnt out in the Chelsea fire. My mother took sick and was taken to the hospital, and we moved from Chelsea to Lynn, where my father worked in a tannery. We were known as the Chelsea refugees.

"Near us there was a Methodist Church, and the Methodist Church people all got together and the night before Christmas they put up a Christmas tree and they made homemade pies and homemade bread and homemade cookies, and they gathered all the toys they had, mended a lot of toys. We were all in bed—there were four of us kids— and when we got up in the morning, that was a wonderful Christmas. 'Cause we lost everything we had in the Chelsea fire, but what we had on. Now that was a nice Christmas."

Alberta Redmond remembered a Christmas Eve vigil in Cape Porpoise for fishermen lost at sea. "Do you remember one Christmas over here at the church?" she asked her daughter. "Everyone was waitin' to hear from Big Mont Sinnett. That's right. That was Christmas Eve.

"They [Big Mont and his son] were lost on the boat and a plane put out from Squantum, Massachusetts, to look for them. They were just ready to quit about three o'clock. I can remember that day. I walked clear to the pier, and that was a long walk for me from up there. We stood there and the boys said they were giving up the search at three o'clock.

"And," Alberta paused, her voice cracking with emotion, "I can remember we stood there, Sammy Wildes was aside me, and I said a little prayer and then it came over [the radio]. Somebody hollered from the house. They come out and they said they were found and the plane was picking 'em up.

"That was just at Christmastime. That's how I happened to think of it. Mont owed my husband a bill for some carpentry work, and he wrote it on the door in the cabin [of the boat]. And he said to my husband, 'Red, now I don't know how much I owe you,' after he lost his boat. 'I'll have to take your word for it.' My husband said, 'Forget it.' He was glad to see him home."

Alberta's great-granddaughter, Wendy Gibson of *Salt,* spoke for all of us. "That was . . . like a Christmas gift," she said.